Feminists in Development ~rga...

Praise for this book

'*Feminists in Development Organizations* is groundbreaking. It illuminates – with rich theoretical insight, passion and creativity – the hidden life and strategic dilemmas of feminists working in and through international and national bureaucracies to try and effect transformational change. Researchers rarely gain access to the quotidian workings of powerful organizations. The book builds upon innovative collaborative action research whereby practitioners reflect critically on their own practice as "institutional entrepreneurs" and "tempered radicals". Through a combination of first-person insider testimonies – and Eyben's creative reimagining of conversations amongst feminist bureaucrats – the book creates a complex and gripping narrative. Eyben and Turquet, and their contributors, take forward our theoretical and practical understanding of the dynamics of political change. The collection demonstrates the strategic agency exercised by feminist bureaucrats, often working below the radar, and at the margins, to bridge the divide between the inside and outside, reframe organizational and political discourse, and exploit bureaucratic contradictions in order to progress a social change agenda. It will be essential reading for academics and practitioners alike.'

Professor Fiona Mackay, Professor of Politics, University of Edinburgh, founder
and co-director, Feminism and Institutionalism International Network

'The book provides a timely and much-needed antidote to the simplistic optimism of earlier reflections on gender mainstreaming and dismissive attitudes and generalizations related to "femocrats". It provides a rich, nuanced, compelling and context-specific analysis of the political process of everyday bureaucratic life. We are provided fresh insights on the many pitfalls, strategic opportunities, trade-offs and strategies used by feminist bureaucrats working politically to transform bureaucracies. Among the numerous and valuable insights offered by the book two points come through with striking clarity. First is the insistence on multiple feminist identities and thus debunking of a single notion of feminism. Second is the sober recognition of the "non-transformative context" of international development bureaucracies while underscoring the importance of "small wins" that accumulatively and over time have the potential to reduce inequity and promote social justice.'

Zenebework Tadesse, long-term activist in the global women's movement,
and board member of DAWN

'This is a brave and much-needed book. Ros Eyben and Laura Turquet have assembled an all-star cast of writers and activists who cast their critical eyes over the future of feminism and development. Nothing could be more important.'

Michael Edwards, Distinguished Senior Fellow, Demos, New York,
and editor of Transformation

'Seldom can outsiders understand the challenges of life-on-the edge within bureaucracies that are ambivalent about employing you for what you believe in and stand for. This volume is a unique and valuable eye opener about how feminists do more than cope with such a tricky position by creatively pursuing their convictions with positive effect. Its practical stories and experiences should convince those who doubt the efficacy of swimming against male-engendered bureaucratic cultures to do just that.'

Alan Fowler, Emeritus Professor of Civil Society in International Development,
International Institute of Social Studies, Erasmus University, South Africa

'While possibly the most transformative and radical of all social justice struggles, feminism and feminists are invariably unwelcome and marginalized actors in almost every mainstream institutional context. But the most unsung heroines of all are feminists working within large development organizations and aid bureaucracies, treated as suspect both by their own hierarchies as well as their "sisters" in women's movements and organizations. This book makes a huge contribution by shedding light on the largely unknown struggles and poignant dilemmas of these "femocrats", and helps us appreciate the value of their impact within these often hostile or resistant institutional settings. The innovative and even subversive strategies these feminist pioneers have deployed to make these institutions more accountable to women is a revelation, with useful insights even for those of us situated in more congenial organizational and movement locations. I applaud Eyben and Turquet for taking us on this unusual journey into these less-travelled frontiers of institutional patriarchy.'

Srilatha Batliwala, Scholar Associate,
Association for Women's Rights in Development (AWID)

'A wonderfully insightful book written by feminist champions for change within the system. The book is important not only for what it says, but how it says it – modelling honest and critical reflection by leading practitioners in the field as another way of knowing.'

John Gaventa, Director, Coady International Institute

Feminists in Development Organizations

Change from the margins

Edited by Rosalind Eyben and Laura Turquet

PRACTICAL ACTION
Publishing

Practical Action Publishing Ltd
The Schumacher Centre
Bourton on Dunsmore, Rugby,
Warwickshire CV23 9QZ, UK
www.practicalactionpublishing.org

ISBN 978-1-85339-804-9 Hardback
ISBN 978-1-85339-805-6 Paperback
ISBN 978-1-78044-804-6 Library Ebook
ISBN 978-1-78044-805-3 Ebook

Book DOI: http://dx.doi.org/10.3362/9781780448046

A catalogue record for this book is available from the British Library.

The contributors have asserted their rights under the Copyright Designs and
Patents Act 1988 to be identified as authors of their respective contributions.

Eyben, R. and Turquet, L. (eds) (2013) *Feminists in Development Organizations:
Change from the Margins*, Rugby, UK: Practical Action Publishing.

Since 1974, Practical Action Publishing has published and disseminated
books and information in support of international development work
throughout the world. Practical Action Publishing is a trading name of
Practical Action Publishing Ltd (Company Reg. No. 1159018), the wholly
owned publishing company of Practical Action. Practical Action Publishing
trades only in support of its parent charity objectives and any
profits are covenanted back to Practical Action
(Charity Reg. No. 247257, Group VAT Registration No. 880 9924 76).

Cover photo: Mika Mansukhani
Cover design: Mercer Design
Indexed by Liz Fawcett, Harrogate
Typeset by Bookcraft Ltd, Stroud, Gloucestershire

Printed in India by Replika Press

FSC
www.fsc.org
MIX
Paper from
responsible sources
FSC® C016779

Contents

http://dx.doi.org/10.3362/9781780448046.000

Preface

People do things better both when they have a chance to reflect on their actions and when they have a chance to learn from others' experiences. These axioms informed a collaborative project between bureaucrats and researchers. We shared common aspirations for social emancipation and gender justice, and a deep anxiety that the organizational arrangements of 'gender mainstreaming' were failing to live up to the promise they offered when agreed at the Beijing Women's Conference in 1995. This book derives from that project and concerns the strategies and everyday tactics of the feminist bureaucrats who collaborated on this project. Although not everyone who contributed to this book was a member of the original project, all the authors write in that same spirit of self-enquiry and honest sharing that characterized the project, and made editing this book such a rewarding experience.

It has also been rather daunting. Necessarily, the authors have shown some caution when explaining what goes on inside their organizations, anxious that published material may be perceived to have damaging effects. In at least a couple of cases, the authors cleared their draft with colleagues or superiors. Another chapter was withdrawn at a relatively early stage because of the author's own anxieties about her organization's possible reaction. Even more unfortunately, a completely finished chapter already in the hands of the copy editor was stopped on the instructions of the author's employers.

However, throughout these travails we continued to receive the warm support of our contributing authors and we are most grateful for their patience during the inevitable delays in the book's publication. We also acknowledge and offer our thanks for the useful advice and constructive feedback we have had on earlier drafts of one or more of the chapters from Itil Asmon, Rosie McGee, Naomi Hossain, Hilary Standing, Patta Scott-Villiers, Alex Shankland, and Fiona Wilson. Thanks also to Jenny Edwards for her great help with seeing the book through to publication and to Andrea Cornwall, director of the Pathways of Women's Empowerment research programme, for all her encouragement and support in making this book happen. Finally, we acknowledge with gratitude the support of the UK Department for International Development whose funding of the Pathways programme made the project possible.

Rosalind Eyben and Laura Turquet

Acronyms and abbreviations

ADB   Asian Development Bank
AWID   Association for Women's Rights in Development
CEB   chief executives board (UN)
CEDAW   Convention on the Elimination of All Forms of Discrimination Against Women
CGA   country gender assessment (ADB)
CIDA   Canadian International Development Agency
CODEV   Working Party on Development Cooperation (EU)
COHOM   Working Party on Human Rights (EU)
CSW   Commission on the Status of Women (UN)
DAC   Development Assistance Committee (OECD)
DANIDA   Danish Agency for International Development
DAW   Division for the Advancement of Women (UN)
DAWN   Development Alternatives with Women in a New Era
DFID   Department for International Development (UK)
DGDEV   Directorate General for Development (EC)
DOC   Department of Children (Ghana)
DOW   Department of Women (Ghana)
ECDPM   European Centre for Development Policy Management
ECOSOC   United Nations Economic and Social Council
EFG   External Forum on Gender (ADB)
ESDP   European Security and Defence Policy
EULEX   The EU's rule of law mission in Kosovo
GADN   Gender and Development Network (UK)
GAP   gender action plan
GDCF   Gender and Development Cooperation Fund
GDO   gender desk officer (Ghana)
GEAP   Gender Equality Action Plan (DFID)
GENDERNET   OECD Network on Gender Equality
GEST   Gender Equality Sector Team (Ghana)
GFP   gender focal point
GRB   gender-responsive budgeting
GTGs   gender theme groups (UN)
IDS   Institute of Development Studies
IFI   international financial institution
INGO   international non-governmental organization
INSTRAW   International Research and Training Institute for the Advancement of Women (UN)
ISSER   Institute of Statistical, Social and Economic Research, University of Ghana

MDBS Multi-Donor Budget Support (Ghana)

MDGs Millennium Development Goals

MFA Ministry of Foreign Affairs (Austria)

MOFEP Ministry of Finance and Economic Planning (Ghana)

MOWAC Ministry of Women and Children's Affairs (Ghana)

NCWD National Council on Women and Development (Ghana)

NDPC National Development Planning Commission (Ghana)

NETRIGHT Network for Women's Rights in Ghana

NGO non-governmental organization

NSGE-DV National Strategy for Gender Equality and Eradication of Domestic Violence (Albania)

OECD Organisation for Economic Co-operation and Development

OSAGI Office of the Special Adviser on Gender Issues and Advancement of Women (UN)

PfA [Beijing Women's Conference] Platform for Action

SAP Structural Adjustment Programme

SG secretary-general

SRHR sexual and reproductive health and rights

UN United Nations

UNCTs United Nations country teams

UNDAF United Nations Development Assistance Framework

UN DESA United Nations Department for Economic and Social Affairs

UNDG United Nations Development Group

UNDP United Nations Development Programme

UNFPA United Nations Population Fund

UNIFEM United Nations Development Fund for Women

UNSCR United Nations Security Council Resolution

UN Women United Nations Entity for Gender Equality and the Empowerment of Women

WAAC women and armed conflict

WB World Bank

WEDO Women's Environment & Development Organization

WGNRR Women's Global Network for Reproductive Rights

WID women in development

WIDE Women in Development Europe

WOCAN Women Organizing for Change in Agriculture and Natural Resource Management

CHAPTER 1

Introduction
Feminist bureaucrats: inside–outside perspectives

Rosalind Eyben and Laura Turquet

Drawing on direct experience, this book is about feminists working politically to promote their organizations' gender equality goals. The aim is that by sharing this experience, the book's contributors can help others in similar positions to debate and reflect on the challenges of their jobs, and that readers from within the wider international women's movement will gain insights to help them engage more strategically with their allies inside development organizations. From a theoretical perspective, the literature stresses the significance of supportive individuals positioned within the bureaucratic system. Thus the book's insider standpoint is its academic contribution – describing and analysing the political processes of everyday bureaucratic life in which feminists assert their agency and creativity.

This book is about feminists reflecting critically on their own experience as gender advisers in large development bureaucracies. The job of such specialists includes reviewing policies and strategies, awareness-raising and skill development, and identifying and introducing systems and incentives for planning and monitoring in support of gender equality (Derbyshire, 2012). Not everyone in these posts is feminist and there are also feminists doing other jobs but – except tangentially – this book is not about them. Its theme is the limits and possibilities for feminist gender specialists to make their organizations capable of promoting and supporting rights-based approaches for social transformation that liberate men as well as women from gendered norms. This book is about bureaucrats working politically to transform bureaucracies, 'so that they become a tool in transforming lives of women' (O'Neill and Eyben, 2013).

Feminists tend to see bureaucrats as preservers of the status quo. A feminist bureaucrat appears a contradiction in terms. Yet, as this chapter will argue, it is this very contradiction that offers them the chance of becoming change agents. The intellectual and emotional rejection of a bureaucracy's hierarchical and controlling character can alienate any feminist employee, but for feminists employed as gender specialists this feeling of not really belonging may be exacerbated by an awareness that their presence is not welcome. The job of gender specialist often exists because of external pressure

http://dx.doi.org/10.3362/9781780448046.001

and prevailing norms more than from any core organizational commitment. Their marginalization – a sense of being on the edge rather than fully integrated into the organization – makes life complicated and full of quandaries. It can sometimes be lonely and the lack of recognition can be depressing. Some find their position untenable and leave to exert pressure for change from the outside; others stay to learn the advantages of being on the edge. As insiders they learn to understand and behave appropriately in the organization that employs them – otherwise they will have no credibility and little influence. As outsiders, they keep their critical distance from the organization, enabling them to challenge 'how things are done around here'. Positively accepting their inside–outside status, they reach out beyond their organizations to the feminist movements in civil society which they understand to be the principal force for transformative change in gender equality. By working politically and exploiting, rather than lamenting, their position on the edge of the organization, feminists employed to work on gender equality issues can change development bureaucracies. In that context, this introductory chapter explains the book's origins, approach and aims, followed by an overview of the other chapters.

Origin, approach and purposes

The book's origins lie in the editors' own experiences as policy practitioners and bureaucrats working in large international organizations. Feminist bureaucrats find it difficult to communicate their experience: they are busy in their jobs, often unfamiliar with academic discourse, and possibly cautious about revealing to the outside world the realities of their workplace. Hence, when Rosalind conceived a research project about feminist bureaucrats working as gender specialists, it made sense to design it not for extracting data from reserved officials, but instead as participatory action research, offering them a safe space to reflect upon and improve their own practice. In 2007, a collaborative project was born in which about a dozen gender specialists (including one man) and researchers shared their common aspiration for social emancipation and gender justice. The project had a conversational approach. Rosalind was doing research with, instead of on, her subjects (Pillow, 2003). This approach made some of those involved want to write in their own voice, and that encouraged others to contribute. Although not everyone contributing to the present book was a member of that original project, all the authors write in its spirit of self-enquiry and honest sharing, and Chapters 4, 8, and 11 capture the reflections and learning of those in the wider group who have chosen to remain anonymous.

Approach

Our approach takes seriously the notion of feminist reflexivity. We ask what is it about our positionality that shapes both how any one of us relates with others and how we choose to act. Hence this book is partial (in the two related senses of this word). First, it makes no claims to represent the situation of all feminist gender specialists in development (although when we have presented our findings to a wider audience of such specialists they have recognized these as their own). Second, the book reflects a certain, necessarily limited, perspective of a small number of professional, educated, (mostly) women, analyzing their own direct experiences of working with gender equality or women's rights units in governments and development agencies. In most cases, the book does not seek to explore the effects of development's bureaucratic politics as these make waves (or ripples) in the lives and prospects of women in general, and in whose name the authors are working. Nevertheless, all the contributors are well aware of the 'long road to walk from victories for women in bureaucratic spaces to gains for women on the ground' (Rao, 2013).

Brigitte Holzner, for example, worries in Chapter 5 whether spending her time on the construction of texts is of any relevance to the real world; Claudia (a disguised character in Chapter 8) agonizes over whether she is making any difference in the lives of 'rural women in Bangladesh'; and in the same chapter, Ratna is concerned that spending all day 'just answering emails and reading stuff … you'll have forgotten what it's like, the reality on the ground for women'.

Indeed, it is this anxiety about whether one's job is worthwhile that led some of the research participants to wonder whether it was self-indulgent to spend time holding up the mirror to themselves. If theirs is not the 'real world', what is the relevance or utility of a book that discusses and analyses their working lives? The answer, and the challenge, is to keep the bigger picture in mind – otherwise reflection is narcissistic – without staying silent on the minutiae in practice of how change is brokered. Silence about such minutiae is politically unhelpful to the real world, because the secrecy of bureaucracies produces a power effect. Weber notes that every bureaucracy will try to hide what it gets up to unless it is forced into revelation, invoking 'hostile interests' if need be to justify the secrecy (Bendix, 1959).

Development bureaucracies may be particularly competent at exercising these privileges of power, whereby power is legitimized by reference to 'the poor' for whose sake the organization exists. Staff commitment to this supreme objective may also make them reluctant to reveal their organization's inner workings and thus expose it to criticism. However, when the blinds stay down, those trying to look in through the window find it hard to see – and therefore to influence – what is going on. Feminist bureaucrats at the threshold between inside and outside are appropriately positioned to pull up the blinds. In the absence of external pressure they cannot secure the institutional change they are seeking. Thus making public their reflexive analysis is not self-indulgent if it contributes, as one of them said, to 'demystifying the bureaucracy'.

As such, this book provides an actor-oriented perspective on organizational politics. By 'actor-oriented' we mean that the book is concerned with how specific individuals 'deal with the problematic situations they encounter' (Long, 2001: 57) and how they act as brokers at the interface of bureaucracy and civil society. Feminists' potential to convert any bureaucracy – even a new one like UN Women – into an engine of social change remains a matter for debate. It is a particularly pertinent question for the complex bureaucratic architecture of international development, whose shared normative discourse is, as the World Bank puts it, 'working for a world free of poverty'.[1] For the authors of the present book, the debate is more than academic. As Aruna Rao (2013) stresses, it is emotional and personal:

> [The] politics around gender equality issues are deeply felt. People who get involved in such intense processes are forced to re-examine their own personal beliefs and behaviours – to walk the talk. And they have to do so in an environment which is rife with politics but where no other issue except human rights is politically framed.

Part of the emotion relates to the discomfort of inhabiting a marginal location in which you are never fully accepted anywhere, either inside or outside the bureaucracy. Yet, when they learn to be comfortable with their position, feminist bureaucrats exploit their marginality through political strategies that include building and balancing internal and external alliances, leveraging outside pressure, and turning dominant discourse on its head.

Accepting rather than worrying about the contradictions inherent in being a feminist bureaucrat means they can discover unexpected pathways of personal and organizational change, discoveries that can help the bureaucracy move closer to achieving its rhetorical aspirations of supporting women's empowerment and gender equality. It is largely a succession of small wins and discouraging defeats that over time turn into bigger victories, such as the feminists' success in securing the establishment of the new United Nations organization, UN Women, in 2010. As Joanne Sandler notes in Chapter 10, the changes that achieved this outcome did not happen quickly, but resulted from years of struggle and many people's efforts. To do this requires above all the commitment and craft of a political strategist.

Political purpose

It is the authors' hope that in sharing their experiences they can help others in similar positions to debate and reflect on the challenges of their jobs. The material from this book has already had a positive reaction from participants at a workshop in Scandinavia for gender specialists from bilateral agencies and development non-governmental organizations (NGOs). Thus the book should first of all prove useful to like-minded colleagues and to those planning a future career in development. For gender specialists newly recruited into development's organizational world, there is little to guide them on effective strategizing in the corridors of power. In addition, another key audience, as just indicated, is the many feminists on the outside who are advocating for development organizations to implement and strengthen commitments they have made. By revealing the inner workings of bureaucracies this book may enable such advocates to become more skilled in supporting their insider colleagues.

From the perspective of a feminist working for a local women's rights organization in an aid-recipient country, a gender specialist in a donor bureaucracy appears self-evidently in a privileged and powerful position. Yet, these two very differently positioned sets of actors need each other. On the one hand, feminist bureaucrats working as gender specialists want to support women mobilizing as a powerful driver for social transformation. On the other hand, women's rights movements cannot ignore donors' policy influence and may make good use of donors' money. In 2011, on a worldwide basis, women's rights organizations received a third of all their funding from donor bureaucracies like those represented in the present book – bilateral and multilateral agencies and international non-governmental organizations (INGOs) (Pittman et al., 2012). This proportion is likely to be significantly higher in poorer countries (the donors in this book do not fund women's rights organizations in richer countries). For example, a study of the effects of the external financing of women's rights organizations in Ghana and Bangladesh (Mukhopadhyay et al., 2011) found their most important sources of funding were bilateral agencies and INGOs.

Yet, as instrumentalist gender equality discourse assumes greater prominence within international bureaucracies, it becomes ever clearer that so much of what should be a fundamentally transformative project is lost in translation. Gender specialists in donor head offices of organizations, including INGOs, and who Rosalind interviewed for the above study, commented that although women's empowerment and gender equality remain central objectives for many donors, it has become a struggle to preserve and fund rights-based approaches. To that end, they stressed their desire to develop a quality relationship with women's rights organizations so they could work better together for a shared objective and ensure their organizations are held to account for their own commitments.

Perhaps it is naive to imagine that there can be solidarity between feminist activists in civil society, some of whom fiercely critique the whole development paradigm, and feminists situated in what one of the feminist bureaucrats in this book described as 'the belly of the beast'. It is a hotly debated issue (Mohanty, 2003; Mullings, 2006). There are, however, women's rights activists that do recognize the strategic value of engaging with those working for change from within international development agencies. The present book should help them do so.

Academic intent

The book's academic intent is to explore how bureaucratic organizations can support real-world change. A parallel stream of research has examined the nature and challenges of gender mainstreaming in international development organizations (Goetz, 2003; True, 2003; Rao and Kelleher, 2005; Prugl and Lustgarten, 2006; and Klugman, 2008) and emphasized the significance of the role of supportive individuals positioned within the bureaucratic system for action on gender justice. However, since most scholars have had little or no insider access to the organizations they study, they have been unable to describe and analyse the political processes of everyday bureaucratic life in which people assert their agency and creativity.

We have to factor in this lack of knowledge about the micro-political strategies of feminist bureaucrats when considering the question, usefully explored by many feminist researchers, of what makes change happen in global policy spaces (Tickner, 2001; Hafner-Burton and Pollack, 2002; Parpart et al., 2002; True, 2003; Moghadam, 2005; Molyneux and Razavi, 2005; Sen, 2006). Case studies about successful instances of policy processes are available, such as securing the UN Declaration on Violence Against Women (Joachim, 2003), and more recently securing Security Council Resolution 1325 (Shepherd, 2008), but studies such as Moghadam's (2005) on feminist policy networks do not sufficiently appreciate the informal and very discreet role of those feminists who support these networks from positions inside official organizations.[2] The role of gender specialists in the development agencies of United Nations member countries is taken into account even less. They may have been supporting campaigns to achieve changes in global policies in favour of gender equality in a number of ways, such as securing the resources to fund a campaign or international conference, influencing their country's delegations, financing the costs of Southern campaigners, and encouraging their own national lobby groups to be active on the issue. However, their own official caution may render these feminist bureaucrats invisible, misleading us about their role and preventing civil society activists and academics from enquiring as to how they could most usefully support them.

A collection of brief memoirs from those active in the 1970s and 1980s provides some fascinating insights into the challenges of establishing 'women in development' sections in organizations such as USAID, the World Bank, and the Commonwealth Secretariat (Fraser and Tinker, 2004). Jain (2005) and Skard (2008) recount how the women who established the Commission for the Status of Women were former WWII resistance fighters, who used that experience to fight their corner in the newly formed United Nations. An exploration of the 'bureaucratic mire' (Staudt et al., 1997) offers a perspective on the years between the 1985 Nairobi Women's Conference and the one that followed 10 years later in Beijing. However, little has been published on what happens inside development bureaucracies[3] since Miller and Razavi's illuminating edited volume of case studies (1998). Knowing more about what happens is not only of academic interest, it can be politically useful.

Walby (2005) argues that unless organizations work through the contradictions between the desire to use gender for instrumental reasons and their desire to promote gender equality in its own right, gender mainstreaming will tend to support the status quo. However, it is more complex than that. As this book will demonstrate, large organizations are heterogeneous and full of contradictions. Politically astute feminist bureaucrats seek to exploit these contradictions rather than resolve them, making small gains as they work towards transformational goals.

Structure of the book

The experience of being a feminist gender specialist, as interpreted through the eyes of an individual, is the focus of most of the book's chapters. In all but one case (Chapter 3, which is about working in a Ministry of Women's Affairs), this is the experience of staff employed in international development organizations: multilateral – the Organisation for Economic Co-operation and Development (OECD), United Nations agencies, and the Asian Development Bank (ADB); bilateral – the Austrian aid department; and non-governmental – Oxfam and ActionAid. The exception to this individual focus is Aruna Rao's chapter, which describes a group process of action-learning and reflective practice undertaken with United Nations country teams. These are similar to the approaches Rosalind used in bringing together a group of gender specialists from Europe, Africa, Asia, and North America, and working in the head offices of these and other international development organizations (including some of the contributors to this book). Rosalind's reflections are captured in three shorter chapters that are different in tone; through the device of conversations that take place between five composite characters – based on a larger group that includes her – these chapters explore relationships, politics, power, coalitions, and discourses, and look at how these shape and inform the practitioner's craft. Importantly, people speak more frankly about their experiences in these conversations than they would as named authors.

Following this introduction, Chapter 2 draws on material from the book's case studies to develop the theoretical arguments about marginality, effectiveness, and strategy. First, Rosalind considers gender mainstreaming as it has ebbed and flowed in the international development system. She then briefly examines some of the inherent contradictions in this system and its associated pitfalls that feminist bureaucrats need to be alert to in their efforts to facilitate social transformation. The focus then shifts to examining more closely the ambivalence of feminist bureaucrats. The chapter considers what it means to be a politically engaged bureaucrat, including motivation and the challenges and opportunities of being marginal. This is followed by a more specific examination of what it means to be feminist in a bureaucracy, and the implications for feminist bureaucrats' most important political strategy – namely constructive relations with feminist movements and networks.

Chapter 3 provides the first of the case studies, setting the scene by linking feminist activism at the country level with donor support for gender mainstreaming in state bureaucracies. Based on conversations with Francesca Pobee-Hayford, a former senior official in Ghana's Ministry of Women and Children's Affairs, scholar activists Takyiwaa Manuh and Nana Akua Anyidoho ask what it means to be a self-confessed 'femocrat' in the state bureaucracy. Francesca's objective was to get the ministry to take up its central management role as the primary implementer of the government's gender mainstreaming agenda. She concludes that despite some achievements, the ministry is still struggling to do this due to a rapid turnover of staff and an inability to develop strong political relationships with other ministries, as well as externally with the women's movement. Frustrated by inadequate political leadership combined with ministerial micromanagement of her job, Francesca eventually resigned from the civil service to take up a post as gender adviser in the country office of a bilateral development agency. Manuh and Anyidoho discover that despite all the institutional challenges they have learnt about from Francesca, they are now more optimistic than before about gender mainstreaming in Ghana.

Chapter 4 describes how in 2007, a group of feminist bureaucrats working as gender specialists in the head offices of international development bureaucracies got together to talk about their approaches. It was an action research process that continued off and on for three years. This chapter is the first of three evocations of some of what was said and discussed. The five characters are based on twelve real individuals but they, and the places they meet, have been heavily disguised (in a way analogous to using fictional characters) to protect the anonymity of those participating and to represent different points of view. This particular chapter explores the theme of feminist identities as discussed over supper in New York.

From her post as gender adviser for the Austrian aid programme in Vienna, Brigitte Holzner considers some of the same challenges in Chapter 5. Feminists face the dilemma of engaging with the state machinery in order to change it, finding that after devoting most of their time to performing the tasks that bureaucracy requires of them, the machinery fails to deliver the hoped-for transformations. Small wins seem the best that can be hoped for. Brigitte describes two instances of engaging with EU development institutions to secure language favourable to women in policy texts: In the first case, by making good use of inter-organizational alliances, she was successful. In the second, the policy topic was more difficult to influence, and she failed. There were certainly some changes in circumstances, but it is possible the principal difference was that the second case (gender and the macro-economy) was more threatening to mainstream EU policy discourse than the first (the role of women in armed conflict).

Chapter 6 is a conversation between Rosalind Eyben and Patti O'Neill, who works for the OECD. Employed in New Zealand's national gender machinery and then in its aid programme, Patti moved to Paris to be responsible for gender issues in the work of the Development Assistance Committee (DAC), which brings together all the bilateral aid agencies in a forum to discuss policy issues, coordinates peer reviews of agencies' aid programmes, and collects statistics. She looks back on her career as a political activist and feminist bureaucrat, stressing the importance of building alliances based on trust and mutual respect within and outside the organization in which the feminist bureaucrat works. These relationships work better if at certain times others are not told about them and when you challenge each other constructively, recognizing and building on complementary roles. Among Patti's other tips for being an effective feminist bureaucrat are creating win–win situations – 'We need to avoid being "the finger-wagging gender police"' – and choosing your battles, which means that strategy must be accompanied by constant scanning of the political environment and readiness to shift tactics in response to emerging opportunities. And, she concludes, when things go wrong, it is essential to keep a positive and optimistic outlook.

Chapter 7 is about working as a gender adviser in an international NGO. Laura Turquet analyses the strategies used and the challenges encountered when she lobbied DFID on its gender equality policy, while struggling to avoid marginalization within her own organization, ActionAid. She argues that building relationships with feminist activists has to be a two-way process. Those on 'the outside' – women's organizations and feminist campaigners – need to appreciate what the insiders are trying to do and reach out to them, and those on the inside must be frank about the challenges of their own bureaucratic location. Like O'Neill, she emphasizes the importance of establishing relationships of mutual trust and respect.

In Chapter 8, we return to the five women we met in chapter 4. This time they are on a weekend retreat in the country. Picking up the threads from their conversation in New York, they ask themselves how they define success. This leads on to talking – and disagreeing – about gender mainstreaming and how to work effectively with an organization's instruments, discourses and procedures.

This is also a strong theme in Chapter 9. Ines Smyth, who works for Oxfam and spent a year as the leading gender specialist at the Asian Development Bank (ADB) – institutions with very different ethoses and priorities – explores how the character of the two organizations shapes their commitment and approach to promoting gender equality in their programmes. Her experience at ADB helps her look at the world of international NGOs in a new light. She concludes that feminist bureaucrats must persist in tackling obstacles and areas of resistance – not a popular approach in NGOs, she comments, where immediate and simple solutions to social problems of intractable complexity are expected.

Chapter 10 takes us into the UN: Joanne Sandler, previously a senior official at UNIFEM in New York, vividly portrays the experience of feminists struggling with the institutional sexism of the UN bureaucratic machine, and shows how this played out in the difficult but ultimately successful negotiations around the creation of UN Women. She writes, 'documenting the types of systemic institutional sabotage that UNIFEM faced throughout its life is a hedge against history repeating itself with UN Women'. UN Women, she argues, must insist on institutional equality if it is to play its role in transforming the UN system as an advocate and instrument of gender justice. What she does not speculate upon is, if the new organization is successful in avoiding the marginalization that UNIFEM experienced, will it still manage to maintain its strong links with global feminist movements that, as outsiders, played such a strong role in supporting the struggles of those inside the belly of the beast?

In Chapter 11, our group of five women find themselves together at an international meeting of gender and development specialists in Berlin. By now, they have got to know each other well, and are able to talk more informally and frankly about their work. What happened at the meeting stimulates a supper time discussion about how power operates in international development processes. How do feminist bureaucrats respond? How subversive do they dare to be?

We leave the head office politics of the preceding chapter to return to the country level – Morocco, Albania, and Nepal – in Chapter 12, where consultant Aruna Rao describes how she and her colleagues worked to strengthen the gender equality programming of three UN country teams (UNCTs) with an action-learning approach for interagency gender theme groups (GTGs). Through the lens of each country context, she examines the importance of inter-organizational cooperation between gender equality staff in UN agencies, and looks at why this has been difficult to achieve in the environment of institutional discrimination that Sandler analyses in the previous chapter. She concludes that 'rather than burdening GTGs with resource manuals focusing on planning and monitoring mechanisms and processes', it may be far more effective to enable them to organize and develop joint solidarity strategies with government and the women's movement, to enhance their voice within.

Finally, in the book's conclusion (Chapter 13), we draw together the common experiences, lessons and strategies of the feminist bureaucrats who have shared their reflections in this book. Without doubt, there are many disadvantages of the marginal position that we occupy – including a sense of powerlessness, lack of visibility both inside and outside our own organizations, conflicted loyalties, and the demands of being held accountable on two fronts. But, if feminist bureaucrats can exploit their marginal position and work politically, they can turn each of these disadvantages into an advantage to advance their own agendas. In order to do so, we identify a checklist of strategies for feminist gender advisers in development agencies: building internal and external alliances, leveraging outside pressure, creating win–win situations, preparing for and seizing opportunities, and coping with bureaucratic resistance.

Notes

1   See the home page of the World Bank <www.worldbank.org>.
2   Except in some cases the roles of UN bureaucrats (for example Ferree and Tripp, 2006) but these do not fully take into account the networking between feminists in multilateral and bilateral agencies (see Sandler, 2013).
3   Other than an interesting study of gender specialists in Canadian development agencies (Hendriks, 2005).

References

Bendix, R. R. (1959) *Max Weber,* London: University Paperbacks, Methuen.

Derbyshire, H. (2012) 'Gender mainstreaming: recognising and building on progress. Views from the UK Gender and Development Network', *Gender & Development*, 20: 405–22 <http://dx.doi.org/10.1080/13552074.2012.731750>.

Ferree, M. M. and A. M. Tripp (eds) (2006) *Global Feminism: Transnational Women's Activism, Organizing, and Human Rights*, New York: New York University Press.

Fraser, A. and I. Tinker (eds) (2004) *Developing Power: How Women Transformed International Development*, New York: Feminist Press.

Goetz, A. M. (2003) 'The World Bank and women's movements', in R. O'Brien (ed.), *Contesting Global Governance: Multilateral Economic Institutions and Global Social Movements*, Cambridge: Cambridge University Press.

Hafner-Burton, E. and M. Pollack (2002) 'Gender mainstreaming and global governance', *Feminist Legal Studies*, 10: 285–98 <http://dx.doi.org/10.1023%2FA%3A1021232031081>.

Hendriks, S. (2005) 'Advocates, adversaries, and anomalies: The politics of feminist spaces in gender and development', *Canadian Journal of Development Studies*, 26, special issue, 620–32 <http://dx.doi.org/10.1080%2F02255189.2005.9669102>.

Jain, D. (2005) *Women, Development and the UN*, Bloomington: Indiana University Press.

Joachim, J. (2003) 'Framing issues and seizing opportunities: The UN, NGOs and women's rights', *International Studies Quarterly*, 47: 247–74 <http://dx.doi.org/10.1111%2F1468-2478.4702005>.

Klugman, B. (2008) 'Advocating for abortion access: Lessons and challenges' *IDS Bulletin*, 39: 10–17 <http://dx.doi.org/10.1111%2Fj.1759-5436.2008.tb00457.x>.

Long, N. (2001) *Development Sociology: Actor Perspectives*, London: Routledge.

Miller, C. and S. Razavi (1998) *Missionaries and Mandarins: Feminist Engagement with Development Institutions*, Rugby, UK: Practical Action Publishing.

Moghadam, V. (2005) *Globalizing Women: Transnational Feminist Networks*, Baltimore: Johns Hopkins University Press.

Mohanty, C. (2003) '"Under Western eyes" revisited: Feminist solidarity through anti-capitalist struggles.' *Signs*, 28: 499–535 <http://dx.doi.org/10.1086%2F342914>.

Molyneux, M. and S. Razavi (2005) '"Beijing plus ten": An ambivalent record on gender justice', *Development and Change*, 36: 983–1010 <http://dx.doi.org/10.1111%2Fj.0012-155X.2005.00446.x>.

Mukhopadhyay, M. and Eyben, R. (2011) 'Rights and Resources: The Effects of External Financing on Organising for Women's Rights' Pathways of Women's Empowerment/Royal Tropical <www.pathwaysofempowerment.org/Rights_and_Resources.pdf> [accessed 2 February 2013].

Mullings, B. (2006) '"Difference" and transnational feminist networks', *International Studies Review*, 8: 112–15 <http://dx.doi.org/10.1111%2Fj.1468-2486.2006.00562.x>.

O'Neill, P. and Eyben, R. (2013) '"It's fundamentally political": renovating the master's house', in R. Eyben and L. Turquet (eds), *Feminists in Development Organizations: Change from the Margins*, pp. 85–100, Rugby, UK: Practical Action Publishing.

Parpart, J., S. Rai, and K. Staudt (eds) (2002) *Rethinking Empowerment: Gender and Development in a Global/Local World*, London: Routledge.

Pillow, W. (2003) 'Confession, catharsis, or cure? Rethinking the uses of reflexivity as methodological power in qualitative research', *International Journal of Qualitative Studies in Education*, 16: 175–96 <http://dx.doi.org/10.1080%2F0951839032000060635>.

Pittman, A., Arutyunova, A., Degiorgis, V., and Shaw, A. (2012) *AWID Global Survey 'Where is the Money for Women's Rights?' Preliminary Research Results from 2011* AWID, June 2012, <www.awid.org/Media/Files/WITM_Preliminary_2011_results%20%20> [accessed 2 February 2103].

Prugl, E., and A. Lustgarten (2006) 'Mainstreaming gender in international organizations', in J. Jacquette and G. Summerfield (eds), *Women and Gender Equity in Development Theory and Practice*, Durham: Duke University Press.

Rao, A. (2013) 'Feminist activism in development bureaucracies: shifting strategies and unpredictable results', in R. Eyben and L. Turquet (eds), *Feminists in Development Organizations: Change from the Margins*, pp. 177–92, Rugby, UK: Practical Action Publishing.

Rao, A., and D. Kelleher (2005) 'Is there life after gender mainstreaming?', *Gender and Development*, 13: 57–69 <http://dx.doi.org/10.1080%2F13552070512331332287>.

Sandler, J. (2013) 'Re-gendering the United Nations: old challenges and new opportunities', in R. Eyben and L. Turquet (eds), *Feminists in Development Organizations: Change from the Margins*, pp. 145–64, Rugby, UK: Practical Action Publishing.

Sen, G. (2006) 'The quest for gender equality', in P. Utting (ed.), *Reclaiming Development Agendas: Knowledge, Power and International Policy Making*, Basingstoke: UNRISD/Palgrave.

Shepherd, L. (2008) 'Power and authority in the production of United Nations Security Council Resolution 1325', *International Studies Quarterly*, 52: 383–404 <http://dx.doi.org/10.1111%2Fj.1468-2478.2008.00506.x>.

Skard, T. (2008) 'Promoting the status of women in the UN system: Experiences from an inside journey', *Forum for Development Studies*, 35: 279–311 <http://dx.doi.org/10.1080%2F08039410.2008.9666412>.

Staudt, K. (ed.) (1997) *Women, International Development and Politics: The Bureaucratic Mire* (2nd ed), Philadelphia: Temple University Press.

Tickner, J. A. (2001) *Gendering World Politics: Issues and Approaches in the Post-Cold War Era*, New York: Columbia University Press.

True, J. (2003) 'Mainstreaming gender in global public policy', *International Feminist Journal of Politics*, 5: 368–96 <http://dx.doi.org/10.1080%2F 14616740 32000122740>.

Walby, S. (2005) 'Gender mainstreaming: Productive tensions in theory and practice', *Social Politics*, 12: 321–43 <http://dx.doi.org/10.1093%2 Fsp%2Fjxi018>.

About the authors

Rosalind Eyben is a Professorial Research Fellow at the Institute of Development Studies, University of Sussex. She is a social anthropologist with a professional background in development policy and practice, and a committed teacher in the IDS doctoral and master's programmes, including on gender and development. She has designed and facilitated numerous workshops for international development practitioners all over the world. Her research interests focus on power and relations in international aid. From 2006–11 she convened the global policy programme of the International Research Consortium on Pathways of Women's Empowerment and is currently developing a new area of work exploring the knowledge/power practices of donors that sustain the invisibility of unpaid care as a development policy issue. In 2010 she launched the Big Push Forward that has created an international network challenging the current audit culture in development. She was awarded a CBE in 2000 and is a board member of UNRISD and ActionAid UK.

Laura Turquet has worked as an advocate and researcher on gender equality and women's rights for the past decade, with experience in diverse settings – from a small feminist campaigning organization to the newly established United Nations Entity for Gender Equality and the Empowerment of Women (UN Women), where she manages the organization's flagship publication, *Progress of the World's Women*. She has published many reports on gender equality issues including violence against women, access to justice, and the Millennium Development Goals. Laura has master's degrees in history and international relations from the Universities of Edinburgh and Sussex.

CHAPTER 2

Gender mainstreaming, organizational change, and the politics of influencing

Rosalind Eyben

This chapter addresses the debates about gender mainstreaming, organizational change, and the politics of influencing, to which the present book aims to contribute. That gender mainstreaming is political has long been accepted, but for this perception to be useful it needs to be transposed onto a much more strategically oriented understanding of feminist bureaucrats' activism. Drawing on material from the book's case studies, theoretical arguments are developed about marginality, effectiveness, and strategy, in the context of the ebb and flow of gender mainstreaming within the international development system.

This chapter starts with an overview of the international development system as the context for a brief historical analysis of gender mainstreaming in development. I then briefly examine some of the inherent contradictions in the development system, and its associated pitfalls, that feminist bureaucrats need to be alert to in their efforts to facilitate social transformation. Thereafter I shift focus to examine more closely the ambivalence of feminist bureaucrats. I consider what it means to be a politically engaged bureaucrat, including their motivation and the challenges and opportunities of being marginal. I then examine more specifically what it means to be a feminist in a bureaucracy – using concepts such as institutional entrepreneur and 'tempered radical' – and the implications for feminist bureaucrats' most important political strategy, namely constructive relations with feminist movements and networks.

The institutional context of 'development'

While development with a small 'd' connotes progress and growth, 'Development' with a capital 'D' refers to the 50-year-old paradigm of planned interventions in 'developing' countries (Hart, 2001) that involves a complex and dynamic institutional nexus of discourses, norms, and organizations into which the contributors to this book have been incorporated. It is a daunting and rapidly changing institutional environment for feminist bureaucrats. The international development sector is composed of thousands of separate organizations. Money, ideas, and people circulate within a web of organizational relationships (Eyben, 2006). Official aid agencies in rich countries finance

http://dx.doi.org/10.3362/9781780448046.002

governments and non-governmental organizations (NGOs) in recipient countries. NGOs in donor countries raise money from voluntary contributions and government budgets to pass on to their counterparts in the South, who are trying to influence their own governments while at the same time seeking to influence donor government policies regarding recipient countries and multilateral organizations that their governments finance. These multilaterals include international finance institutions such as the World Bank and regional banks like the Asian Development Bank (ADB); United Nations agencies such as the United Nations Development Programme (UNDP) and UN Women; and the European Commission. The multilateral organizations transfer resources to recipient country governments and NGOs, while seeking to influence them and everyone else. And all this mutual influencing and jockeying for position is performed by trans-organizational, formal and informal networks of policy actors pursuing particular agendas in a multitude of global arenas.

In 2000, this institutional nexus committed itself to the Millennium Declaration and, a few years later, the Millennium Development Goals, which included a goal relating to gender equality. The OECD Paris Declaration on Effective Aid of 2005 was designed to achieve these goals through harmonization of effort in support of recipient country poverty reduction strategies (O'Neill and Eyben, 2013). Civil society in those countries was framed as the watchdog of the state – to hold it accountable to the country's citizens – and international NGOs were encouraged to build local capacity to that end (Mercer, 2002). But soon after the millennium highpoint, some countries in Asia and Latin America began to change their status from recipients to donors, providing bilateral aid to poorer countries and financing multilateral organizations. These changes have led many to conclude that 'the West and the international development institutions, founded and controlled by [it] will gradually lose their exclusive competence in development strategies' (Six, 2009: 1118).

So far there is little evidence about how this major shift in the development paradigm will play out in relation to global development policies on gender (Eyben, forthcoming). However, as the political stance of the 'emerging powers' is non-interference in the domestic policies of their aid recipients (Mawdsley, 2011), and as their aid becomes more influential, traditional donors' support of women's rights may fall further out of fashion. Meanwhile other, new institutional actors are already making their mark. On the one hand, philanthro-capitalists like the Gates Foundation see development as a technical matter that can be effectively achieved through employing the approaches of business management expertise (Edwards, 2008), and are noted for their absence of interest in gender equality. On the other hand, the corporate sector is entering into partnerships with donor governments and multilateral agencies on the premise that the private sector is more efficient and effective at achieving development objectives, including those associated with gender. Organizations like the Nike Foundation, in partnership with the UK Department for International Development (DFID), are promoting their own instrumental brand of gender equality (Eyben, 2011).

Against this backdrop I briefly review the history of gender mainstreaming as the more immediate shaping force of feminist bureaucrats' activism in development organizations, and then identify some of the problems and pitfalls they face when working as feminists from inside the development system.

Gender mainstreaming in development

Between the first World Conference on Women in Mexico in 1975, and the fourth such conference in Beijing in 1995, women in development (WID) became part of the standard discourse of global development policy. 'A good working definition of WID is simply the taking of women into account, improving their status, and increasing their participation in the economic, social and political development of communities, nations and the world' (Fraser, 2004: ix). In the 1970s, the WID lobby argued that women, as well as men, should be beneficiaries of development. Hard-nosed, neo-liberal male economists interpreted this argument to regard women as consumers, rather than producers, of wealth. Women, when thought about at all, were a category of the population that had specific needs, such as water and firewood (men apparently never being thirsty or hungry). Women, not men, had babies. They were wealth consumers, not producers. Men had to make economic growth happen for consuming women to reap the benefits. Then in the 1980s, what seemed a bold and radical shift in discourse at the time, a new argument was introduced: women were not only potential beneficiaries – they were also agents of development. Thus began the era of instrumentalist advocacy to persuade male decision-makers that that they should invest in women to secure faster development. To include women in development projects led to greater efficiency and effectiveness.

In the early 1990s came a further breakthrough: The United Nations Conference on Human Rights recognized that women's rights are human rights. The instrumentalist/efficiency agenda moved into the shadows as the preparations for the 1995 Beijing Women's Conference developed a vision of global social transformation. Amartya Sen said that development was freedom and women were claiming it. Beijing marked the apex of twenty years of sustained endeavour, helped in the second half of that period by the international climate becoming more favourable to women organizing than before. The end of the Cold War led to the return of parliamentary democracy in many countries and an increased international emphasis on human rights. The macroeconomics of the Washington Consensus and the associated structural adjustment policies of the 1980s did not disappear, but they ceased to be the unique preoccupation and site of contestation among international development organizations. The negative impact of structural adjustment combined with the new enthusiasm for civil society and democracy following the end of the Cold War led to people – and their participation – becoming important. The coalition of grassroots activists, politicians, and bureaucrats that met at Beijing was emboldened by this positive climate.

By then, it was no longer just the radical fringe who argued that systemic improvement to the status of women could only be achieved by transforming gender relations and the historically derived structures that sustained these relations (Miller and Razavi, 1995). This had become a mainstream agenda that included transforming bureaucracies, because they were seen to have historically institutionalized the unequal power relations between men and women. Public administration was not delivering gender equitable policies because of how gender structured the 'power and opportunity within administration' (Goetz, 1992: 6). Rao and Kelleher's work with BRAC, from the early 1990s onwards, demonstrated the challenges for organizations with gender equity goals to change the way they worked in order to meet these goals (Rao and Kelleher, 1995). Hence, paragraph 290 of the Beijing Platform for Action (PfA) states that 'effective implementation of the Platform will also require changes in the internal dynamics of institutions and organizations, including values, behaviour, rules and procedures that are inimical to the advancement of women'. The PfA (chapter IV) also requires organizations to 'promote an active and visible policy of mainstreaming a gender perspective'.

Gender mainstreaming, as defined at Beijing, was thus both a strategy for infusing mainstream policy agendas with a gender perspective and for transforming the institutions associated with those agendas. Its radical promise has since dimmed, as it became increasingly evident that the desired results were not being achieved. The run-up to the 2005 'Beijing Plus Ten' provoked a moment of significant reflection among international development researchers and practitioners. The overall conclusion was that the transformational promise of Beijing had failed to bring about a policy shift in favour of women's empowerment. By 2006, a spate of negative evaluations had further depressed feminists working inside large development bureaucracies. These evaluations confirmed a failure to sustain the development sector's interest in women's empowerment. Had they been too ambitious, feminists asked, when they were seeking to transform their bureaucracies? Would more modest objectives have achieved more? Some feminist bureaucrats argued that buying into the prevailing discourse of efficiency and effectiveness might, after all, be a quicker route than a rights-based approach for getting their organizations to take 'women's empowerment' seriously.

By 2010, the mood had shifted yet again. 'Gender equality and women's empowerment' have re-established themselves as important goals in international development agencies, and senior managers appear to be paying them serious attention. The vote of the United Nations General Assembly to establish a UN 'gender entity' was an impressive result (Sandler, 2013). Three years earlier, many – including the editors of this volume – would not have predicted that so many governments would have lobbied so hard in the UN corridors to secure such a change. Yet while the new, avowedly feminist executive director of UN Women Michelle Bachelet spoke about women's rights, the World Bank continued to promote ever more vigorously its 'gender is smart economics' approach. There were also ominous signs of how right-of-centre donor governments were framing their work on gender equality. Influenced by the Nike Foundation, DFID returned – in its 2011–15 business plan – to the language of the British government of the early 1980s, with its commitment to lead international action to 'empower and educate girls, recognize the role of women in development, and help to ensure that healthy mothers can raise strong children'.[1]

Problems and pitfalls for feminist gender specialists

Despite the changes to the institutional system of international development described earlier, there are certain historical characteristics of the paradigm that are still recognizable and that continue to shape notions of gender mainstreaming and feminist bureaucrats' strategies. It is a problematic paradigm (see for example Grillo, 1997; Hart, 2001; Rist, 2002; Kothari and Minogue, 2002) which creates interlinked pitfalls that feminists must circumvent to avoid reinforcing the very thing they are trying to change.

Although the effect is diminished when staff are assigned to country offices, there is first of all the pitfall of a spatial, cognitive, and social distance between the staff in development agencies and the people for whom they are designing or advocating policies. The racist legacy of colonial attitudes shaping international development practice is still evident in the structures of authority, relations, and hierarchy (Crewe and Fernando, 2006; Kothari, 2006). Joanne Sandler (2013) highlights how development agencies expect aid-recipient countries to do things which their own agencies often fail to achieve. Canada's export of gender-based analysis to developing countries has been criticized for 'marketing a model that has yet to be successfully implemented at home' (Hanson, 2007).

The detachment from diverse and complex local realities can make international development policy struggles self-referential and disconnected from the experience and views of the people in developing countries that such policies are meant to help. It contributes to, and is reinforced by, a process of 'othering' which entails the invention of categories and stereotypes – 'the poor', 'Moslem women', etc. (Moncrieffe and Eyben, 2007). This is the second pitfall. Feminists in development organizations risk making essentialist claims about women's lives to demonstrate the correctness of their policy prescriptions (Smyth, 2013). Arguments become depoliticized and turned into myths – 'essentialisms and generalizations, simplifying frameworks and simplistic slogans' (Cornwall et al., 2007: 1). When those making such claims receive or expect privileges and authority based on their whiteness, or on their ability to allocate financial resources, we would expect tensions in the relations between them and those they are making claims for (Mohanty, 1988). In a Pathways of Women's Empowerment study, five women's rights organizations in Bangladesh highlighted what makes a good donor: mutual respect, solidarity, responsiveness, and helpfulness. Donors' negative qualities, on the other hand were: being top-down; not giving the organization a 'decent hearing'; no transparency in decision-making; wanting too much publicity; imposing their decisions; being bureaucratic and inflexible; and thinking too much of themselves (Nazneen and Sultan, 2011).

Another legacy from the time of European imperial expansion is the pitfall of expertise, in which 'the universal [is asserted] over the particular, the travelled over the placed, the technical over the political, and the formal over the substantive' (Craig and Porter, 2006: 120; cited in Mosse, 2011). Gender analysis is part of and contributes to a broader body of development expertise characterized by Mosse (2011: 7) as 'travelling orthodoxies' that apply universal policy models to diverse contexts. The distinctive character of development institutions ensures that manuals and policy guidance notes, reporting templates, and planning frameworks have more power than in other bureaucracies to standardize judgements and promote particular diagnoses and solutions (Mosse, 2011). In promoting the tools and procedures of 'gender mainstreaming', a feminist bureaucrat may unreflectingly reproduce the inequitable power relations that she is seeking to change.

Finally, there is the pitfall of failure of accountability. Unlike national bureaucracies in democratic contexts, international development organizations are unaccountable to those for whom they exist. UN Women, for example, is not accountable to rural women in Bangladesh. It is easier to promote policy interventions inspired in global policy spaces, and detached from local realities, in a development aid context than in a domestic context, where citizens in a democracy can use public protest, the media, and eventually their vote to show policymakers that they are out of touch. Nor is this just a syndrome of government bilateral development agencies and multilateral organizations. International NGOs also risk succumbing to belief in their own simplistic messages, designed to raise money from voluntary contributions by making development projects sound easy. Like the donor governments on whom they partly depend, they can fall prone to funding projects that are easy to implement with measurable outcomes, but may have no socially transformative effect.

In her overview of gender mainstreaming in the EU, Sylvia Walby (2005) discusses instances of policy change in EU countries in which expert gender knowledge intertwines with, and is balanced by, democratic voice and accountability. In development institutions, the absence of democratic accountability to those for whom the institutions exist distorts how academic evidence is used, and leaves it open to abuse, to satisfy one-way demands for accountability back to those funding the system. Extraordinary demands are being made by some bilateral agencies, governments, and foundations in terms of reporting against quantifiable achievements – what can be counted – that bear little relation to how social transformation happens. These demands are having an effect on UN agencies, on development research institutes, and on international NGOs, all of whom pass donor government demands down to the organizations they are partnering with in developing countries.

I have briefly sketched some pitfalls of power and knowledge that feminist gender specialists in development organizations must learn to steer clear of, to stay faithful to their transformative cause. However, they cannot escape another, deeper trap, namely that they are strategizing for social transformation from a location in a global institution – international development – that post-development criticism argues sustains inequitable power relations more than it succeeds in changing them (see for example Crush, 1995; Escobar, 1996; Pieterse, 2000). If they cannot avoid this trap, they must learn to turn it to their advantage by using the inequitable power their location gives them. Bourdieu (1985: 731) comments, those with the most power to make change happen are 'on the whole … least inclined to do so'. However, he adds, there is also a minority among those with power who do want to change things. These are the people who feel marginalized because of an identity which places them in a relative position of subjection despite their powerful position in the bigger scheme of things. This experience of relative oppression motivates them to transform the power structures that oppress others much more seriously. Thus, changes to power relations occur through the agency of this minority whose relative institutional powerlessness motivates them to help those with very little power and with whom they perceive they have a common identity of oppression, such as, for example being black or female.[2]

The next section elaborates this argument, namely that feminist gender specialists are motivated by their relative powerlessness to work for social change, taking advantage of their marginal position inside powerful institutions to capitalize on their dual identity as bureaucrats and feminists.

Being a bureaucrat

Feminist officials' potential to support social transformative action depends on them having a feminist commitment and motivation combined with a political ability to operate strategically, both within and beyond the confines of the bureaucratic system. To do this they have to be good bureaucrats. The feminist agenda appears to sit uneasily with the caricature of pen-pushing bureaucrats, content with the status quo, whose only political manoeuvring concerns personal career advancement. However, while 'feminist bureaucrat' sounds like a contradiction in terms, concepts such as 'institutional entrepreneur' and 'tempered radical' – employees who are able to make their organizations think and act differently – are useful in helping us understand how they operate effectively and take advantage of the contradictions in their identity.

Evolving bureaucracies

The ideal bureaucratic form of organization is rational. Decisions are based on objective evidence, and scrutinized by experts working in a hierarchical system where all obey the established procedures (Courpasson and Reed, 2004). The first thing I noticed when I started working 25 years ago at the British aid ministry (now DFID) was its hierarchy, visually established through the organization of space. The size of one's room, the number of windows, the type of furniture, and the presence or absence of carpeting were all signals of status. Clerical staff were crowded into large rooms, while those of higher rank sat isolated, each in their own room, behind closed doors. Today in DFID nearly all staff sit in an open-plan arrangement; only the most senior ones have kept separate offices. Meetings are held in rooms designed and designated for that purpose, rather than, as it used to be, in the office of the most important person attending. In some large international NGOs like Oxfam and ActionAid, even top management no longer have their own offices.

The disappearance of these outward signs of status is part of an evolution from the traditional bureaucratic model into what has been described as 'post-bureaucracy', in which organizations have increasingly fuzzy boundaries with greater mutual interdependence (Hajer and Wagenaar, 2003). There is a new emphasis on entrepreneurial spirit, transformational leadership, and charismatic visioning (Clegg at al., 2006). As a result, it is argued, values such as impartiality, due process, and the strict separation of the public and private domains are under attack (Hogget, 2007). The old hierarchies have to a large extent dissolved and been replaced by networks of power and information, mirrored by other emerging networks of civil society (Castells, 1997). Without fixed status and job purpose, the networked organization – exemplified by organizations like Google – is more dynamic and action-oriented (Mazlish, 2000). Policymaking is no longer contained within the bureaucracy; it is a networked process involving advocacy coalitions and epistemic communities that straddle the divides between politicians, bureaucrats, and non-state actors (Rhoades, 2006). The feminist arguments that classic bureaucracy is an essentially patriarchal form of organization (Alvesson and Thompson, 2005) might point towards post-bureaucracy as more sympathetic to feminist interests, and to the potential for gender mainstreaming to be transformative. In the post-bureaucratic era, policy is no longer the privileged domain of technical experts behind closed doors, but involves a diverse set of actors whose voice is significant in setting agendas rather than just influencing already established policy themes (Walby, 2005).

However, many aspects of classic bureaucracy have remained (Alvesson and Thompson, 2005). Although email and open-plan offices may encourage greater collaboration and more democratic ways of working, the underlying structure of authority, including associated salary differentials, may not have shifted. Joanne Sandler observes that the most powerful means used to keep UNIFEM politically weak was the low grade of its executive director, 'which suppressed all other post levels, so UNIFEM directors in the field were often one or two ranks lower than their counterparts' in other institutions (2013). Moreover, organic systems and flexibility, as opposed to established procedures, can make it harder than in a rules-based bureaucracy to locate where decisions are made and thus more difficult to engage with decision-making processes. Hidden power (Gaventa, 2006) grows as formal power – observable spaces of decision-making – shrinks. Conspiracy theorists might even suspect that post-bureaucracy – with the apparently 'feminine' values of rela-tionships and networking – has been a wily patriarchal response to reduce the impact of the increasing numbers of professional women who have entered the management structures of large organizations.

The reconfiguring of the bureaucratic idiom has coincided with an ideo-logical development in which public sector management is judged as less efficient and effective than private sector management. In many countries, just when the state has started employing proportionately more women in senior positions and introducing more gender-responsive policies and services, its overall reach and authority have shrunk. Takyiwaa Manuh and her co-authors (2013) make this startlingly clear in their analysis of what has happened to Ghanaian public sector bureaucracy following more than 20 years of structural adjustment during which civil servant capacity has eroded. They point out that this dismantling of the civil service coincided with the Ghanaian government signing up to the Nairobi and Beijing confer-ence commitments for gender justice, so that 'its power and capacity to inter-vene directly to bring about social justice was being eroded as power shifted to market forces, donors, and NGOs' (Manuh et al., 2013). At the same time, at least one characteristic of the bureaucratic ideal – evidence-based policy – has strengthened through the quasi-hegemony of the New Public Management regime (Kantola, 2010). NPM's claim, that devolved decision-making leads to the empowerment of those lower down the hierarchical pyramid, is question-able. Top-down authority is reinforced through the increased demands of performance or results-based measurement that NPM imposes (Clegg et al., 2006). Surveillance is framed as 'accountability' and the increase in planning and reporting requirements, accompanied by demands for quantification, all represent a return to the original spirit of modern bureaucracy as formulated by its principal founder, Bentham (Hare, 1981).

In Chapter 8 of this volume (Eyben, 2013), Karin has to design a gender equality plan with 'monitorable indicators and tangible results'. Laura Turquet (2013) struggles to come up with quantifiable 'asks' for policy advocacy because 'women's rights' is 'too fluffy'. Patti O'Neill (O'Neill and Eyben, 2013) decides to use the statistical evidence of how much each donor agency spends on women as a political tool that each agency's gender specialist could use 'to make a real difference to the priority their agency gives to gender'. Evidence-based policy discourse is used ever more frequently to justify investing in women. 'Asked to produce a clear evidence base for strengthening commit-ments to women, we feel inadequate that we could not present the magic piece of evidence that would convince our colleagues. … We fail to realize that no such evidence would do so', warns Joanne Sandler (2013).

The motivation of bureaucrats

Anna Marie Holli (2008: 169) remarks that 'issues concerning women's mutual cooperation, coalition-building and joint activities for achieving their goals seem to have become somewhat passé' in feminist political studies, along with such ideas as 'sisterhood' and 'women's interests'. She argues that despite theoretical post-structuralist advances in feminist scholarship, it would be a mistake however to ignore the empirical importance of cooperative efforts. This same point applies to the feminist bureaucrats in this volume. Their sense of solidarity is a fundamental driver in seeking to make their bureaucracies promote the rights of women who are in very different circumstances from themselves. Feminist gender specialists are committed to improving the condition of women; 'We have a moral duty to occupy these spaces', one said recently to me.

Yet pursuing such a strong political agenda incurs a risk because in many state bureaucracies civil servants are not expected to have a personal motivation. The bureaucratic ideal of 'impartiality' is a discourse that can frame concern for women's rights as special pleading and out of place (Chappell, 2002). On the other hand, the literature on the discretionary power of individuals in bureaucracies demonstrates that, as well as feminists, others too are partial. In the ideal bureaucracy, people lower down the hierarchy obey orders handed down from on high. However, this is not necessarily what happens in real life. Classic studies such as 'Street level bureaucracy' (Lipsky, 1997) look at how frontline workers continuously exercise their discretion in their relationships with citizens and clients of public services. Rational choice theory uses the principal–agent concept to explain how agents – public sector officials – pursue their individual interests, subverting policy intentions determined by the legislature or ministers (the principals). Hence to ensure alignment of agents/actors' interests with those of the organization, positive and negative incentives are introduced to encourage individuals to contribute to the principals' desired outcomes. Behavioural control through incentive structures such as performance-related pay and promotion prospects has become so 'naturalized' that it is almost a hegemonic discourse. One of the 'guiding principles' of the World Bank's action plan, *Gender Equality as Smart Economics* (World Bank, 2006: 3), is 'incentives rather than mandates and obligations'. In Chapter 8 of this volume (Eyben, 2013), 'Claudia' explains how she helped introduce an incentives scheme, as part of her organization's gender equality action plan, by offering bonuses to senior staff to encourage them to implement the plan.

Other organizations use different means. Smyth (2013) writes that she was struck by the contrast between Oxfam and the ADB. The latter is more of a traditional bureaucracy that controls staff behaviour through standard operating procedures. Staff are meant to follow detailed instructions for incorporating gender issues in ADB's projects and programmes. Oxfam, a more informal and less hierarchical organization, has largely relied on winning over staff 'hearts and minds' in favour of gender equality. However, because it is an organization in which systematic application of established procedures is still relatively weak, 'gender requirements can be ignored without much fear of sanction' (Smyth, 2013). Smyth notes ruefully that although most ADB staff are largely indifferent to gender issues, the organization does actually apply its gender equality policy systematically – something that Oxfam is still struggling to do.

Oxfam started up as a small group of committed volunteers and its continuing dependence on 'hearts and minds', and its culture and ethos, remain influenced by its organizational history, despite it having become a large bureaucracy. Nevertheless, it demonstrates that not all organizations subscribe to a view of bureaucrats as self-interested individuals, who have to be controlled either through orders from the top or through incentives. Moreover, some scholars of bureaucracy have viewed bureaucrats as people with a moral commitment to ensuring that the state delivers on its respon-sibilities (Du Gay, 2000). Skocpol (1997) provides historical examples from around the world in which state officials are portrayed as autonomous actors pursuing ideological goals and transformative strategies even in the face of indifference or resistance from their own political masters or the wider society (Skocpol, 1997). So, are bureaucrats 'knaves' to be managed through incen-tives, or 'knights' managed through their own self-motivation to work for the public good? (Le Grand, 2003). As we have seen, the balance between the two varies from one organizational culture to another, but feminist bureaucrats – 'knights' almost by definition – are surprised when they find they have to work with colleagues who are 'knaves'.

Change comes from the margins

Sandler (2013) argues that feminist bureaucrats' psychological state is shaped by the patriarchal institutional cultures in which they work. Many are in a state of denial about institutional sexism and blame the lack of change on their own personal inadequacies – and feel guilty for these. 'It's not that gender mainstreaming has failed, but that we have failed gender mainstreaming' was the comment that I heard at a meeting of the Development Assistance Committee (DAC) GENDERNET (O'Neill and Eyben, 2013). Nevertheless, Sandler suggests that some feminist bureaucrats achieve a stage when they leave denial and guilt far behind and are empowered. 'Empowerment', she once said to me, 'is more than just about power. It is about using power with vision, integrity, and inclusiveness'. Feminist bureaucrats are effective when able to analyse their severe operational constraints and combine this analysis with a willingness to use power.

Several contributors to this volume emphasize that when feminists find themselves in potentially oppressive, patriarchal institutions, the neces-sity of regular and careful political analysis is essential. Aruna Rao and her colleagues encouraged UN gender specialists to make organizational maps of power. By observing where decisions were made, 'they learnt that power was not located in just one place', but 'circulates and is exercised rather than held, and that power exercised to dominate or exclude needs to be effectively countered, and structures and practices built to allow "transgressions" (Rao, 2013). Equipped with their regularly updated power analyses, how do feminist bureaucrats engage with the bureaucracy? A pair of actor-oriented concepts is useful in answering this question. These are 'institutional entrepreneur' and 'tempered radical'.

'Institutional entrepreneur', a concept borrowed from organizational studies, can be used to throw light on the interplay between structure and agency, through paying attention to the institutional values, norms, discourses, and practices that shape bureaucratic action (Garud et al., 2007). Institutional entrepreneurs are working for change from a location within the institution. They develop and transform what is available to them. 'I looked at the core areas of the DAC work – peer reviews, statistics, aid effectiveness', says Patti O'Neill, 'and thought really long and hard about what we could do with these' (O'Neill and Eyben, 2013). Feminist bureaucrats take advantage of existing rules, procedures, and discourses to make new wine in old bottles, in the hope of eventually throwing the old bottles away. This does not always work. Sometimes the new wine loses its originality and begins to taste much like the old. 'Old ways of doing things stick and settle down, deeply sedimented, in both consciousness and organization, irretrievably there' (Clegg et al., 2006: 323). How to prevent this happening to UN Women is Joanne Sandler's preoccupation in Chapter 10 (Sandler, 2013).

The notion of institutional entrepreneur is useful because it broadens our perspective from the organization to the wider institutional context in which the organization is situated. Feminist bureaucrats recognize they cannot change their own organizations without tackling this wider context, and thus reach out beyond their employers to engage more widely in the development sector. Hence, a strong theme in this volume is the building of inter-organizational alliances between different development bureaucracies. For example, Holzner (2013) describes how she organized agreement within the EU on a controversial policy text concerning women in armed conflict – one in which she sought to change the discourse from 'women as mothers' to 'women as actors'. A phone call to a colleague in Sweden started a snowballing process, by which Holzner was able to get in touch with a succession of other like-minded bureaucrats scattered across EU member countries, eventually influencing the EU itself.

Arguably, a gender specialist's capacity to change things depends on two factors (Grindle and Thomas, 1991: 187). The first is the institutional environment (as well as the actor's quality of analysis of that environment), including the person's own character and resources; the second is the character of the policy issue itself. Grindle and Thomas propose that 'systematic thinking about the interrelationships and consequences of context, circumstance and policy characteristics therefore provides both an analytic tool ... and a first cut at developing strategies ... for change'. This is a helpful framework for feminist bureaucrats, enabling them to identify what is realistically possible and encouraging them to become self-aware in practice (Clay and Schaffer, 1984). Here the notion of 'tempered radical' (Meyerson, 2001) proves useful. Whereas institutional entrepreneurs are expected to 'institutionalize the alternative rules, practices or logics they are championing' (Garud et al., 2007: 962), tempered radicals appear more modest in their ambitions. Tempered radicals, explains Meyerson, learn to rock the boat without ever falling out of it. They achieve change through a succession of small wins. Small wins, rather than big, may be all that is possible in relation to a feminist bureaucrat's agenda, bearing in mind that their agenda of societal transformation is profoundly radical. However, accumulatively, small wins may make a big difference:

> A small win is a concrete, complete, implemented outcome of moderate importance. By itself, one small win may seem unimportant. A series of wins at small but significant tasks, however, reveals a pattern that may attract allies, deter opponents, and lower resistance to subsequent proposals. Small wins are controllable opportunities that produce visible results. (Weick, 1984: 43)

In their classic essay on being effective in a bureaucracy, Clay and Schaffer (1984: 192) stress, 'All is to be questioned. Nothing is to be taken for granted. Nothing is innocuous'. Both 'tempered radicals' and 'institutional entrepreneurs' must be successful in avoiding being so institutionalized that they stop questioning how the world works, thus making it impossible to imagine alternatives. Undoubtedly, as has been the case with this book's contributors, moving around from one location to another helps. Seeking out and being comfortable with marginality is important. It can also be cultivated, not just through a deliberate change in one's institutional location – as was the case for Ines Smyth (2013) – but also through reflective practice, as with the action research project on which this book is based. Not succumbing to the taken-for-granted is a key element of reflective practice. Based on theories of transformative learning, it requires the individual to enquire into her assumptions concerning why and how she understands the world in a certain way. Conscious and sustained reflective practice helps feminist bureaucrats to tolerate their marginal position and not to worry whether they fit. I have focused so far on how they respond to the challenges and opportunities from their role as insiders – that is, as bureaucrats. But when we think of feminist bureaucrats as 'institutional entrepreneurs' we must be careful to avoid thinking of them as lone champions (Clegg, 2010), to the neglect of looking at the social movement from which they have sprung, and which provides their motivation and shapes their agency. In that light, I now look at how they manage their role as feminists engaging with the bureaucracy, crafting their most important political strategy of building relations with feminist movements and networks.

Feminist engagement with bureaucracy

There are multiple and contested understandings of feminism. Rather than discuss these in any detail, I shall follow Mazur (2002) in understanding feminism as being firstly, solidarity with other women, while recognizing and responding to the enormous diversity among women along lines of class, ethnicity, religious belief, etc.; secondly, a commitment to advancing women's rights; and thirdly, changing the patriarchal institutions that keep women subordinated. To these I would add two more elements: that feminism is about social transformation that liberates men as well as women from gendered norms, and that it involves collective action informed by values of horizontal and democratic modes of organizing.

Because bureaucratic disinterestedness does not privilege certain individuals or points of view, it can be seen as admirable (Courpasson and Reed, 2004; Du Gay, 2000). However, for many feminists the hierarchical power of a bureaucracy has 'a tremendous capacity to hurt people, to manipulate, twist and damage human possibility' (Ferguson, 1984: xii). Ferguson contrasts bureaucracy, which sees people as objects to be manipulated, with egalitarian structures, which permit individual autonomy and self-development. But, argues Riger (1994: 288), 'implying that bureaucracy is masculine and dominating, while collectivity is feminine and humanizing, stereotypes not only gender but also organizational structures ... Indeed, the accountability permitted by bureaucracy can provide a check on abuses of power that may not be possible in a non-bureaucratic organization'.

In terms of its functions, a bureaucracy can be seen as sustaining the values and power relations of the wider society of which the bureaucracy is a part, and thus as an accessory to institutionalized racism or gender discrimination, albeit in a non-emotional and objective fashion (Bauman, 1989). State bureaucracies, it is argued, reflect and reproduce wider societal patterns of the systemic subordination of women. As the institutional arm of male dominance, the bureaucratic form of organization is by its very nature oppressive to women (Calas and Smircich, 1999; Ashcraft, 2006). Thus, it is pointless to seek to influence laws and policies within existing state structures, because 'the master's tools will never dismantle the master's house' (Lorde, 1997: 112). There is however a contrary view, specifically in relation to development institutions, that 'engagement in the master's house is one among many valid political strategies in contemporary development enterprises' (Staudt, 2002: 57, cited in Bedford, 2007a: 104). This view is shared by Patti O'Neill, who is not worried if the master's house cannot be dismantled, provided it can be sufficiently altered through renovation, with rooms added on, and the view improved (O'Neill and Eyben, 2013).

O'Neill is reflecting a more optimistic view of bureaucracies as sites of contest in which change occurs through the construction of new meanings and ways of seeing the world. From this 'tempered radical' perspective, policy advocacy for women from within the bureaucratic machinery becomes a possibility (Stetson and Mazur, 1995; Outshoorn and Kantola, 2007). In certain circumstances and conditions, strategic alliances between feminist politicians, bureaucrats, and activists can get state bureaucracies to effectively implement pro-feminist policies – a view that gave birth to the notion of 'femocrat' (Sawer, 1990). This introduces a more actor-orientated approach to the institutionalization of feminism within the bureaucracy, analysing the feminist staff responsible for taking forward this agenda, their strategies, and the challenges facing them. Yet, in the present volume, only Francesca Pobee-Hayford, previously a senior official in Ghana's Ministry of Women's and Children's Affairs, is 'a self-described femocrat' (Manuh et al., 2013). The other contributors dislike the term, possibly because it is used pejoratively by feminists outside the bureaucratic machinery, who see those on the inside as 'selling out the women's movement and profiting from women's disadvantage' (Chappell, 2002: 86). This challenge of insider–outsider relationships and communication about what feminist bureaucrats can achieve crops up in almost every chapter of this book, indicating its importance for feminist bureaucrats in the strategic exploitation of their marginal location.

Insider–outsider relationships

From her experience of influencing government policy from outside the state machinery, Laura Turquet (2013) argues strongly for a networked approach in which bureaucrats on the inside and campaigners on the outside mutually recognize and respect each other's positionality. Francesca Pobee-Hayford comments on the failure of her ministry to engage with women's organizations, and to create alliances with them, to influence other parts of the state bureaucracy (Manuh et al., 2013). For Patti O'Neill, alliances beyond the bureaucracy are 'one of the most powerful things we can do' (O'Neill and Eyben, 2013), although they require mutual trust and the relationships may not be easy ones. Very practically, if such inside–outside strategies are to be pursued, all those involved need to recognize that large organizations are not monolithic, and within them champions, even soulmates, may be found. Advantage can be taken of cracks or contradictions in organizational identity. The World Bank, for example, is both a bank and an international development agency, leaving space for pockets of resistance in which alternative policy models can be developed to challenge the dominant neo-liberal paradigm (Goetz, 2003). Unfortunately, such internal contradictions may also work against a feminist bureaucrat's agenda. She may secure the support of top management, and get women's rights into speeches and policy documents, but still encounter passive resistance from colleagues (Rao, 2013).

The majority of this book's contributors have, over time, moved from one marginal location to another in the development world. For example, Laura Turquet and Ines Smyth moved from international NGOs to very different kinds of multilateral agencies; Patti O'Neill from national machinery to a bilateral aid agency and then to a global policy organization; Joanne

Sandler from a women's rights organization to the UN machinery; and Brigitte Holzner from academia to a bilateral aid agency. In her 'velvet triangle' analysis of gender policy processes in EU institutions, Woodward (2003) discovers a similar pattern of femocrats, academics/consultants, and those from organized women's movements changing places. She argues that it is the personal, informal networks resulting from this process – combined with strong linkages within the institutional machinery – that have made gender mainstreaming successful within the EU, and which the experience of the feminist bureaucrats in the present volume confirms. The more marginalized they find themselves in terms of power and resources, Woodward argues, the more they must rely on informal networking. Social movements, suggests Clegg (1989), are successful when they mobilize their resources through networks and alliances and manage to communicate with each other effectively. However, such alliance-building is not easy to achieve. Rao (2013) looks at how feminist bureaucrats can learn to balance investing in relationships on the inside with those on the outside, and discuss how their commitment to collaborative ways of working with those outside the organization can be frustrated by their organizational identity, and the need to be loyal to that identity, on which their internal credibility depends.

Contacts with former colleagues are not lost, but fluid relations are not always easy. Some of the distrust between those on the inside and those on the outside may be due to misperceptions. Like chameleons, feminists who become bureaucrats have to change how they look and behave. Even what you wear – 'a jacket with big shoulder pads and a pair of high heels' – helps you get into role (O'Neill and Eyben, 2013). In analysing the success of Swedish state feminism, Kabeer (2007) observes that feminist activists working inside the state machinery operated with apparent pragmatism and careful lack of passion – like any typical bureaucrat. Insiders are possibly even being quiet about their feminism (Chappell, 2002). Yet although they have become 'mandarins', in their heart they remain 'missionaries' (Miller and Razavi, 1998). Nevertheless, even if those on the outside realize that feminist bureaucrats are wearing camouflage, they still might not want to engage if they view them as liberal feminists who have failed 'to contest neo-colonialism and capitalism' (Bedford, 2007b: 293).

Thus if 'development' is seen as the handmaiden of neo-colonialism and capitalism, a feminist bureaucrat's self-identification as an activist may be contentious for those whose activism is at the grassroots, or in Southern civil society, and who are deeply suspicious of the development paradigm. Laura Turquet (2013) was surprised to discover that, because she worked for a big international NGO, she was viewed not as part of the global women's movement, but as a 'donor'. Ines Smyth (2013) notes how feminist organizations have been reluctant to engage with the ADB, whose ideology and practices they judge to be damaging to women. By claiming an activist identity, feminists in development bureaucracies may be presuming an unwelcome solidarity between North and South, between privileged and marginalized – a supposed sisterhood that is problematic and possibly even oppressive when, with the best of intentions, their resources and access to policy spaces squeeze out other perspectives and voices (Kantola and Squires, 2008).

The controversy about whether feminists are irretrievably compromised by working for the development machine mirrors the debate between those who see bureaucrats as located across an unbridgeable divide between the state and society, and those who appreciate the political strength of overlapping networks cutting across formal, organizational state–society boundaries. Banaszak (2005) takes the latter stance, arguing that the number and location of activists within the state significantly shapes feminist movements' strategies and achievements. According to Beckwith (2007), such an effect is only likely to occur when liberal feminist movements, rather than more radical feminist movements, strategically collaborate with insiders. At the same time, however, while a liberal feminist movement

> might employ a state-involved/insider strategy to pressure the state for improved access to women's healthcare, a radical or socialist component of the larger movement might employ an outsider/state-involved strategy, targeting members of parliament to produce new legislation, employing mass demonstrations and other disruptive tactics. Furthermore, different components of a women's movement may coordinate their different strategies in the same movement campaign, engaging the same target but employing different strategies and tactics for achieving the same end. (Beckwith, 2007)

Feminist gender specialists can take advantage of the radicalism of other parts of the movement, without necessarily having to risk their insider status by entering in direct contact with them. The overall challenge is to seek support from feminists outside the bureaucracy and to engineer this in a manner that works 'with the grain' of the organization employing them (Eyben, 2013). This means understanding its politics, cultures, and ethos – as the contributors to this book do.

Notes

1   See   <www.dfid.gov.uk/About-DFID/Finance-and-performance/DFID-Business-plan-2011---2015/>.
2   Although, those with whom they are sympathizing may very well reject any notion of shared oppression based on a perception of common identity – a point well made in Mohanty's classic piece (1988).

References

Alvesson, M. and P. Thompson (2005) 'Post-bureaucracy?', in S. Ackroyd, R. Batt, P. Thompson and P. S. Tolbert (eds), *Oxford Handbook of Work and Organization Studies,* Oxford: Oxford University Press.

Ashcraft, K. (2006) 'Feminist-bureaucratic control and other adversarial allies: Extending organized dissonance to the practice of "new" forms', *Communication Monographs,* 73: 55–86 <http://dx.doi.org/10.1080%2F0363 7750600557081>.

Banaszak, L. (2005) 'Inside and outside the state: Movement, insider status, tactics and public policy achievement', in D. Meyer, V. Jennes, and H. Ingram (eds), *Routing the Opposition: Social Movements, Public Policy, and Democracy,* Minneapolis: University of Minnesota Press.

Bauman, Z. (1989) *Modernity and the Holocaust,* Cambridge: Polity Press.

Beckwith, K. (2007) 'Mapping strategic engagements: Women's movements and the state', *International Feminist Journal of Politics,* 9: 312–38 <http://dx.doi.org/10.1080%2F14616740701438218>.

Bedford, K. (2007a) 'Governing intimacy in the World Bank', in S. Rai and G. Waylen (eds), *Global Governance: Feminist Perspectives,* Basingstoke: Palgrave Macmillan.

Bedford, K. (2007b) 'The imperative of male inclusion: How institutional context influences World Bank gender policy', *International Feminist Journal of Politics,* 9: 289–311 <http://dx.doi.org/10.1080%2F14616740701438200>.

Bendix, R. R. (1959) *Max Weber,* London: University Paperbacks, Methuen.

Bourdieu, P. (1985) 'The social space and the genesis of social groups', *Theory and Society,* 14: 723–44 <http://dx.doi.org/10.1007%2FBF00174048>.

Calas, M. and L. Smircich (1999) 'From the woman's point of view: Feminist approaches to organization studies', in S. Clegg and C. Hardy (eds), *Studying Organization, Theory and Method,* London: Sage.

Castells, M. (1997) *The Power of Identity,* Oxford: Blackwell.

Chappell, L. (2002) *Gendering Government,* Vancouver: UBC Press.

Clay, E. and B. Schaffer (1984) *Room for Manoeuvre: An Exploration of Public Policy Planning in Agricultural and Rural Development,* London: Heinemann.

Clegg, S. (1989) *Frameworks of Power,* London: Sage.

Clegg, S. (2010) 'The state, power, and agency: Missing in action in institutional theory?' *Journal of Management Inquiry,* 19, 1: 4–13 <http://dx.doi.org/10.1 177%2F1056492609347562>.

Clegg, S., D. Courpasson, and N. Phillips (2006) *Power and Organizations,* Los Angeles: Sage.

Cornwall, A., E. Harrison and A. Whitehead (2007) 'Gender myths and feminist fables: The struggle for interpretive power in gender and development', *Development and Change,* 38: 1–20 <http://dx.doi.org/10.11 11%2Fj.1467-7660.2007.00400.x>.

Courpasson, D. and M. Reed (2004) 'Introduction: Bureaucracy in the age of enterprise', *Organization,* 11: 5–12 <http://dx.doi.org/10.117 7%2F1350508404039656>.

Craig, D. and D. Porter (2006) *Development Beyond Neoliberalism?,* London: Routledge.

Crewe, E. and Fernando, P. (2006) 'The elephant in the room: Racism in representations, relationships, and rituals', *Progress in Development Studies,* 6: 40–54.

Crush, J. (1995) *Power of Development,* London: Routledge.

Du Gay, P. (2000) *In Praise of Bureaucracy: Weber, Organization, Ethics,* London: Sage.

Edwards, M. (2008) *Just another Emperor? The Myths and Realities of Philanthrocapitalism,* New York: Demos.

Escobar, A. (1996) *Encountering Development: The Making and Unmaking of the Third World,* Princeton: Princeton University Press.

Eyben, R. (2006) *Relationships for Aid,* London: Earthscan.

Eyben, R. (2007) 'Gender myths in the British Aid Programme', in A. Cornwall, E. Harrison and A. Whitehead (eds) *Feminisms and Development: Contradictions, Contestations and Challenges,* London: Zed Press.

Eyben, R. (2011) 'What is happening to donor support for women's rights?' *Contestations* 4, <www.contestations.net/issues/issue-4/what-is-happening-to-donor-support-for-women's-rights/>.

Eyben, R. (2013) 'Finding our organizational way', in R. Eyben and L. Turquet (eds), *Feminists in Development Organizations: Change from the Margins,* pp. 117–26, Rugby, UK: Practical Action Publishing.

Eyben, R. (forthcoming) 'Promoting gender equality in the changing global landscape of international development cooperation' in A. Coles, L. Grey and J. Momsen (eds) *A Gender and Development Handbook,* London: Routledge.

Eyben, R. and Turquet, L. (eds) (2013) *Feminists in Development Organizations: Change from the Margins,* Rugby, UK: Practical Action Publishing.

Ferguson, K. (1984) *The Feminist Case against Bureaucracy,* Philadelphia: Temple University Press.

Fraser, A. (2004) 'Preface', in A. Fraser and I. Tinker (eds), *Developing Power: How Women Transformed International Development,* New York: Feminist Press.

Garud, R., C. Hardy, and S. Maguire (2007) 'Institutional entrepreneurship as embedded agency: An introduction to the special issue', *Organization Studies,* 28: 957–69 <http://dx.doi.org/10.1177%2F0170840607078958>.

Gaventa, J. (2006) 'Finding the spaces for change: A power analysis', *IDS Bulletin,* 37: 23–33 <http://dx.doi.org/10.1111/j.1759-5436.2006.tb00320.x>.

Goetz, A. M. (1992) 'Gender and administration', *IDS Bulletin,* 23: 6–17 <http://dx.doi.org/10.1111%2Fj.1759-5436.1992.mp23004002.x>.

Goetz, A. M. (2003) 'The World Bank and women's movements', in R. O'Brien (ed.), *Contesting Global Governance: Multilateral Economic Institutions and Global Social Movements,* Cambridge: Cambridge University Press.

Grillo, R. D. (1997) 'Discourses of Development: The view from anthropology', in R. D. Grillo and R. L. Stirrat (eds), *Discourses of Development, Anthropological Perspectives,* Oxford: Berg.

Grindle, M. and J. Thomas (1991) *Public Choices and Policy Change,* Baltimore: Johns Hopkins University Press.

Hajer, M. and H. Wagenaar (2003) 'Introduction' in M. Hajer and H. Wagenaar (eds), *Deliberative Policy Analysis, Understanding Governance in the Network Society,* Cambridge: Cambridge University Press.

Hanson, C. (2007) 'Canadian gender-based analysis training in South Africa', *International Feminist Journal of Politics,* 9: 198–217 <http://dx.doi.org/10.1080%2F14616740701259853>.

Hare, L. (1981) *Bentham and Bureaucracy*, Cambridge: Cambridge University Press.

Hart, G. (2001) 'Development critiques in the 1990s: Cul-de-sacs and promising paths', *Progress in Human Geography*, 25: 649–58 <http://dx.doi.org/10.11 91/030913201682689002>.

Hogget, P. (2007) 'A service to the public: The containment of ethical and moral conflicts by public bureaucracies', in P. Du Gay (ed.) *The Values of Bureaucracy*, Oxford: Oxford University Press.

Holli, A.-M. (2008) 'Feminist triangles: A conceptual analysis', *Representation*, 44: 169–85 <http://dx.doi.org/10.1080%2F00344890802080407>.

Holzner, B. (2013) '"It's just a text – who cares?" Construction of texts in the context of EU policies', in R. Eyben and L. Turquet (eds), *Feminists in Development Organizations: Change from the Margins*, pp. 67–84, Rugby, UK: Practical Action Publishing.

Jain, D. (2005) *Women, Development and the UN*, Bloomington: Indiana University Press.

Joachim, J. (2003) 'Framing issues and seizing opportunities: The UN, NGOs and women's rights', *International Studies Quarterly*, 47: 247–74 <http://dx.doi.org/10.1111%2F1468-2478.4702005>.

Kabeer, N. (2007) 'Passion, pragmatism, and the politics of advocacy: The Nordic experience through a "gender and development" lens', in E. Magnus, N. Kabeer and A. Stark (eds), *Global Perspectives on Gender Equality: Reversing the Gaze*, London: Routledge.

Kantola, J. (2010) 'Shifting institutional and ideational terrains: The impact of Europeanization and neoliberalism on women's policy agencies', *Policy & Politics*, 383: 353–68 <http://dx.doi.org/10.1332/030557310X521053>.

Kantola, J. and J. Squires (2008) 'From state feminism to market feminism?', paper presented at the International Studies Association Annual Convention, San Francisco, 26–29 March.

Kothari, U. (2006) 'Critiquing "race" and racism in development discourse and practice', *Progress in Development Studies*, 6: 1–7 <http://dx.doi.org/10.1191/1464993406ps123ed>.

Kothari, U., and M. Minogue (eds) (2002) *Development Theory and Practice: Critical Perspectives*, Basingstoke: Palgrave.

Le Grand, J. (2003) *Motivation, Agency, and Public Policy: Of Knights and Knaves, Pawns and Queens*, Oxford: Oxford University Press.

Lipsky, M. (1997) 'Street level bureaucracy, an introduction', in M. Hill (ed.), *A Policy Reader*, London: Prentice Hall.

Lorde, A. (1997) 'Age, race, sex and class: Women redefining difference', in A. McClintock, A. Mufti, E. Shohat (eds), *Dangerous Liaisons: Gender, Nation, and Postcolonial Perspectives*, Minneapolis: University of Minnesota.

Manuh, T., N.A. Anyidoho and F. Pobee-Hayford (2013) '"A femocrat just doing my job": working within the state to advance women's empowerment in Ghana', in R. Eyben and L. Turquet (eds), *Feminists in Development Organizations: Change from the Margins*, pp. 37–54, Rugby, UK: Practical Action Publishing.

Mawdsley, E. (2011) 'The changing geographies of foreign aid and development cooperation: Contributions from gift theory', *Transactions of the Institute of British Geographers*, 37: 256–72 <http://dx.doi.org/10.111 1%2Fj.1475-5661.2011.00467.x>.

Mazlish, B. (2000) 'Invisible ties: From patronage to networks', *Theory, Culture and Society*, 17: 1–19 <http://dx.doi.org/10.1177%2F02632760022051086>.

Mazur, A. (2002) *Theorizing Feminist Policy*, Oxford: Oxford University Press.

Mercer, C. (2002) 'NGOs, civil society and democratisation: A critical review of the literature', *Progress in Development Studies*, 2: 5–22 <http://dx.doi.org/10.1191%2F1464993402ps027ra>.

Meyerson, D. (2001) *Tempered Radicals*, Harvard: Harvard Business Publishing.

Miller, C. and S. Razavi (1995) 'From WID to GAD: Conceptual shifts in the women and development discourse', Occasional Paper 1, Geneva: UNRISD.

Miller, C. and S. Razavi (1998) *Missionaries and Mandarins: Feminist Engagement with Development Institutions*, Rugby, UK: Practical Action Publishing.

Mohanty, C. (1988) 'Under Western eyes', *Feminist Review*, 30: 61–88 <http://dx.doi.org/10.2307%2F1395054>.

Moncrieffe, J. and R. Eyben (eds) (2007) *The Power of Labelling in Development*, London: Earthscan.

Mosse, D. (2011) 'Introduction: The anthropology of expertise and professionals in international development', in D. Mosse (ed.), *Adventures in Aidland*, Oxford: Berghahn Books.

Nazneen, S. and M. Sultan (2011) 'Mobilising for women's rights and the role of resources: Synthesis Report Bangladesh', Brighton and Dhaka: Pathways of Women's Empowerment and BRAC Development Institute <www.dfid.gov.uk/r4d/Output/189221/Default.aspx>.

O'Neill, P. and R. Eyben (2013) '"It's fundamentally political": renovating the master's house', in R. Eyben and L. Turquet (eds), *Feminists in Development Organizations: Change from the Margins*, pp. 85–100, Rugby, UK: Practical Action Publishing.

Outshoorn, J. and J. Kantola (2007) *Changing State Feminism*, Basingstoke: Palgrave Macmillan.

Pieterse. J. (2000) 'After post-development', *Third World Quarterly*, 21: 175–91 <http://dx.doi.org/10.1080%2F01436590050004300>.

Rao, A. (2013) 'Feminist activism in development bureaucracies: shifting strategies and unpredictable results', in R. Eyben and L. Turquet (eds), *Feminists in Development Organizations: Change from the Margins*, pp. 177–92, Rugby, UK: Practical Action Publishing.

Rao, A. and D. Kelleher (1995) 'Engendering organizational change: The BRAC case', *IDS Bulletin*, 26: 69–78 <http://dx.doi.org/10.1111%2Fj.1759-5436.1995.mp26003008.x>.

Rhoades, R. (2006) 'Policy network analysis' in M. Moran, M. Rein, and R. E. Goodin (eds), *The Oxford Handbook of Public Policy*, Oxford: Oxford University Press.

Riger, S. (1994) 'Challenges of success: Stages of growth in feminist organizations', *Feminist Studies*, 20: 275–300 <http://dx.doi.org/10.2307%2F3178153>.

Rist, G. (2002) *The History of Development: From Western Origins to Global Faith*, London: Zed Books.

Sandler, J. (2013) 'Re-gendering the United Nations: old challenges and new opportunities', in R. Eyben and L. Turquet (eds), *Feminists in Development Organizations: Change from the Margins*, pp. 145–64, Rugby, UK: Practical Action Publishing.

Sawer, M. (1990) *Sisters in Suits: Women and Public Policy in Australia*, Sydney: Allen & Unwin.

Six, C. (2009) 'The rise of postcolonial states as donors: A challenge to the development paradigm?', *Third World Quarterly*, 30: 1103–21 <http://dx.doi.org/10.1080%2F01436590903037366>.

Skocpol, T. (1997) 'Bringing the state back in', in M. Hill (ed.) *A Policy Reader*, London: Prentice Hall.

Smyth, I. (2013) 'Values and systems: gender equality work in different organizational settings', in R. Eyben and L. Turquet (eds), *Feminists in Development Organizations: Change from the Margins*, pp. 127–44, Rugby, UK: Practical Action Publishing.

Staudt, K. (2002) 'Dismantling the master's house with the master's tools? Gender work in and with powerful bureaucracies', in K. Saunders (ed.), *Feminist Post-Development Thought: Rethinking Modernity, Post-Colonialism and Representation*, London: Zed Press.

Stetson, D. and A. Mazur (eds) (1995) *Comparative State Feminism*, Thousand Oaks, CA: Sage Publications.

Turquet, L. (2013) 'Who is the better feminist? Negotiating the middle ground', in R. Eyben and L. Turquet (eds), *Feminists in Development Organizations: Change from the Margins*, pp. 101–16, Rugby, UK: Practical Action Publishing.

Walby, S. (2005) 'Gender mainstreaming: productive tensions in theory and practice', *Social Politics*, 12: 321–43 <http://dx.doi.org/10.1093/sp/jxi018>.

Weick, K. (1984) 'Small wins: Redefining the scale of social problems', *American Psychologist*, 39: 40–9 <http://dx.doi.org/10.1037%2F0003-066X.39.1.40>.

Woodward, A. (2003) 'Building velvet triangles: Gender and informal governance', in T. Christiansen and S. Piattani (eds), *Informal Governance in the EU*, Cheltenham: Edward Elgar.

World Bank (2006) 'Gender equality as smart economics: A World Bank Group gender action plan', Washington DC: World Bank.

About the author

Rosalind Eyben is a Professorial Research Fellow at the Institute of Development Studies, University of Sussex. She is a social anthropologist with a professional background in development policy and practice, and a committed teacher in the IDS doctoral and master's programmes, including on gender and development. She has designed and facilitated numerous workshops for international development practitioners all over the world. Her research interests focus on power and relations in international aid. From 2006–11 she convened the global policy programme of the International Research Consortium on Pathways of Women's Empowerment and is currently developing a new area of work exploring the knowledge/power practices of donors that sustain the invisibility of unpaid care as a development policy issue. In 2010 she launched the Big Push Forward that has created an international network challenging the current audit culture in development. She was awarded a CBE in 2000 and is a board member of UNRISD and ActionAid UK.

CHAPTER 3

'A femocrat just doing my job': working within the state to advance women's empowerment in Ghana

Takyiwaa Manuh and Nana Akua Anyidoho
with Francesca Pobee-Hayford

Following the round of UN Conferences on Women from the 1970s to the 1990s, many states in the developing world established national machineries to first 'integrate women into development', and later to spearhead the task of gender mainstreaming adopted in the Beijing Platform for Action. Analyses of these national machineries in different African countries suggest their effectiveness is constrained by, among other things, inadequate conceptualizations of mandates and functions and inadequate resources, including personnel. In this chapter, we analyse Ghana's Ministry of Women and Children's Affairs (MOWAC) to understand how gender issues have been conceptualized and treated institutionally. To anchor our analysis, we include reflections by a former senior bureaucrat within the ministry, to understand the challenges and possibilities of working to advance gender equity within the Ghanaian state.

We [Takyiwaa and Nana Akua] met Francesca while working on a research study on 'policy discourses around women's empowerment' as part of the Pathways of Women's Empowerment research programme. For that study, we were interested in the main institutional policy actors in Ghana, in respect of women's empowerment. As the Ministry of Women and Children's Affairs (MOWAC) is the lead policymaking agency on this issue, we had a series of interviews with a number of ministry staff, including Francesca who was at the time the director of the Department of Women of MOWAC. Out of that engagement came the idea to co-author this chapter on what it means to be a 'femocrat' in the state bureaucracy, from both insider and outsider perspectives. The chapter is based on primary data (including interviews with MOWAC staff, staff from other ministries, and donors; observation of MOWAC meetings; and document analyses – all between 2008 and 2010) and on Francesca's experiences and insights working within MOWAC from 2002.

This chapter discusses the possibilities for and challenges in influencing the government and its agencies in the direction of gender equality and women's empowerment. Through Francesca's reflections on her time at

http://dx.doi.org/10.3362/9781780448046.003

MOWAC, we explore the institutional structures that exist to promote gender equality within the Ghanaian state; the understandings within the bureaucracy of what serves to promote women's empowerment and gender equality; the skills and knowledge base required of bureaucrats mandated to promote women's empowerment and gender equality; the room for manoeuvre for self-described feminist policy actors; the extent to which their actions support or contradict the work of the broader women's movement in Ghana; and, finally, the possibilities for alliances between femocrats and activists outside of the state, towards the goal of women's empowerment.

Becoming a femocrat

Francesca Pobee-Hayford began her working career in the government bureaucracy in 1990. With a bachelor's degree in planning, she took up a position in the Ministry of Health as a planning officer. During her tenure at the ministry, she completed a master's programme in population studies. Her return to work coincided with the decision by the government to adopt the Affirmative Action Policy Guideline, through which it committed to appoint 40 per cent representation of women into positions of public decision-making. Through a directive, the government also introduced the concept of gender desk officers (GDOs) who were expected to be part of senior management positions and to influence policymaking on gender mainstreaming and gender equity. Francesca was appointed GDO at the Ministry of Health. As she recalls, she got the job because she had taken a course in gender and development during her master's programme, and was thus perceived by her boss to have enough knowledge and interest for the position, even though she was not in senior management. Indeed, the majority of GDOs who were appointed in the wider bureaucracy had been in junior positions, which suggests the low importance that the various ministries attached to these positions. However, the Ministry of Health funded a short course for Francesca in gender and health at Manchester University, and this training marked the beginning of her journey to becoming a self-described 'femocrat'. As she states:

> The training deepened my understanding of feminism as it exposed me to feminist literature. Thus I would describe myself as a 'femocrat'; that is, a feminist working within a bureaucracy or working with the state. I am a feminist because, through my studies, I began to appreciate and acquire values of working towards the achievement of women's rights, gender equality, social justice, and transformation. This emboldened me further to speak up for gender equality, to stand up for my beliefs, and be passionate about them. However, even before becoming a femocrat, as a civil servant/bureaucrat I would say that I considered myself an outsider, in the sense that I didn't really conform to the norms of the civil service. I was a person who spoke up for what I believed in. Right from the start

of my working life I found myself championing causes, and acting as a spokesperson on behalf of my peers, when issues arose that required taking up with senior management for action to be taken.

Having taken up this new cause of gender equality, Francesca's goal was to influence the Ministry of Health to be more gender responsive, in terms of both the content of their programmes and the structure of the ministry, particularly in regard to women's career progression in a male-dominated government bureaucracy. By the end of her tenure in the ministry, among other achievements, she had completed a draft of a Health Sector Gender Policy (completed in 2002 it was eventually launched in 2009, long after Francesca had left the ministry).

In 2002, Francesca applied for the position of gender adviser, funded by the Danish International Development Agency (DANIDA), on a programme to build the capacity of staff in the newly established MOWAC. After that contract ended in 2004, MOWAC made a request to the Ministry of Health for Francesca to be seconded to its Department of Women (DOW) as acting director.

An investigation of the nature of the task of promoting gender equality and women's empowerment in MOWAC and the state bureaucracy must account for two interrelated contexts. One is the context of global discourses that permeate national-level policies. Gender equality and women's empowerment have emerged as important goals in national and international development, as indicated by the rounds of UN World Conferences on Women and their review processes (1975–2010), to the Millennium Development Goals (MDGs) adopted in 2000 by all 192 UN member states and at least 23 international organizations. The principle of gender equality is enshrined in Article 17 of Ghana's 1992 Constitution, although women's rights are narrowly construed in Article 27 to cover only protection of maternity rights and equal rights to training and promotion. The Ghanaian state has assumed several other obligations to advance gender equality and women's empowerment through its passage of national legislation and the adoption, signature, and ratification of several continental and international treaties and conventions. For instance, Ghana was one of the first countries (in 1985) to sign on to the Convention on the Elimination of All Forms of Discrimination Against Women (CEDAW). Ghana's formal policy stance on gender equality stems in part from its membership of the United Nations and the increasing commitments that the world body has made on gender equality, particularly since the landmark Beijing Conference and the adoption of the gender mainstreaming strategy. But it also derives from the activism and organization of the women's movement at home, and its mobilization to hold the state and its agencies to account (Tsikata, 2009). This is against the backdrop of a growing influence of the women's movement in Africa that has succeeded in getting the African Union to make commitments to advancing gender equality (African Union, 2003, 2004).

The second relevant context is that of the state bureaucracy in Ghana; the ability of MOWAC to move on the question of women's empowerment and gender equality is greatly influenced by the structures established to take up these issues. It is to this question, of the organization and capacity of the state bureaucracy, that we now turn.

The state, development and gender equity in Ghana

From its inception, the modern Ghanaian state was expected to play a catalytic role in delivering the gains and benefits of independence to the population at large. Indeed, that had been a major argument for decolonization, and under the first post-independence government, the Ghanaian state (1957–66) saw itself as developmentalist, intervening greatly in economic and social life (Killick, 1978; Mkandawire and Soludo, 1999). The new state carried out these interventions on the back of a well-equipped bureaucracy – staffed by competent Ghanaians, tasked to craft and implement policies.

Changes in ideology and practice of development have led to a diminishing of the state's dominance in this arena. Nonetheless, Ghana's Constitution affirms the responsibility of the state to ensure equitable development and commits it to delivering social goods to the population, under the directive principles of state policy (Republic of Ghana, 1992). However, such commitments have been made in the face of a bureaucracy that has weakened following more than two decades of reforms implemented as part of structural adjustment programmes (SAPs) (Daddieh, 1999; Olukoshi, 2004; Mkandawire, 2009). An important component of the SAPs was the programme of 'rationalization' of the public sector, which resulted in retrenchments and freezes on employment as part of the de-emphasis of the role of the state and thus of the role and capacity of the public bureaucracy. As a corollary, there was growth in the numbers of NGOs and their functions, backed by donor funding, while the establishment of parallel structures within government ministries and departments allowed some staff to moonlight as consultants. This eventually resulted in the exodus of hundreds of skilled staff into these alternative positions outside the government, and dampened the commitment of those who remained. It further meant that the public bureaucracies were no longer the primary sites of knowledge, influence, and sponsorship of development. The austerity measures of the structural adjustment period and their debilitating impact on bureaucracies coincided with the World Conferences on Women and increasing commitments by states to address growing gender disparities and inequities. Thus, ironically, the state was increasing its commitments through subscription to these conventions, at the same time as its power and capacity to intervene directly to bring about social justice were being eroded as power shifted to market forces, donors, and NGOs.

Institutional structures for gender equality in Ghana

The Ghanaian state institutionalized its commitments to women through the establishment of the National Council on Women and Development (NCWD) in 1975 as the national machinery for women. Much has been written on the NCWD and its changing fortunes as it lost staff to better-financed NGOs and its political clout declined, due to cooptation by the state and the competing force of a women's organization supported from within the state (Manuh, 1993; Tsikata, 1989; Mensah Kutin et al., 2000). In recognition of the NCWD's important role, and its growing deficit in skills, the UNDP in Ghana developed a capacity-building programme for the NCWD in the early 1990s. As is well known, the 1990s were generally a time of training and 'workshopping' to increase knowledge and skills in recognition that gender and development are learned activities (Tsikata, 2001). Nonetheless, the fortunes of the NCWD did not improve significantly.

The decade closed with the serial killing of women in the capital city, Accra, and an increase in reported violence against women (Manuh, 2007; Tsikata, 2009). This led to increasing mobilization of women who demanded an end to the violence and urged state action on its many declared commitments to women (Manuh, 2007; Tsikata, 2009). It is these events that formed the immediate backdrop to the creation of MOWAC in 2001. The establishment of this ministry was meant to more fully articulate the government's commitment and intentions on issues related to women and children, harness the expertise relating to their specific area, and link up with partners in multilateral and bilateral agencies, and civil society.

Functionally, MOWAC has two service arms – the Department of Women (DOW) and the Department of Children (DOC). These subsumed the implementation function previously performed by the NCWD and the Ghana National Commission on Children, respectively, while MOWAC itself is charged with policy formulation and coordination.

The political leadership of MOWAC is provided by a minister and a deputy, both of whom are appointed by the president. In common with other civil service bureaucracies, the technical work of the Ministry occurs in four main units: finance and administration; policy, planning, budgeting, monitoring, and evaluation; human resources and development; and the statistics, research, and information directorate. Each unit is headed by a director, with a chief director overseeing all the directorates.

In general, civil service bureaucracies operate at national, regional, and district levels. However MOWAC, the newest and smallest of the ministries, only operates down to the regional level.[1] At this level, it is expected to have a core staff of four – consisting of a regional director supported by a programme officer, and two other staff – but acquiring the full complement of staff has not been possible due to difficulties in receiving clearance from the Ministry of Finance and Economic Planning to recruit staff, even when technical clearance has been given by the Office of the Head of the Civil Service. In addition, there appears to be some resistance on the part of some members of regional bureaucracies to include DOW regional directors in the meetings of the Regional Coordinating Council even though all ministries, departments, and agencies have representatives in the coordinating and planning units at the regional and district levels. The reason advanced by the ministers and senior administrators is that there has been no written directive from the Ministry of Local Government and Rural Development, although the needed justification is provided in the National Development Planning Commission planning guidelines (Act 480). At the district level, the story is similar for most GDOs: they have been marginalized and their office politicized to the extent that in some districts they are replaced after a change in government following elections.

This is the broader context of the bureaucratic and political environment in which Francesca set to work to transform gender relations in Ghana.

In the trenches with Francesca – working in the Department of Women

Coming in as the head of the DOW, Francesca's objective was to empower MOWAC, and specifically DOW, to take up the central management role as the primary implementer of the government's gender mainstreaming agenda. Francesca tackled these goals on a number of fronts – by restructuring DOW through training and capacity building for staff, through forming alliances and eliciting buy-in from actors within and outside the government bureaucracy, and by actively seeking a place at the table. These efforts are discussed in turn, beginning with the basics of the physical working space.

The DOW is housed in the premises of the former NCWD, in a four-storey building, along with three other departments/agencies. The building is in the capital city, near its busy commercial centre, and is surrounded by many people doing business – selling small goods, providing photocopying services in small kiosks, and generating a lot of activity and noise for premises that are supposed to conduct government business. Francesca had the DOW office spaces painted and she replaced old equipment and furniture – when the budget permitted – to create a more conducive working environment.

Setting the agenda

MOWAC was one of eight ministries designated as central management agencies. The importance of this designation is that the mandate and work of the ministry are recognized as cross-cutting and requiring collaborative sector efforts to achieve the desired goals. As explained in 2009 by the then sector minister Akua Sena Dansua, MOWAC's description as a central management agency with cabinet status provides it with a comparative advantage with the role and responsibility to monitor policy implementation and programme in the sector areas, coordinate cross-sector issues and evaluate the impact of sector policies on women and children. Its specific mandate is to initiate and formulate policies and promote gender mainstreaming across all sectors to lead to the achievement of gender equality and empowerment of women, and the survival, development and growth of children, as well as ensuring the protection of the rights of women and children. (Dansua, 2009)

From the minister's statement and from the *National Gender and Children Policy* launched in 2004 (Government of Ghana, n.d.), it is clear that MOWAC's main directive is to 'mainstream' gender issues in the workings of other ministries as a way to achieve *gender equality*, a term that is used synonymously with *women's empowerment* in the quote above.

In Francesca's opinion, one of the weaknesses of MOWAC is that it is unable to fulfil its mandate of policy formulation and engagement. For instance, the 2004 MOWAC gender policy was not developed in a very participatory manner, in part because MOWAC was unable to convene a policy dialogue on the document that could have made it a point of reference for implementing women's empowerment and gender equality priorities within various sectors. The document also did not contain any clear directives for gender mainstreaming, neither were there an accompanying strategic document and accountability framework for tracking gender equality results.

Francesca's job as acting director of DOW was to implement policy, not to formulate it. However, there were no institutionalized weekly, monthly, or quarterly internal meetings during which the ministry could have taken a stance on gender equality issues and then tabled them at other policy dialogues. This situation limited Francesca's ability to influence policymaking processes. Moreover, the failure of MOWAC to convene regular annual policy discussions with other units within the government bureaucracy was a big drawback because it meant that there were few opportunities for actors outside MOWAC – whether within the government bureaucracy or outside it – to contribute to shaping the agenda on women's empowerment.

Shut out of the policymaking process at the highest level, there was little opportunity to engage in a discussion about the meaning and usefulness of gender mainstreaming as a means of advancing women's empowerment. Instead, Francesca strategized to build up the ability of her department to carry out this assigned task.

Getting the institutional set-up right

By her own accounts, Francesca's main preoccupation at DOW was to create institutional structures that would effectively support gender mainstreaming. This could also be seen as an effort to legitimize and empower MOWAC/DOW, which appears to have been a reasonable preoccupation given the situation of MOWAC. The ministry has little stature or power within the government bureaucracy. This is largely a reflection of scepticism about, and a lack of real commitment to, gender equality among both administrative cadres and politicians, and which means that MOWAC is not given sufficient budget resources, human resources, or voice. Even among development partners that ostensibly have an interest in supporting MOWAC to push the 'gender agenda', there is a palpable lack of confidence in the ministry's capabilities to take the lead in these efforts within the government and society-wide. In order to be able to fulfil its mandate of influencing other units of the government, MOWAC needed to better position itself as having the institutional capacity. Francesca describes her approach:

> I realized early on that the mandate of MOWAC could not be achieved on the weak institutional base I found and therefore I sought to strengthen the institutional capacity of DOW. I began first by placing my staff into the five approved units of the directorate, namely finance and adminis-tration, projects and programmes, counselling, research, information and advocacy, and monitoring and evaluation. In a participatory manner, I provided them with job descriptions and linked these up with a scheme of service I developed with the Office of the Head of Civil Service. I assigned members of staff responsibility for various areas related to women's empowerment and gender equality based on the 12 critical areas of the Beijing Platform for Action.
>
> I believed that for MOWAC to take up more effectively its role as a central management agency, its four directorates would have to work in concert to make the ministry more gender responsive. Because I viewed gender main-streaming as a planning function, I saw that as the core business of the plan-ning and budgeting directorate. This unit was to provide a gendered analysis of various sector policies in terms of content and potential impact on the lives of women and men, and develop monitoring and evaluation mecha-nisms. Secondly through the statistics and research directorate, the ministry was to be able to undertake or commission research, and in particular to assure that data would be sex-disaggregated so as to support gender analysis. Through its human resources directorate, the ministry was also to be capable of training its own staff, as well as training other staff within the civil service bureaucracy, so that women's empowerment and gender mainstreaming would become an integral component of their planning processes.
>
> I made sure that we produced annual work plans and strove to imple-ment them in the face of frequent budgetary cuts. I also instituted – initially – weekly meetings and subsequently, fortnightly meetings with my senior staff. This was done to ensure that the department had staff that could be referred to as specialists in those areas and to provide for continuity through transfer of knowledge. However, my influence did not extend to the structures within the regions and districts because of the ministry's peculiar set-up, which has been discussed.

Building capacity

A persistent challenge to the institutional structures for women's empowerment in Ghana has been that of obtaining an adequate number of skilled
staff (see TWN series, 2000). Staff members of MOWAC and DOW were transferred in from other ministries within the civil service. The majority of such
staff had been administrators without any training[2] in planning or gender,
and the expectation seemed to be that they would be trained by the ministry
or would 'pick up' knowledge and skills in gender issues as they went about
their work. Of course, MOWAC is not the only civil/public sector organization that lacks the needed competencies; in fact, this is a major reason for
the ongoing public sector reforms to improve public/civil service efficiency
and service delivery. However, in some other ministries such as finance,
agriculture, and health, there is a technical core of staff that have sector-
specific training. Even if some of those technocrats are transferred or shuf-
fled around, they are often still in the sector or in other capacities in the
service. This cannot be said about MOWAC. Moreover, even though over the
last three decades there has been some politicization of the Ghanaian civil
service overall, with the careers of persons in the service being impacted by
their perceived political leanings, there is a perception that it has been worse
in the women's machinery than in other ministries. In view of this reality,
Francesca describes her approach to capacity building of MOWAC staff:

> As acting director, my response to this shortfall in expertise in DOW was
> to institute in-service training through regular seminars. Members of staff
> were also sent to international conferences and workshops concerning
> issues in their designated areas of specialization. Again, I used the oppor-
> tunity of the biannual regional directors and senior staff meetings to build
> the capacities of these staff to do gender analysis. During these meetings,
> I would have either resource persons make presentations or staff who had
> benefited from training and international conferences share their knowl-
> edge. Outside of DOW, I contributed to training GDOs and staff of other
> ministries and agencies on gender mainstreaming and gender-responsive
> budgeting. I am pleased to say that as a result, after my first year I was able
> to delegate a lot of work to members of staff. I was also gratified to hear
> from my staff through the grapevine that I had contributed a great deal to
> building their capacity and levels of confidence.

The expected benefits of capacity building for persons in the state bureaucracy are clear, but we note two conditions under which these benefits can
be subverted. One is when technocrats have the knowledge but not the
ideologies that illuminate and energize their ideas. Previously, much of the
knowledge about gender (as well as about human rights, participation, and
other potentially transformative discourses and strategies) was located in civil
society. These ideas have now been taken up into mainstream policy speak

and practice, but in a technocratic manner that divorces these approaches from the politics of gender equality. The second circumstance is the voluntary and involuntary exit of people from the government bureaucracy. MOWAC is a good illustration of the reasons for, and the effect of, these staff movements in the government bureaucracy. At different periods of time, staff of MOWAC (and its forerunner, NCWD) have either been made redundant as part of a rationalization exercise, have chosen to leave for other opportunities, or have been transferred from their primary units to other parts of the bureaucracy because of the perception that their loyalty lay with a previous administration.[3] Most recently this happened at the beginning of the tenure of the third MOWAC minister in 2009, whose predecessor was in the opposition. These movements out of the bureaucracy effectively denude the critical capacity of the civil service in general and of MOWAC in particular. One might say that the movement of MOWAC staff to other areas has the potential to diffuse 'gender expertise' to other units of government. The problem is whether those other units are receptive to what a gender-knowledgeable person might have to say. One can imagine such a person in a sector such as finance or energy being told, 'We are here to do budget support, not gender' (to paraphrase a response given to Francesca herself by fellow bureaucrats in the finance ministry). This is to say that, as weak as MOWAC might presently be, in garnering the respect and attention of other ministries, it provides at the very least an institutional space for a femocrat to speak and work in. Outside this arena, it is even harder for feminist actors to make an impact.

Influencing policy actors

In this section we discuss Francesca's attempts to shape the women's empowerment and gender equality agenda by influencing major policy actors. These include the minister, the chief director, policymakers in key positions in the government bureaucracy, and development partners.

As of 2011 MOWAC has had four ministers, all women. Not surprisingly, each minister's background, political affiliation, and general orientation has driven the direction of the ministry and particularly its relations with donors and civil society actors, who are co-actors in shaping understanding and approaches to advancing women's empowerment. Francesca reports:

> The minister is the primary policy actor in a ministry. It was challenging to work with different ministers because each had a different background and varying understandings of gender issues. Even though I believe they were all committed to working towards women's empowerment, I perceived that they were also motivated by personal and ideological perspectives. As an instance, the first minister made it clear that her own orientation, and that of her government, was economic empowerment equated to the provision of microcredit, as opposed to, for instance, a focus on research, advocacy, and policy dialogue or engagement on issues such as trade or

practices of international financial institutions. In contrast, I was able to get the buy-in of the second minister to run policy coordination meetings. I believe this succeeded because of her planning background and exposure to gender issues as an active member of the women's movement previous to her entry into government.

I also realized that the ability of ministers to work to push the ministry's agenda was partly a result of their personal clout in cabinet and their party's orientation towards gender equality. I surmised from conversation with one minister that she had encountered considerable resistance to these issues from her peers within her own party. Again, the party's political interests were always an important consideration. For this reason, it was not always easy to get the minister's political buy-in to programmes that were in the long-term interests of women's empowerment and gender equality, such as building institutional structures and instituting policy dialogues with other ministries, departments and agencies. Ministers were more amenable to signing-off on projects to provide microcredit to women's groups, which were likely to result in election votes for their political parties. Thus some initiatives that I proposed, such as engaging civil society organizations and women's organizations, or utilizing a non-partisan approach to increasing women's participation in local governance, did not receive support.

Looking beyond the minister, it is important to acknowledge the influence of technocrats within the civil service bureaucracy in charting the policy course of their ministry, department, or agency. Given the critical role of directors, it is especially problematic that they are valued almost exclusively for their administrative skills rather than for sector-specific knowledge, so that they might not perceive a need to acquire the conceptual and technical knowledge that would make their indirect policymaking role more beneficial for the process of women's empowerment. Francesca reports:

> It was challenging working with the different chief directors, as their ability and willingness to integrate gender into policies and programmes were questionable. The absence of strategic leadership on how the women's ministry as a collective ought to engage, what positions it should take and contributions to make at policy fora, contributed to making MOWAC appear incoherent and incompetent. Save for a few policy coordination meetings, MOWAC was unable to institutionalize regular review meetings because of its inability to keep up an institutional policy coordination programme. This greatly undermined the clout of MOWAC as a central management agency, able to influence policy formulation and its implementation across sectors.

In her quest to chalk up some successes for MOWAC, Francesca manoeuvred to attend high-level policy meetings such as the Multi-Donor Budget Support meetings. She reflects on her experience:

Initially we faced resistance from some of our colleagues in the Ministry of Finance and Economic Planning and were told even by female colleagues that these meetings had 'nothing to do with women's empowerment and gender equality'. On some of these occasions, I 'named and shamed' those female colleagues who were highly placed in that ministry and who were instrumental in convening these policy meetings, calling them 'gender insensitive' to their faces. However, over time I realized that their attitudes stemmed from a lack of appreciation of the importance of gender equality. This meant that I had to change tactics. I lobbied the minister at the time to sponsor some of these senior management persons to attend international meetings which were in their line of work, such as the World Bank's Gender and Economics seminar held in Ghana in 2007, where the bank finally asserted that 'Gender is Smart Economics', and which had a bearing on women's empowerment and gender equality. We also took advantage of an international trade meeting that was held in Ghana in 2007 to have the Commonwealth Secretariat organize gender training for GDOs and some female staff members of the Ministry of Finance and Economic Planning (MOFEP). After these programmes they became gender advocates in their own ministry and later formed the core group for the gender-responsive budgeting initiative. We also took advantage of moments such as the Commonwealth Finance Ministers and Women's Ministers meetings on financing for development in the same year, to lobby the MOFEP about the link between the themes of these conferences and gender equality and mainstreaming.

On the whole, I would say that MOWAC was more successful at working on a more sustained basis with development partners than with other departments within the government bureaucracy. One main reason was that development partners (both multilateral and bilateral agencies) organized themselves, on their own initiative, into working groups to engage in policy dialogue with the government.[4] The Gender Equality Sector Team (GEST) began working with MOWAC in 2004 and lobbied for MOWAC's inclusion in 2005 in policy discussions with the government. GEST would tip off MOWAC when these meetings were to take place so the ministry attended uninvited, initially as observers, but subsequently through lobbying and negotiations it became a full member of these meetings.

With the active support of GEST, MOWAC has been able to influence the Multi-Donor Budget Support process (MDBS). This happened while I was the co-chair for the GEST group from 2006 to 2008. Now gender equality targets such as sex-disaggregated data, gender-responsive budgeting, and action on domestic violence have been inserted in the performance assessment framework for the MDBS. MOWAC has also been able to participate in the Consultative Group annual partnership meetings, which are high-level policy discussions between the government and development partners, where donors pledge the amount of development assistance for the country.

Building alliances

Another important question that this chapter seeks to address is the possibilities of alliance-building by femocrats with individuals and groups working within civil society for similar ends of women's empowerment. Civil society activists working on gender issues in Ghana seem to be ahead of MOWAC in championing policy and reform issues, but it is not clear how femocrats can link up with them to push an empowerment agenda and create synergies with their own work. Francesca reports:

> In terms of establishing links with civil society MOWAC – through the GDOs at the district level and the regional director at the regional level – is supposed to work with civil society/NGOs and networks of women's groups organized around trades and vocations. This was supposed to happen through regular meetings explaining government policies to them and eliciting feedback from them into the policymaking process. This worked well for some time under the NCWD, when there was hardly any independent organization by women. However, due to lack of resources, these meetings started to occur on an ad hoc basis.
>
> The rise of women's NGOs and independent movements and coalitions of women, led by well-educated, middle-class women able to articulate their own positions and engage in policy advocacy and discourse, also meant that the mediatory role of the NCWD and now DOW did not seem necessary. Attempts at revitalizing meetings through updating an inventory of groups registered with the DOW and by instituting regular visits to them proved futile (see Pobee-Hayford and Awori, 2008).
>
> At DOW, I tried to build visibility and credibility through actions in support of women's empowerment and gender equality. In my visits to community and trade-based women's groups during the monthly meetings, I tried to nurture support for their programmes, but these efforts could not be sustained because of inadequate resources. I also tried to strengthen the groups by being inclusive and democratic during the women's organizations' monthly meetings, and I believe I was able to demonstrate that I was non-partisan – that I was just a femocrat doing my job.

From its inception, MOWAC had a tense relationship with women's rights groups who protested the establishment of the ministry[5] and were subsequently involved in public stand-offs with the first minister over her opposition to domestic violence legislation which was being pushed by these activists.[6] In effect, women's organizations have been critical of the ministry from the start, and this history may explain why there is little evidence of collaboration at an institutional level between DOW and feminist activists.

Aside from this history, there are other reasons femocrats may fail to connect with feminists in civil society. Within the government bureaucracy there appears to be a sense of the boundaries of the possible, which one might be reluctant to contravene for the sake of maintaining one's place in the bureaucracy. In Ghana, it would be fair to assume wariness among many bureaucrats of being labelled as activists, unlike for example bureaucrats under Lula in Brazil, or feminist bureaucrats working within the UN system. Many Ghanaian bureaucrats would be cautious about close identification with the women's or other social or political movements because of the possibility of being seen as disloyal to the state, or being labelled a 'troublemaker'. It is also conceivable that some femocrats might have a distrust of, or distaste for, the activists and activism of the women's movement in particular. All of this may produce a bureaucrat and even a femocrat who might maintain a distance from feminists in civil society.

Another challenge to building alliances for women's empowerment is that there is a tendency for government bureaucrats on the one hand, and practitioners, activists, and researchers in academia on the other hand, to operate in separate and seemingly unbridgeable spheres. This is partly a result of the different ethoses of these groups in terms of their mandate, their accountability systems, and their incentives structures. It may even be that the personalities and orientations of the people who enter and stay within the bureaucracy are different from those in civil society.

However, there are encouraging signs of alliance-building. An instance is of NETRIGHT inviting female government bureaucrats and technocrats, including Francesca, to do presentations for NETRIGHT members at a learning workshop on gender budgeting. While this may not demonstrate the sustained engagement that is needed, it may be a starting point to providing femocrats with access to constituencies of women with whom they can share ideas, and to whom they can be accountable, at the same time that these constituencies can push the government and its bureaucracy to work at delivering the many commitments it has assumed on gender equality and women's empowerment. Finding and being part of such a network might also prevent the frustrations felt by femocrats who may respond by leaving the bureaucracy to join donor organizations, thus further impoverishing the state bureaucracy and its ability to work for women.

'Why I left'

Francesca tendered her resignation at the end of 2010, after working in MOWAC for six years. She reflects on her time there and her reasons for leaving:

> From the outset, my appointment to the position of acting director of the DOW was perceived by some to be a political appointment, since it did not follow the bureaucratic procedure. I was assured this would be rectified in the course of time, but this situation did not set the right tone for my tenure. Moreover, some of my predecessors, who had been appointed

through the normal bureaucratic process, had been reassigned within a year of their appointment following a change in government, and so I psyched myself up to be ready for any change that came along.

The constraints to my being able to bring change to DOW and MOWAC included, first and foremost, the lack of political will at all levels, from the regional to the national, and the lack of accountability for women's empowerment and gender equality results, which made it difficult to achieve any lasting and significant results. Over the years, this led to a situation where I felt that this might, after all, be an exercise in futility, as there was really no commitment on the part of the government.

On a more personal level, the feeling of knowing what to do and not being allowed to do it was irksome. For example, after being in charge of a department and having a free rein to initiate and implement programmes, it was not easy to be micromanaged by a newly appointed minister. It was particularly stifling to find that I needed to get clearance for every activity in a programme that I had initiated and completed a work plan and budget for, and that clearance sometimes took three months to secure. Then I would be blamed if the programme was not implemented on schedule. It was frustrating as well, to offer advice that was not taken, only to be confronted later with an embarrassing situation which could have been prevented if the advice had been heeded. This happened on a number of occasions, making me – as a femocrat – feel very uncomfortable, since it made me look incompetent. In addition I felt unappreciated, and the dim prospects of being confirmed in the position as director made me feel demoralized, as I realized that my career goals and expectations were not going to be met because of the politicization of issues. Eventually, I left because of what I perceived to be political interference in my work and in the ministry. The mass transfers of my colleagues, and of other staff whose capacity I contributed to building, and seeing the systems I had put in place over the years disrupted, meant that I would have to reinvent the wheel if I stayed. This signalled to me that it was time to move on.

Working within any bureaucracy is challenging; working within a weak bureaucracy, within which partisan politics are palpably at work, is even more difficult. Francesca left DOW to work with the Canadian donor agency, CIDA, as senior gender adviser. Ironically, it is possible that as senior gender adviser for a major donor, Francesca may exert a greater influence on MOWAC than she did as its acting director. In Ghana donor agencies are powerful policy actors, not least because of their substantial financial support of the government's budget. In this sense, CIDA arguably has more real clout than MOWAC. Again, working within CIDA, and outside the political sphere of the state bureaucracy, Francesca can be more critical of MOWAC and more asser-tive in influencing the ministry's policies and practices.

On the other hand, Francesca's exit is a significant loss to the state bureau-cracy. We are concerned here with MOWAC and its ability to perform its role as the lead agency in policymaking on gender equality and women's empowerment. At the beginning of our research on policy discourses, our perception – as members of the women's movement – of government bureaucrats and of MOWAC staff in particular, was jaundiced by the oppositional relationship MOWAC's first minister had set up between the ministry and women's groups, as well as by our understanding of the historical attrition of human resources and skills in the state bureaucracy, as we have described in this chapter. We revised this view in the course of our work and particularly in our interaction with Francesca. Her commitment to her work, coupled with a clear-eyed assessment of the potentials and deficiencies of her department, inspired in us some optimism about the state bureaucracy. Her subsequent exit brought up again the question of what it is possible for a femocrat to achieve within such a setting. We shall allow Francesca the last word on this important question:

> From my experience I would say that with the requisite institutional structure, along with adequate operational systems, bureaucracies can act as a pathway for women's empowerment and gender equality, but it requires perseverance and fortitude on the part of the femocrat. While resistance can be expected, it is also possible to have allies and there is a need to seek out these potential allies. Above all, I learned not to assume that every bureaucrat, even female bureaucrats, knows about women's empowerment and gender equality issues or will be prepared to teach or facilitate a process where they can be taught.

Notes

1   MOWAC has attempted to have GDOs placed within the district assemblies, which form the lowest level of Ghana's decentralized government system. However, the actual appointment of GDOs is by the Ministry of Local Government rather than MOWAC, and therefore the appointed GDOs are not considered core staff of MOWAC.
2   A partial explanation for this lack of gender 'expertise' is that there are few institutions in Ghana offering specialized gender-related courses, especially at the graduate level.
3   It seems to matter little whether the previous administration of the ministry was located in the same or a different political party.
4   This initiative evolved out of the Paris Declaration with its emphasis on aid effectiveness.
5   The opposition was not so much to the creation of an institution that would attend to women's concerns but to the vehicle that had been chosen. A statement put forward in 2001 by the Network for Women's Rights in Ghana (NETRIGHT) had proposed the establishment of a body with a constitutional mandate to reach into all parts of government and other institutions, which might be more effective at tackling the multi-dimensional and multi-sector nature of gender issues than a ministry.

Another major concern was the coupling of women and children within one ministry.

6   Despite the fact that MOWAC was technically the sponsor of the Domestic Violence Bill, its first minister was a public critic of the Bill, which was passed during the tenure of her successor.

References

African Union (2003) 'Protocol to the African Charter on Human and Peoples' Rights on the rights of women in Africa'. Maputo: Adopted by the 2nd Ordinary Session of the Assembly of the Union. 11 July.

African Union (2004) 'Solemn declaration on gender equality'. Addis Ababa: Third Ordinary Session of the African Union Assembly of Heads of State and Government, July.

Daddieh, C. (1999) 'Beyond governance and democratization in Africa: Toward state building for sustainable human development', *Journal of Sustainable Development in Africa*, 1, Available at: <http://www.jsd-africa.com/Jsda/Winter%201999/articlespdf/ARC-beyond%20governance%20and%20democratization%20in%20Africa.pdf>.

Dansua, A. S. (2009) 'Address by Hon. Minister of Women and Children's Affairs, Akua Sena Dansua, MP'. The Meet-the-Press Series. Accra: Ministry of Information Conference Room, 12 May.

Government of Ghana (n.d.) *National Gender and Children Policy*, Accra: Ministry of Women and Children's Affairs [MOWAC].

Killick, T. (1978) *Development Economics in Action: A Study of Economic Policies in Ghana:* London: Heinemann Educational Books Limited.

Manuh, T. (1993) 'Women, state and society under the PNDC', in E. Gyimah-Boadi, E. (ed.), *Ghana under PNDC Rule*, pp. 176–95, Dakar: CODESRIA Books.

Manuh, T. (2007) 'The passage of domestic violence legislation in Ghana', *Pathways of Women's Empowerment*. Available at: <www.pathwaysofempowerment.org/GhanaDV.pdf>.

Mensah Kutin, R., Tsikata, D., Ocran, S., Mahama, A., Ofei-Aboagye, E., and Okine, V. (2000) *The National Machinery for Women in Ghana: An NGO Evaluation*, National Machinery Series No. 3, Accra: Third World Network.

Mkandawire, T. (2009) *Institutional Monocropping and Monotasking in Africa*, Geneva: United Nations Research Institute for Social Development (UNRISD).

Mkandawire, T. and Soludo, C. (1999) *Our Continent, Our Future: African Perspectives on Structural Adjustment*, Dakar: Council for the Development of Social Science Research in Africa (CODESRIA).

Olukoshi, A. (2004) 'Democratisation, globalisation and effective policymaking in Africa', in C. Soludo, O. Ogbu, and H. Chang (eds) *The Politics of Trade and Industrial Policy in Africa: Forced Consensus?*, Trenton and Ottawa: Africa World Press/IDRC.

Pobee-Hayford, F. and Awori, T. (2008) *Aid Effectiveness and Gender Equality in Ghana 2004-2006*, Accra: EC/UN Partnership on Gender Equality for Development and Peace.

Republic of Ghana (1992) *Constitution of the Republic of Ghana 1992,* Accra: Assembly Press of Ghana Publishing Corporation.

Third World Network (2000) *National Machineries Series,* Accra: Third World Network.

Tsikata, D. (1989) 'Women's political organizations 1951–1987', in E. Hansen and K. Ninsin (eds) *The State, Development, and Politics in Ghana,* pp. 73–93, Dakar: CODESRIA.

Tsikata, D. (ed.) (2001), *Gender Training in Ghana: Politics, Issues and Tools,* Accra: Woeli Publishing Services.

Tsikata, D. (2009) 'Women's organizing in Ghana since the 1990s: From individual organizations to three coalitions', *Development* 52: 185–92 <http://dx.doi.org/10.1057%2Fdev.2009.8>.

About the authors

Takyiwaa Manuh retired in 2011 as Professor of African Studies at the University of Ghana, Legon, where she also served as director of the Institute of African Studies from 2002–9. She was the convenor of the West Africa hub of the Pathways of Women's Empowerment research programme where she worked on conceptualizations of women's empowerment in Ghana and women's political participation. Her research interests are gender and women's rights, contemporary African migrations, and higher education in Africa, and she has published extensively in these areas. She has also served on the boards of several national, continental, and international organizations.

Nana Akua Anyidoho is a Senior Research Fellow at the Institute of Statistical, Social and Economic Research (ISSER), University of Ghana. She has a BA in psychology from the University of Ghana and a PhD in human development and social policy from Northwestern University. Nana Akua studies the intersection of policy processes and people's everyday lives. Her recent research focuses on policy discourses on women's empowerment; the work aspirations and prospects of young people; and the informalization of women's work.

Francesa Pobee-Hayford currently works as a consultant senior gender adviser in the Canadian International Development Agency's project support unit. Prior to this, she was acting director of the Department of Women in Ghana's Ministry of Women and Children's Affairs from 2005 to December 2009. She initially joined MOWAC as a gender adviser on a DANIDA capacity-building project in 2002. Prior to this she worked in the Ministry of Health for 13 years, in the policy, monitoring, and evaluation division, until becoming a principal planning officer. She was also the gender desk officer.

CHAPTER 4

Feminist identities

Rosalind Eyben

This is the first of three chapters that analyse the research findings from the Pathways project, using the device of five fictionalized characters to preserve the anonymity of participants. Each chapter finds the characters meeting in a different venue – this first time in Ratna's flat in New York. The theme of the conversation is feminist identity: whether they are open about their feminism and how others in the wider movement may not see them as such.

Every day, in development organizations large and small, feminist bureaucrats make use of strategy, tactics, wisdom, and skill to act for their principles. Most of their strategies are invisible and their tactics subtle. They draw on networks of friendships and relationships that create ripples of effect in enabling their organizations to be pathways of women's empowerment. In 2007 a group of feminist bureaucrats – mainly women – from Europe, Africa, Asia, and North America, and working as gender specialists in head offices of international development bureaucracies – got together with me, to talk about their approaches. It was an action research process that continued on and off for three years. This chapter is the first part of three evocations in this book (see also Chapters 8 and 11 (Eyben, 2013a, 2013b)) of some of what we said and discussed. I am present in these discussions as narrator and a participant observer. The other five characters and the places where they meet are heavily disguised: an amalgam of more than a dozen people participating in the project. I do this to protect their anonymity and as a device to represent different points of view (Etherington, 2004). What they say, however, is entirely drawn from transcripts of my conversations with them and from records of the workshops. Students and practitioners in reflective learning circles might like to treat the dialogue as a play script, each taking the role of a different character and developing from the text their own thoughts and arguments.

Meeting the characters

Let me start by introducing Marianne. Now in her early sixties, she served an apprenticeship with a grassroots movement and saw that the issues of poverty reduction and women's rights are a daily struggle for the majority of people, but finds it hard to keep this in mind when working at head office. Marianne then got a job as policy adviser in a women's international NGO. Since 1994

http://dx.doi.org/10.3362/9781780448046.004

she has been employed in the gender unit of her country's aid ministry. 'I think if you see life politically, you see it's about contestation – it's about alliances, it's about influencing things in the way that you've decided you'd like them to go, and plotting how to do that. And what's wrong with politics anyhow?'

Karin, the youngest member of our group – she is in her late thirties – also works in her country's aid programme. Until four years ago, she taught gender and development studies at a university and has been excited about what she has been able to achieve since starting at the ministry. 'I came in at a time when gender equality was once again coming back up the agenda and people were beginning to take it a little more seriously. It was a question of just networking and pushing and knowing who to talk to when.'

Claudia is a senior policy adviser for a multilateral organization with its head office in Europe. Her early career was as an agricultural extensions specialist and that was when she first became interested in gender. Since getting a job in her current organization she has held a number of different policy briefs but was delighted to move into the gender equality section when a post became vacant. She describes a meeting she attended where some present were very much at the far end of the feminist-activist continuum. 'And held up against that light, I felt myself pale considerably. I was a bureaucrat just doing a job. But I think, again, that I may not have done enough networking with feminist activists generally.'

Ratna works for the United Nations. She is hosting the first meeting of the group, that this present chapter describes. Ratna has been in her job for the last 15 years. Before that she worked for her own country's Ministry for Women's Affairs. Ratna sees the civil service as an avenue for making change happen. 'You can work as a feminist, even if it is only in subtle ways within the confines of what is possible within your organization. It's about room for manoeuvre, compatibility, building up alliances, creating space. That's all ... kind of ... quite subtle. And it's about craft.'

Gillian, the last in our group, is women's rights officer at an international NGO and is in her early forties. At the 1995 Beijing Women's Conference she was a young activist from the South. Three years later she got her first job as the sole women's rights officer in the NGO she still works for. 'I think that my knowledge derives from my experience. Well, it's kind of a combination. I am quite a reflective person and I think that's the aspect ... well, there are many aspects of my job that I find interesting but that's one of them. So from each thing you're doing, you're learning something different and thinking and reflecting on that, thinking how does that influence what I say and what I do and trying to move things forward.'

Why this project?

I too used to be a feminist bureaucrat in an international development agency. It was my friendships from that time, with people like those just described, that made possible the action research project I initiated with them to learn about our craft. Altogether a dozen people signed up for the project. Although their responsibilities and working environments varied, they shared a passionate commitment to shaping these environments – both within and beyond their organizations – to better support the realization of women's rights.

Soon after becoming one of two social development advisers in the British government aid ministry, I attended a training course on 'negotiating skills'. My childhood, like Laura Turquet's (see Turquet, 2013), was one in which we lived and breathed politics. My father had been a trade union leader and when I visited him shortly after this training course, I told him about the techniques I had learnt. 'You mean someone actually told you how to do it?' asked my father. 'Do you think *that* is how you are going to become a good negotiator? Nobody ever told me what I should do. I wouldn't have wanted them to – it wouldn't have helped me. I just did it, that's all, and if I say so myself, I was bloody good at it.'

My father was a passionate reader but nowhere on his crowded shelves was a book about crafting union leadership. Just as craft cannot be explicated in a training course, so he would have argued it cannot be reduced to written text. This is partly true, but books and explicit enquiry can also help. As a feminist bureaucrat, I discovered that some of what came naturally to me was less obvious to colleagues who had not absorbed notions of political strategy at the family tea table. Yet, feminists from less political backgrounds can and do learn to be effective strategists. All participants hoped the project would help them improve their strategic skills, as well as be useful to readers in equivalent situations and who might learn from their reflections.

The project for me was an opportunity to interrogate my own past experience. When I started at the ministry, I saw myself as a feminist in my personal life but not in my work. I was not enthusiastic about what was then (in 1986) called the women in development (WID) element of my job – one that also included participation, poverty, and social policy issues. The other social development adviser was a man. I worried that because I was female I would be told to do the 'women part' – and *he* would get what I thought would be the more interesting, politically significant assignments. However, an incident in my first week led to a gradual change of mind. A recently appointed and progressive minister had instructed his officials to meet a group of NGO representatives and feminist academics who had long been critical of the ministry for its lack of any WID policy (Eyben, 2007). I knew nothing of this. Before my new job I had been living in various parts of Africa and Asia for twenty years; both the lobbyists and the lobbied were equally strange to me.

Four male officials sat on a little dais at one end of the room, warding off with evasive, non-committal replies the challenging questions and pointed remarks of the women lobbyists. It was an uncomfortable atmosphere. When the chairman saw me standing at the back of the room observing this unfruitful exchange, he asked me forward. 'At last,' he must have thought, 'we have a woman in the office who can handle these wearisome matters.' With some embarrassment – I felt I was being taken advantage of – I said a few inane words and the meeting drew to a close. Thereafter, my superiors made it clear that among my WID responsibilities was keeping the women's lobby under control, to ensure it did not cause any difficulties for them. Whatever the minister's intentions might have been, his officials viewed his interest in 'women's issues' as something to which only a symbolic response was required. I began to be irritated. I disliked being cast in the role of the token woman.

Soon after this encounter, I went to a conference where many of the lobbyists were present. I had no reputation as a WID specialist – indeed no reputation at all, as I had been out of the country since I was a student. I knew no one in the UK academic and NGO circles to which those women belonged. One of them approached me and said, 'You know, we're going to put a lot of pressure on.' Without thinking, and to my own and her apparent surprise, I replied, 'Please do, please do! The more pressure the better – if we are to change things.' I spoke spontaneously. I was 'thinking in action'. I appreciated the significance of my words only after I had spoke them. Then I discovered where my heart lay. Later, I came to see that unplanned moment as the start of a conscious strategy to change the ministry – a strategy that relied heavily on making friends with the lobby group, as I recount in the final section of Chapter 11 (Eyben, 2013b).

Meanwhile, I became fascinated by how other feminist bureaucrats were trying to make gender equality and women's empowerment a more central feature of international development agendas. We exchanged hints and tactics in the coffee breaks of international meetings, but had neither time nor support for more systematic and critical reflection on our craft. Nor were those outside our organizations able to give us as much help. This is because, knowing little about the reality of our position, they were ignorant about how best to ally with us in a common cause. It is risky for bureaucrats to divulge their more subversive tactics to enquiring academics. When one such researcher interviewed a number of DFID staff, including me, in the 1990s, I was very cautious and guarded. The 'Ms Mandarin' of the published text (Kaufman, 1997) was a very pale shadow of my real self. When years later I started work at the Institute of Development Studies (IDS), I found that academic colleagues' ignorance of the internal processes of development bureaucracies resulted in them seeing us as faceless, uniform automatons. How to bridge this reality gap?

Rather than interviewing the bureaucrats, what about supporting their reflective practice? Reflective practice is about being aware of the processes of thinking-in-action, which are the essence of any craft (Schön, 1983). By making that craft visible to oneself, it can more easily be shared and improved. Reflective practice can be strengthened through action research, whereby practical knowledge is constructed and communicated through mutual questioning, learning, and support. These are methods that encourage individual and collective critical reflections on how we live our lives and relate to others. As Reason and Bradbury (2001) emphasize, the *process* of enquiry may be more important for those directly involved, than any published research product – as some participants discovered. One of them said to me, 'Do not underestimate the effect of this project,' citing instances of solidarity when fellow participants had found themselves together in global policy spaces.

I therefore proposed an approach known as 'first- and second-person enquiry' (Reason, 1999). 'First-person enquiry' means consciously observing our own daily professional experiences and seeking to explain instances of success and failure. 'Second-person enquiry' involves collectively setting questions and sharing findings among those researching themselves. Andrea Cornwall and colleagues took such an approach with a group of staff at Sida, the Swedish bilateral agency (Arora-Jonsson and Cornwall, 2006). Unlike focus-group methods – where the researcher is in control – everyone in a 'second-person inquiry' has a say in deciding what questions are to be addressed and the conclusions the group might reach.

We were scattered all over the world and met together – at workshops – only three times between 2007 and 2010. In between, I had separate, semi-structured conversations with participants. Those conversations, the workshop discussions, and my observations of meetings where one or more of the participants were present, are the evidence for what follows. Through the device of conversations that take place between these five women, this chapter, and Chapters 8 and 11 (Eyben, 2013a, 2013b), explores relationships, politics, power, coalitions, and discourses and looks at how these shape and inform the feminist bureaucrat's craft.

New York

I now invite the reader to the first of three moments in the life of our project. We are gathering in Ratna's open-plan loft in downtown Manhattan. She has cooked a large casserole of fish stew and left it on the stove to heat up for when I arrive in the early evening to get things ready. It is late February and the first week of the annual meeting of the United Nations Commission on the Status of Women. The CSW formal proceedings are accompanied by many parallel activities, including discussion panels and showcase events, but above all, it provides the opportunity for people from all over the world to meet informally, exchange ideas, and plot strategies. Along with civil servants from women's national machineries, and activists from grassroots organizations and global networks, our feminist development agency bureaucrats also come to New York. It is an ideal opportunity for our group to meet.

Claudia is the first to arrive. She has had a demanding day. She has persuaded some of her colleagues from the Washington office of her organization to come up to New York to meet a global civil society network that has been criticizing her organization's economic policies and their impact on women. Claudia has managed to facilitate successfully the meeting with both parties and is feeling that it was useful and constructive. Karin arrives a few minutes later, looking surprisingly perky. Because she flew in from Europe only two days earlier, she took advantage of jet-lag to get up at four o'clock that morning and to work in her hotel room on the draft of a revised gender strategy for her bilateral agency; a draft that must go for ministerial approval later that week, once her boss – the head of the gender equality and human rights department – has approved it. Karin still finds it challenging to write in the style of a civil servant rather than that of an academic.

The last two members of our group arrive together as they have been at the same meeting. Marianne's government's mission to the United Nations provides a daily evening briefing to NGOs based in its country, about the CSW negotiations to which Gillian has been. As a member of her government's delegation to the CSW, Marianne is having a hard time making her civil servant colleagues in the women's affairs ministry understand gender and development issues. In the taxi to Ratna's place, Marianne and Gillian have had a good laugh about the delegation's mixed messages to the NGO lobby. She tells Gillian about the time she was part of her government's delegation to the Beijing Women's Conference. She had to persuade the delegation leader that just because in their own country the monarchy was based on primogeniture, this should not mean that the government should oppose the paragraph in the draft Platform for Action about inheritance rights. 'I told them, "For goodness sake! This should not mean that we are not in favour of women in Africa having equal rights to inherit land!" In the end they agreed to stay silent rather than oppose the paragraph, but I was still very embarrassed. I had a quiet word with the Zambians who were leading the fight to keep this paragraph in and told them that my own ministry was on their side, even if the rest of my country's government was not.'

Being, feeling and doing feminism

Ratna twists her wine glass between her fingers, looks around, and asks, 'What does it mean to be a feminist within a global policy institution and stay connected to what drove me there in the first place – to do this work?'

'It's important to me – as a feminist,' Marianne replies, 'to ground myself in external alliances and constituencies, to stay real, to stay connected. My connections – particularly with the feminist lobby – are distanced, not just geographically, but distanced in terms of the email traffic I have and the conversations I have with people … They are ad hoc. The last time I felt energized and connected was when I went to the African Feminist Forum, which was almost two years ago. And then there was some email traffic, but it's fallen away, and now I need to try again.'

Claudia picks at her salad and worries she does not know enough theory to qualify for the epithet 'feminist'. Then she draws in a breath: 'But if a feminist is someone interested in changing power relations, then yes, I'd hold my hand up on that one.'

'Identity is complex', says Karin. 'It is about knowing who we are, about others knowing who we are, and us in turn knowing who those others think we are.'

Karin mentions Jenkins (2008), who she read while still an academic, and talks about his discussion of identity – that how we see ourselves might not be the same as how others see us. And of course there are many different feminist identities. Everyone agrees. Indeed, feminist bureaucrats have a responsibility to recognize and respond to multiple feminist identities. 'For all these reasons', says Karin, 'I find it simpler and more effective to sidestep rather than embrace the feminist label.'

'I'm not sure about it. I am a feminist but should I label myself as one?' Gillian asks. Her NGO colleagues share her social transformation goals without recognizing themselves as feminists, and Gillian is careful not to alienate them. She adds, 'I think you can become so entrenched in your identity as an activist against a dominant structure that you don't see the opportunities. You're just painting an entire field of people a particular colour ... Maybe that's why a lot of people are turned off by feminism, because it's become reified in some way.'

'Well keeping quiet about our feminism doesn't mean we have abandoned our identity,' says Karin.

'The problem', says Gillian, carefully picking out a bone from her spoon of fish stew, 'is that how we label ourselves matters – not only for our own sense of purpose and how we relate with our colleagues, but also for how we are perceived by other feminists.'

'There are, of course, people', Marianne observes, 'who are natural feminists.' She explains that she means those who do not see themselves as part of a movement, but are nevertheless good allies within the organization.

'But there is another kind of woman bureaucrat', says Ratna, emptying her wine glass, 'who's happy to admit to her feminism in her personal life but who abandons it at work. I have a colleague who, when it comes to trying to persuade her to do stuff in her team on women's rights, doesn't feel that it's going to help her do her job'.

'Equally depressing', says Gillian with a sigh, 'are those feminists whose self-proclaimed "feminist" practice is just not very good and who act in a way that reinforces the negative stereotypes of feminisms.' She recounts an incident that sticks in her mind of going to a meeting of an international civil society network. The chairperson started the meeting by announcing she was a feminist and that she was going to adopt a feminist approach to running the meeting. 'Which', says Gillian, 'in her interpretation seemed to mean no chairing at all. The meeting was a shambles!'

Karin jumps up to help Ratna serve out second helpings of fish stew. We swap recollections of civil society activists whom we have invited to meetings with senior officials in our organizations. The activists dress in a manner likely to reinforce the anti-feminist prejudices of the officials that we had hoped the activists might be able to influence. Claudia laughs and takes off her formal navy blue jacket. 'We have to be conscious of how others perceive others. It matters to project the right image.' She unscrews her pearl choker and pops it in the pocket of the jacket. 'We have to dress like bureaucrats not like feminists.'

Working together

Ratna puts down her napkin and fetches more wine. 'But what really matters is working with others. And trust. I remember working with a colleague and how we politically and morally supported each throughout the battles with the executive.'

Karin has had a similar experience. She recounts how a strong bond between her manager and the head of country operations meant that together they were able to carve out a permissive space for Karin to pursue a feminist agenda.

Ratna frowns. She was not so lucky, when young, like Karin is now. 'There are in-crowds and out-crowds, and if you are part of the out-crowd it is difficult to know how decisions get made, even those made by senior feminists.'

'The alliances you form, or the inspiration you get, or the partners you work with, are rarely found among your own colleagues', says Claudia, who is also not convinced by the possibility of making strong ties across the organizational hierarchy. 'You know, in my previous job I had a great outreach, but it was either to civil society organizations or other like-minded people in development agencies. And similarly now, I probably find much more understanding talking to UNIFEM or even to the gender section of the World Bank, than I would find in my own office. Let me tell you ...'

'What really matters', Gillian interrupts, 'is how to build solidarity relations with the feminist groups in the South that we are financing.'

Karin, the ex-academic, agrees and cites the 'under Western eyes' critique of feminists in the North imposing their frames of reference on the South (Mohanty, 1986). Claudia, folding her napkin neatly, concurs, '... because my "subordinate" position as a woman is in many ways counteracted or overshadowed by the power I hold as Northern, white, middle-class.'

'No one wants to be seen as belonging to an elite ... everyone wants to be seen as a subaltern,' says Gillian, our group's ironist.

'Race is an important factor in a multilateral organization like mine, yet nobody talks about it,' says Ratna, following her own train of thought.

'But it is not just a question of race or nationality,' says Claudia. 'I was a working-class child from the post-second world war welfare state. I went to grammar school, university, everything was paid for us. The next generation – they aren't us. Life is more difficult for the younger ones.' Karin nods with agreement and makes a thumbs up sign.

'The other thing', Claudia continues, 'is that I, as a working-class woman, am associating every day with highly elite women from the South. Isn't that funny? Things aren't that simple, are they?'

'And age also matters', says Karin. 'I am tired of the women lobbying my agency reminding me I don't have behind me their history of a 30-year struggle.'

This reminds Marianne of a young woman who used to work with her. 'We were at a workshop in Zimbabwe and she took me aside to tell me she had heard I had separated from my husband. And she was crying. I asked why she was crying and she said, "I really want to do this work but it kills me, the number who are divorced or not married, or don't have children. Is that the price you have to pay?" And she said, "at least you seemed to be, like, married – now even *you* are getting separated." And I thought, Oh my God, this is horrible. This is the next generation. I mean, why would they ever do this work if that is what they see?'

'Well that's it', says Gillian. 'I am not able to draw a line between my paid job and what I do outside work. It's been a life choice, not an approach to work.'

Does that make us different, we wonder, from others equally passionate – environmental activists, for example? We think it does. By being women, we have a sense of solidarity with other women – different from the feelings an environmental campaigner might have for trees.

'The personal is political. It still resonates', says Marianne. 'At the same time, do we set ourselves too-high standards?' she continues as she helps clear away the plates. Someone who recently got a job in another agency told Marianne of her disappointment in finding her colleagues in the gender equality unit failing to live up to her expectations of a feminist collaborative way of working. The problem, Marianne tells us, is that leaders in 'women only' units are often excessively criticized and challenged by their colleagues within the unit. 'I remember being part of what I considered a fairly high-performing organization but always imagined what we could do if we could get rid of that level of dysfunction.'

'Aha', says Ratna, 'but what does high performance mean? What *is* success?'

We are too tired now to answer. That's for next time we meet. Karin, having got up so early that morning, is nodding off. The evening is drawing to an end.

Conclusion

Feminist identity is complex. There is no single feminism, indeed feminist bureaucrats working in development have a responsibility to recognize and respond to multiple feminist identities. It is a difficult balancing act. On the one hand, many people in the women's movement may not even perceive such bureaucrats as feminists – should they even declare themselves publicly to be so – while on the other hand, colleagues at work would be put off, if feminists explicitly labelled themselves as such.

It is important to be aware of, and manage, the effects on others; otherwise there is the risk, not only of diminishing influence within the organization and in wider networks, but also of letting down allies. Being conscious of how one is perceived by others, and creating a persona that influences these perceptions, is an aspect of the job. It relates to communication and the strategic use of language, including getting the message across simply and clearly. At the same time, and underneath all this, the purpose does not change; although what can and cannot be done depends on location. While working from inside a bureaucracy leads to certain constraints, as well as opportunities, this does not mean abandoning feminist identity, nor the value attached to solidarity as part of that identity. While very challenging, most important is how to build solidarity relations with the feminist groups in the South, that development agencies are financing.

References

Arora-Jonsson, S. and Cornwall, A. (2006) 'Making connections: learning about participation in a large aid bureaucracy', in R. Eyben (ed.) *Relationships for Aid*, pp. 80–93, London: Earthscan.

Etherington, K. (2004) *Becoming a Reflexive Researcher: Using Ourselves in Research*, London: Jessica Kingsley Publishers.

Eyben, R. (2007) 'Gender myths in the British aid programme', in A. Cornwall, E. Harrison, and A. Whitehead (eds), *Feminisms and Development: Contradictions, Contestations, and Challenges*, London: Zed Press.

Eyben, R. (2013a) 'Finding our organizational way', in R. Eyben and L. Turquet (eds), *Feminists in Development Organizations: Change from the Margins*, pp. 117–26, Rugby, UK: Practical Action Publishing.

Eyben, R. (2013b) 'Intimate knowledge of the material at hand', in R. Eyben and L. Turquet (eds), *Feminists in Development Organizations: Change from the Margins*, pp. 165–76, Rugby, UK: Practical Action Publishing.

Heron, J. and Reason, P. (1997) 'A participatory inquiry paradigm', *Qualitative Inquiry* 3: 274–94 <http://dx.doi.org/10.1177%2F107780049700300302>.

Jenkins, R. (2008) *Social Identity*, Abingdon: Taylor & Francis.

Kaufman, G. (1997) 'Watching the ethnographers: A partial ethnography' in R. Grillo and J. Stirrat (eds), *Discourses of Development*, Oxford: Berg.

Mohanty, C. (1988) 'Under Western eyes: Feminist scholarship and colonial discourses', *Feminist Review* 30: 61–88 <http://dx.doi.org/10.2307%2F1395054>.

Reason, P. (1999) 'Integrating action and reflection through cooperative inquiry' *Management Learning* 30: 207–26 <http://dx.doi.org/10.1177%2F1350507699302007>.

Reason, P. and Bradbury, H. (2001) 'Introduction: Enquiry and participation in a world worthy of human aspiration', in P. Reason and H. Bradbury (eds) *Handbook of Action Research: Participative Inquiry and Practice*, pp. 1–14, London: Sage.

Schön, E. (1983) *The Reflective Practitioner*, New York: Basic Books.

Turquet, L. (2013) 'Who is the better feminist?', in R. Eyben and L. Turquet (eds), *Feminists in Development Organizations: Change from the Margins*, pp. 103–16, Rugby, UK: Practical Action Publishing.

About the author

Rosalind Eyben is a Professorial Research Fellow at the Institute of Development Studies, University of Sussex. She is a social anthropologist with a professional background in development policy and practice, and a committed teacher in the IDS doctoral and master's programmes, including on gender and development. She has designed and facilitated numerous workshops for international development practitioners all over the world. Her research interests focus on power and relations in international aid. From 2006–11 she convened the global policy programme of the International Research Consortium on Pathways of Women's Empowerment and is currently developing a new area of work exploring the knowledge/power practices of donors that sustain the invisibility of unpaid care as a development policy issue. In 2010 she launched the Big Push Forward that has created an international network challenging the current audit culture in development. She was awarded a CBE in 2000 and is a board member of UNRISD and ActionAid UK.

CHAPTER 5

'It's just a text – who cares?' Construction of texts in the context of EU policies

Brigitte Holzner

*This chapter illustrates – with two examples – the procedures applied for the formu-
lation of politically negotiated texts that guided international policies in the field of
women, gender, and development. The challenges in the preparation and negotiation
process that ultimately led to a formal position of the European Union are described
from the perspective of a gender adviser to a member state's Ministry of Foreign
Affairs. The chapter also articulates the individual experience of the switch from
a rather self-determined academic task toward the accommodation of the rules of
bureaucratic environments. Finally, some critical questions about the impact of such
policy texts are raised.*

A development bureaucracy is required to engage in gender mainstreaming
as a strategic demand, backed by gender equality goals stipulated in national
law and international declarations and conventions. This strategic demand
allows the opening of discursive spaces. However, bureaucracies also function
as disciplining forces that restrict individual actions.

I present an example of successful use of discursive space that was built
on contemporary debates and insights by feminist development studies. As a
contrast, an example of failure will also be discussed, demonstrating the limits
to policy when politics interfere. This chapter should help other novices to
the world of international policy and politics to reduce their feeling of culture
shock when they move from university to a government institution. It should
also show the academic world how policy/political texts are constructed, and
by what processes, leading to final political consensus on texts that are in
the end called 'communications', 'declarations', 'conclusions', or 'resolutions'.

Coming from the academic world to the world of development bureaucracy, I had no idea that the creation of public texts had to pass through a
validation process of negotiation and consensual agreement. An academic/
scholar composes the text herself, which then undergoes a review process
by professional experts on the topic. The comments of the review are seen
as recommendations, and she herself can decide on the final version to be
delivered to the publisher of the journal or book. It is only the publisher

http://dx.doi.org/10.3362/9781780448046.005

who makes the decision as to whether the text will be published or not. An academic/scholar owns her text, and her qualifications are judged by the quality of her published texts. Being socialized in the world of universities and consultancies for teaching, training, and research – and then in an international institute as a lecturer in gender and development studies – I had no idea of the alienation I would experience in the hierarchical structure of government bureaucracy and diplomacy. Carving out a personal space in this new world was an art I could only learn by observation, participation, and – not least – trial and error.

When taking up the position of gender adviser at the Austrian Development Agency, the operative institution of Austrian development cooperation, one of my tasks was to advise the Ministry of Foreign Affairs (MFA) on gender mainstreaming issues at the international level, along with gender-mainstreaming tasks related to development cooperation programmes and projects. I was confronted with requests to contribute to the minister's speeches, to advise on my country's position regarding international agreements, and to report on advances regarding developmental governance frameworks such as the Millennium Development Goals or the Monterrey Consensus on Financing for Development. I was also invited to be a member of government delegations and to speak 'on behalf of the Government', a role hitherto unknown to me. For those tasks, I needed to learn that my texts were not mine any more; that they won't appear on my CV under the 'publications' section, and that anything I wrote for the public had to undergo a process of authorization. My texts were no longer, for example, dealing with family farms in postsocialist environments or the potentials and problems of Bourdieu's concepts as applied to gender in development.

Rather, the texts I wrote were descriptions of successful development projects the agency had been funding, and were used as a PR instrument to advertise the relevance of development cooperation. Other types of texts were political: briefs for the minister or statements for the ministry on the occasion of international events – multilateral meetings at the level of the United Nations (e.g. the 2008 Doha conference on Financing for Development) or the European Union. It was not peer academics, with the same professional expertise, who were deciding on the quality of my texts, but ministerial staff – driven by the need to give the country a good international reputation or to cater to the expectations of an undefined 'public' that should be convinced of the merits of development cooperation. Political reason overtook academic reason; simplicity overtook complexity; the 'quick fix' overtook careful investigation.

Texts from international bodies such as the European Union (EU) landed on my desk for comment. Unknown persons had drafted those texts, which were channelled into a commenting process in order to give all member states the opportunity to add or delete words, sentences, or paragraphs. I was unaware that expressions such as 'sexual and reproductive health and rights' were still highly politically loaded phrases. Abbreviated as SRHR, this phrase appeared in the final document of the UN's 1994 Cairo Conference on Population and Development.[1] The inclusion of SRHR represented a success of the international women's movement against conservative, religious governments who object to women's rights to decide on partner choice, fertility control, and pregnancy. In my former university teaching I had explained the genesis of this phrase, which departed from earlier family planning rhetoric, and had worked with students to operationalize sexual and reproductive rights in the practice of quality of care; an exercise that could not create controversy, as it was rooted in empirical observations and interviews (Holzner et al., 2002).

To my surprise, in the world of international development policy, SRHR – despite the Cairo Programme of Action – remained politically highly charged; defended by certain European countries and opposed by others. Defenders attentively scrutinized draft development documents and communications to examine whether SRHR appeared in the text at all, whether SRHR was embedded unambiguously in sentences, or left unseen in text passages that dealt with women's health or human rights. If so, defenders – i.e. like-minded colleagues – emailed or phoned each other, proposed alternative wordings, and promised each other to agree on the insertion of the four words in the text. Texts were a product of support, dissent, negotiation, and finally of consensus and thus compromises, and through that process became political. Texts were infused with the political orientation of the member states, although the ideological orientation of the ruling political party (Social Democrat, Christian Democrat, Liberal) was nowhere explicitly mentioned. The member state had a certain official position towards SRHR, but it was civil servants who brought that position into the texts. As a novice in the policy world of international relations, I had to learn that such texts received the status of 'conclusions' or 'agreements'.[2] Their authorship remained anonymous; it was 'the Council', 'the Commission' or even 'the United Nations' that became the owner. And that ownership was then also the property of all European member state populations, or even of the whole world in the case of the United Nations. Sometimes I felt happy when I could discover some words of mine in a segment of a sentence or even a whole sentence of mine in those official texts. But only I knew, and only I could tap myself on the shoulder with a silent 'well done'.

In this chapter, I intend to show some of the dynamics that lead to the adoption of policy texts by consensual agreement. I select a positive and a negative example and will show which steps are taken in the preparation and negotiation; how informal relationships are used for formal decision-making processes; and how the politics of international relations might interfere with feminist concerns. I'll show the process of generating texts and the bureaucratic rituals necessary for their negotiation. My reflections are based on personal notes in a work diary and on discussions with the peer group of the Pathways project.

Both examples deal with the role of individual member states in the European Union.[3] The EU wants to speak with one voice in international bodies such as the United Nations, and naturally – with 27 diverse members – this requires consensus-seeking in advance. Similarly the G77, as the representative body of around 130 developing states today, intends to harmonize the diverse positions of its members at the United Nations.[4]

An example of success: women in armed conflict and the EU response

Every EU presidency focuses on certain policy themes during its half year of responsibility. For example, concerning the women's agenda: the respective presidency uses a topic from the Beijing Platform for Action and elaborates indicators for its measurement in EU member states. Preparations for pursuing the policy themes start six months before the actual start date of the presidency, in close interaction with the preceding and subsequent presidencies in a so-called 'troika' arrangement. EU presidencies also prepare council conclusions during their half-year term, which are circulated for comments by member states before adoption by the Council. During this process government officials can suggest and negotiate among member states, adding, deleting, and correcting the paragraphs of the draft. The presidency consolidates the changes and forwards the draft to the Council, where a final round of discussions provides the opportunity for further formulations. However, common practice is that during the official discussion at the Council meeting no substantial amendments are made, so that the Council conclusions can be adopted.

In what follows, I want to present a special experience in which I can show a process of preparation for Council conclusions that allowed for the combination of academic and policy work. Four months before the start of the Slovenian EU presidency (January – June 2008), the Austrian secretary-general (SG) of development cooperation met with her Slovenian colleague, who informed her about the plan to prepare Council conclusions regarding women and children in armed conflict. A specialized Dutch consultancy firm, European Centre for Development Policy Management (ECDPM), had already been asked to prepare a study regarding the EU response to women and children in armed conflict. Austria offered support for the Slovenian effort; Slovenia accepted; and I was asked by the Austrian SG to follow up on the offer. I contacted my Slovenian colleague and expressed our willingness to support, asking what kind of support she would like to receive. She proposed that I should comment on the study. Reading the draft, I saw that it focused, in an imbalanced way, on children; and that, women were seen, primarily, as mothers and caregivers – not as individuals having their own agency. I suggested that one study should focus on children and armed conflict and a separate study should focus explicitly on women and armed conflict (WAAC). I communicated this proposal to the Austrian Ministry of Foreign Affairs, received its backing, and managed to secure funding from our agency for a second such study. I also communicated this proposal to

ECDPM, which shared my concern that putting women and children together in one study would overload the topic and would not do justice to women's special concerns in situations of armed conflict, independently of whether they were mothers or not. One useful argument was that the United Nations already had two separate Security Council resolutions on the subject: Security Council Resolution 1325 (UNSCR 1325) devoted to women, peace and security (2000), and Security Council Resolution 1611 (UNSCR 1611) focusing on children in armed conflict (2005). I then suggested to Slovenia the Austrian Ministry's offer to finance a separate study, which Slovenia accepted. Having the political support in place, I drafted the new terms of reference before Christmas, with the intention that work on the study could start immediately after the holiday break.

Support for the Austrian offer was also given at the EU Gender Experts Meeting in autumn 2007, during which Slovenia presented its plan for a study of children and women in armed conflicts. Participants at that meeting questioned the usefulness of associating women with children and requested a separate discussion, which was the Austrian position exactly. Thus I could inform the meeting of the Austrian support for a separate study.

In communication with the Dutch consultancy firm, I proposed that the author of the children study should also conduct the women study – as he was already entirely familiar with the EU structures, and briefing a new author would take too much time and effort. Choosing the same author also assured a similar structure for the two studies. We agreed that a specialist on women and armed conflict from an international NGO would assist the author with some literature, and I sent him the Brussels Call to Action to End Sexual Violence Against Women of June 2006. (The Brussels Call was a result of a joint UNFPA–EU conference during the Austrian EU presidency at which, as presidency representative, I gave a speech drafted by me and approved by the ministry.) I also informed him of the special issue of *Forced Migration Review* (2007) that had covered the conference, and included a short article by a colleague and myself, and added other literature references.

My ideal was that after the studies on children and women in armed conflict, a sound study on gender in armed conflict would be undertaken by the next presidency. I thought that UNSCR 1325 lacked a gender perspective (nowhere is 'gender' mentioned in the text of the resolution), and that looking at armed conflict from a gender perspective would go beyond the conceptualization of 'women as victims' and 'women as peace builders' – the two notions that permeate that resolution. A gender perspective would also broaden the analysis from inclusion of women in peace talks and would allow the identification of processes of women's inclusion in war as fully fledged agents. (In many wars and armed conflicts women were and are consciously among the fighting forces.) Similarly, a gender perspective would also allow addressing men as peace-seekers and builders, and would articulate their victimization, including sexual assaults that men suffer in war. Furthermore, a true gender perspective could address the complexity of intersectionality

– a differentiation of people along several lines of power such as nationality, ethnicity, religion, caste, and certainly also by economic status or class – interwoven with gender relations of different kinds. But I could not get such a proposal through; during the Slovenian presidency there was no more scope for it, and the French presidency that followed had other priorities and, in any case, was too far removed from my network.

After the Christmas break, the Slovenian Ministry of Foreign Affairs phoned to inform me that Germany was also willing to contribute to the WAAC study. After several phone calls, the German official and I agreed on shared financing; Austria would finance the study and Germany would finance the Dutch firm for all tasks related to logistics and coordination. The author of the study on children was also willing to write the study on women and asked for the assistance of a versatile NGO expert on the topic. Although the author did not have much time, through outstanding efforts he was able to finalize the study within two months, by mid-March.

The next policy step was to lobby for Council conclusions that were recommended by the study. This was difficult. At that time I received unofficial information that two EU member states would be against Council conclusions on WAAC because they would include SRHR, to which they objected. Maybe Slovenia succumbed to their pressure, and therefore wanted presidency conclusions only, to be released at the end of its term. I informed the director of the international relations department of the Ministry of Foreign Affairs and asked for permission to contact my Swedish colleague and others from the gender experts' network to discuss this matter. Austria would certainly want to include SRHR in the council conclusions. The terms of reference clearly stated that the study should serve as a basis for council conclusions.

The next day, a meeting of development ministers was scheduled at which the Slovenian development minister would be present so that she could be approached for clarification of the Slovenian position regarding Council conclusions on WAAC. That meeting could also be used to offer her support. Through several phone calls with colleagues in like-minded countries, support was secured to highlight, in that meeting, the importance of special Council conclusions regarding WAAC. Nevertheless, due to the overfull schedule, the topic was relegated to the end of the meeting and hardly got any attention.

In April, Slovenia presented the study publicly in Brussels to the EU, UNIFEM, and various NGOs,[5] and invited several panellists for comments: representatives from the troika presidencies (Slovenia, Portugal, and Germany from the previous presidencies, and France as the next presidency), Austria as co-funder, the European Commission, and NGOs. Our common ground was the necessity for a strategic approach concerning the EU response to women and armed conflict. The director-general for development cooperation at our foreign ministry asked me to represent her at the presentation of the WAAC study in Brussels in the Slovenian embassy. I arrived in the evening in order to prepare a statement together with the

Austrian mission's representative. The statement emphasized the importance of the study; the necessity for coherence among development, security, and foreign policy objectives of the EU; and for continuation of the topic under the following presidencies. The last point was the explicit wish of our Ministry. We boiled down my more extensive statements to these two points: coherence and continuity. My colleague advised me that only very few things should be emphasized – because they stay in people's minds; long and elaborate comments presented at a panel risk evaporating when they overstretch the audience's capacity to absorb them.

At the meeting, I heard from earlier acquaintances that international NGOs working for reproductive health had joined together for a statement regarding the importance of SRHR – always a sensitive topic due to the standpoints of predominantly Catholic EU countries. The study was received very well and the follow-up process began. After the presentation meeting, our mission was invited to an informal lunch which was attended by France (which was to hold the next EU presidency after Slovenia), Germany, Belgium, the Netherlands, Denmark, the EC, and two persons from the Working Party on Human Rights – but unfortunately not by Slovenia. At that meeting, follow-up of the Council conclusions and actions of solidarity among like-minded member states was to be discussed. The new director of the Social and Human Development Department at the Directorate-General of Development Cooperation (DGDEV), with whom I had spoken earlier, aired the idea that NGOs from Austria and other countries should create lobby bases with progressive NGOs in conservative member states. At that meeting we agreed that the EU should not be taken hostage, in important matters of human rights and women's rights, by a few of the 27 member states.

The discussion concentrated on the follow-up to the study. Preference was given to Council conclusions – which are discussed at the Council meeting and should be approved by the European Parliament. However, Slovenia did not want to prepare Council conclusions regarding women and armed conflict, due to lack of capacity, but intended to include some phrases in the presidency's conclusions at the end of its term.[6] France affirmed that it would continue to focus on women and armed conflict, but probably only in the Working Group on Human Rights (COHOM),[7] and not in the Working Group on Development Cooperation (CODEV),[8] where development topics are discussed broadly which was what we wanted. The French idea was to formulate a 'Comprehensive Approach to Implementing UNSCR 1325 and 1820 on Women, Peace, and Security'. It was good to feel solidarity for the importance of the topic. My realization was that the creation of an informal policy space – like a lunch – among like-minded actors at a medium–high level, is an important strategy.

Two months later, when Slovenia presented its presidency's conclusions, our diplomatic mission in Brussels was very quick – involving me by email and phone – to formulate questions for the Foreign Ministers' Meeting in which Council conclusions were to be discussed. How SRHR would be reflected was included in our catalogue of questions; this is one way to ensure that a policy-relevant issue – in this case SRHR – receives attention, as the questions must be answered by the presidency and the discussion is recorded and published.

Six months later in December 2008, at the end of the French EU presidency, the Council conclusions regarding the European Security and Defence Policy (ESDP) did mention the WAAC study and its recommendations – indicating our efforts had been moderately successful. Council conclusions can be commented upon by EU member states and are discussed at the Council. So although during the Slovenian presidency no special Council conclusions regarding women and armed conflict were launched, the next presidency did take up the baton. Sometimes one fights a particular front, while on another, favourable things happen away from one's attention. In addition, the French did formulate, at the end of their presidency, a 'Comprehensive Approach to the EU Implementation of the United Nations Security Council Resolutions 1325 and 1820 on Women, Peace, and Security',[9] which also mentioned the WAAC study. Since then, this document has guided the EU's Common Security and Defence Policy in regard to gender mainstreaming.

In early 2009, at the next EU Gender Experts Meeting at the Directorate General for Development (DGDEV), the French representative presented the comprehensive approach issued in December 2008. At that occasion, participants raised some criticisms that the DGDEV had been excluded from the preparatory discussions, and that armed conflicts were framed only as a human rights and external relations issue, and not as a development issue. The importance of also seeing armed conflicts as a development issue was finally recognized in the June 2010 council conclusions on the Millennium Development Goals for the United Nations High-Level Plenary meeting in New York and Beyond, where Objective 9 of the annexed EU Gender Action Plan says: 'Support partner countries in fully implementing UNSCR 1325 and 1820, 1888, and 1889', and one action would be to 'Operationalize the EU Comprehensive Approach on Implementing UNSCR 1325 and 1820 on Women, Peace and Security from the perspective of development cooperation and other external assistance'.[10]

Alliances – formal and informal – are crucial

Changing the discourse from women as mothers to women as actors was a considerable success. It was a change from a conservative position to a progressive one, from considering women only in the context of 'women and children' to women as rights holders. This had the consequence that EU institutions had to lay special emphasis on women affected by armed conflict, irrespective of whether they were mothers or not. Another insight is that discourses flutter around and vibrate in people's minds. In this case, the institutional frames of working parties and departments for human rights, development, and external relations have taken up those ideas in their mandate and channelled them into public announcements.

The triangulated cooperation based on mutual information and consensus-seeking between the Austrian MFA, the Brussels mission, and me resulted in the WAAC study. The text of that study created even more consensus-seeking among officials from the EU and its member states, as well as from feminist NGOs, and became the basis for further documents dealing with women affected by armed conflict.

We may conclude that alliances among officials, thematic experts, and NGOs can bring good results. It is important that the influential persons in the bureaucracy create political space, even beyond national boundaries. Identifying rapport through common language, study at the same school, residence in the same country, etc. is an important path for finding understanding and support.[11] Lunches and dinners put everyone in a good mood and provide an informal space for lobbying and advocacy. Such hospitality events are a good base for dialogue and not an unnecessary luxury as outsiders might criticize.[12]

Having shown how a discourse can be changed by quick, coordinated actions and carefully chosen alliances, I present below a negative example, where my attempt to influence a discourse failed due to lack of solidarity, weak alliances, and the formalized rules of negotiation at the highest level of policy – the United Nations.

An example of failure: negotiating the EU position for the agreed conclusions of the Commission on the Status of Women

Since the foundation of the UN Commission on the Status of Women (CSW) in 1946, a ten-day session managed by the Division for the Advancement of Women (DAW) has been held nearly every year, around 8 March – International Women's Day. In 2010, the 54th session of the CSW was held.

The Commission on the Status of Women (hereafter referred to as 'CSW' or 'the commission') is a functional commission of the United Nations Economic and Social Council (ECOSOC), dedicated exclusively to gender equality and advancement of women. It is the principal global policymaking body in matters concerning women. Every year, representatives of member states gather at the United Nations headquarters in New York to evaluate progress on gender equality, identify challenges, set global standards, and formulate concrete policies to promote gender equality and advancement of women worldwide. The commission was established by ECOSOC resolution 11(II) of 21 June 1946 with the aim of preparing recommendations and reports to the council on promoting women's rights in political, economic, civil, social, and educational fields. The commission also makes recommendations to the council on urgent problems requiring immediate attention.[13]

Expert group meetings are organized on every continent to prepare the commission's sessions. At the sessions, experts are invited to present an overview of the current knowledge and debates concerning the current theme. These form the basis of the agreed conclusions, which are the output of the annual session. Agreed conclusions contain an analysis of the priority theme and a set of concrete recommendations for governments, intergovernmental bodies and other institutions, civil society actors, and other relevant stakeholders, to be implemented at the international, national, regional, and local levels.[14] In addition, some member states propose resolutions (e.g. on the situation of Palestinian women or on HIV/AIDS). These are negotiated and adopted as well, and are brought together with the agreed conclusions to ECOSOC for adoption. Since 1997, agreed conclusions are negotiated as follow-up to the 12 areas of concern in the Beijing Platform for Action of the Fourth World Conference on Women of the United Nations.

Drafts of the agreed conclusions and resolutions are usually sent out one month prior to the session, allowing member states to prepare comments that are then negotiated during the session and agreed on. The negotiations often last until midnight or longer. They require knowledge of earlier agreements and resolutions as well as of the CEDAW and Beijing Platform for Action texts, because 'agreed language' from those texts is less controversial. Controversies arise around 'new language' in which the insights of scholars, demands of NGOs, and political positions of governments need to be reconciled in new formulations. In order to reach compromises faster, the EU and the G77 prepare their consolidated version of comments to the draft agreed conclusions during the first week of the session. But this consolidation can fall apart when national interests take priority during the negotiations of the second week, in which all member states come together to agree on the final text.

After the opening speeches by the representative of the secretary-general and the representative bodies of women's affairs at the UN (Division for the Advancement of Women [DAW], Office of the Special Adviser to the secretary-general on Gender Issues and Advancement of Women [OSAGI], United Nations Development Fund for Women [UNIFEM], and International Research and Training Institute for the Advancement of Women [INSTRAW][15]), the CSW offers an update by the best feminist theoreticians on the topic under discussion. This is followed by a panel discussion with the audience, which consists of government representatives. The next day is partly devoted to two-minute speeches by the women's affairs/gender equality ministers. (These are usually not so exciting as they mostly present very brief overviews of achievements.) The EU and the G77 speak on behalf of their members. Negotiations on the draft conclusions run parallel in the morning session. During the whole two weeks of the session several UN bodies (mostly UNIFEM), some national governments, and many NGOs hold workshops related to the general topic.

In spring 2008 I was government delegate to the 52nd session of the CSW, which was titled 'Financing for Gender Equality'. During my preparations at home for commenting on the draft agreed conclusions, I liaised with feminist NGOs and received some comments from a feminist economist. For discussion with our delegation, I included the collected comments in the draft agreed conclusions, which I retrieved from the CSW website a few weeks before the start of the session. Most delegates arrive on Saturday afternoon, as on Sunday morning they need to queue for their visitor's pass – sometimes for several hours – at a small office opposite the UN building, where their photos are taken and passes are printed. In the evening prior to the start of the Monday morning session, I presented my comments and suggestions for changes at the preparatory meeting at our mission office in New York. No other delegate had been able to prepare any comments, which put me in an advantageous position; all of my comments were accepted by our delegation and by our mission representative – who would negotiate with the other member states.

It is always the EU presidency that leads the discussion of comments on the draft, and that incorporates – mostly during long evening meetings – comments that have been made during the discussion or have been sent later via email to the respective embassy. In the EU's well guarded mission on the 20th floor, East 41st Street in New York – only accessible by visitor's pass – the member state delegates came together in the meeting room. Each of the 27 member states had one seat at the table, which was occupied by its mission representative in New York. In front of each was a black plastic standard called 'flag', with the country's name printed on it, and smart mobile phones, which the representatives used for instant consultations with their ministries back home. The other delegates 'from the capital' sat behind the table, on chairs that were lined up along the walls. This closeness permitted quick, whispered information exchanges.

The coffee breaks allowed bilateral encounters to achieve support, if necessary, on certain wordings. Those negotiations were held in the mornings during the first week of the session, starting at 9 and continuing until 11 a.m. Afterwards, we delegates walked twenty minutes to the UN building, to attend various sessions and workshops.

The Slovenian chair (Slovenia held the EU presidency during the first half of 2008) led the negotiations very strictly, not allowing much discussion. Most of the inputs, including mine, were accepted without discussion, but the one addition that I had prepared – regarding coherence to a paragraph about trade policies – was difficult to push through. I explain the details regarding the text in question below.

Original text:

11) k.: Incorporate gender perspectives in the formulation, implementation and evaluation of trade policies *by taking into account coherence between trade policies, macro-economic policy frameworks and human development policy*, and facilitate the active participation of women decision-makers and women's organisations in national, regional and international trade decision-making structures and processes; (Based on E.CN.6/2008/2, para. 88(i))

The part in italics was the addition that my delegation had suggested, but as I could not refer to 'agreed language' my defence was weak. I thought that creating a coherent link between trade policy, macroeconomic policy, and human development policy would make sense, and respond to a demand, which had been put forward by feminist NGOs for a long time. All participants in the negotiations had already agreed to the addition. But in a moment of silence, a member of a Nordic country raised her flag saying that her ministry of women's affairs had, just now, instructed her by phone to object to the phrase. Then to my surprise other flags went up – Germany, the United Kingdom, Spain ... Speakers said that they supported the Nordic country, and the Austrian representative, deciding that we could not hold on to our proposal, withdrew the suggested formulation. I felt disappointed – nearly sad – and a bit angry that my point about coherence between economic and social policy was discarded by those whom I had believed to be 'like-minded'. Was I too much an academic, too much an activist? After four years, was I still an alien in the world of bureaucracy and diplomacy? I started to reflect ...

This was a defeat of a clear feminist position that emphasizes the need to look at the human development impacts (including gender impacts) of trade liberalization. My position on the relevance of a critical look at structural adjustment policies and macroeconomic policies was inspired, first, by my function as chair of the feminist network Women in Development Europe (WIDE), that had concentrated on gender and trade as well as on follow-up to the Beijing Platform for Action; and second, by my academic work as a lecturer on women, gender, and development, where I had taught economic restructuring policies and their impact on poor women, raising concerns about human development.

I speculated about the causes of this defeat. In 2006, the Nordic country had elected a centre-right majority government that was inclined to give preference to economic arguments over social ones. Although that country's representative personally supported my suggestion, someone sitting in a ministry of her country had decided that a link between trade and human development was unacceptable. Another cause might have been the nature of the representatives at such negotiations. Most of them were not academic gender studies experts, nor economists, and only a few were feminists. Such delegates are mostly bureaucrats, who hold a certain function for some years, until they move on – or are moved on – to other functions. Their knowledge of feminist standpoints is by and large limited, and they are usually quite far away from NGOs in general and feminist NGOs in particular.

Finally, my own lobbying was not convincing enough. During the breaks I had not created alliances, thinking that specific support would not be necessary. At the table I could not directly communicate with the negotiators, but was sitting as resource person behind my country's representative – a diplomat at the Austrian mission who had been meeting regularly with the other country representatives during the run-up to the CSW in the preceding weeks. He acted as a diplomat; assessing the majority and minority positions, wanting to avoid resistance, and probably trying to prevent any antagonism towards Austria at the moment that it was applying for membership to the Security Council.

I hoped then, that member states of the South would challenge the EU position and that the final conclusions would include what was excluded by the EU. Our delegate from a women's NGO network observed that process, and I encouraged her to contact other NGOs from the South who might want to take up the topic. I felt that out of loyalty to my government I could not do more, and anyway, I thought that perhaps the wording of a particular paragraph was not so important, as in the process of negotiations during the second week of the CSW it would most likely be turned upside down.

So what did happen to that paragraph? I did not attend negotiations during the second week, when the EU discussed the text with the G77 and other countries of both the South and North, as I had permission from my agency only to stay during the first week of the CSW. Instead, I screened the final text of the CSW on the website and found the paragraph later in the document, with the following formulation:

> 11) w.: Identify and address the differential impacts of trade policies on women and men and incorporate gender perspectives in the formulation, implementation and evaluation of trade policies, develop strategies to expand trade opportunities for women producers, and facilitate the active participation of women in national, regional and international trade decision-making structures and processes; (AGREED AD REF)

Thus the final formulation did not refer to coherence but emphasized the differential impacts of trade policies of women and men, and added a phrase regarding the expansion of trade opportunities to women producers. I consoled myself that one could read 'differential impacts' as referring implicitly to 'human development', as I had suggested.

Later, I coped with this failure by questioning the meaning of those CSW conclusions – Who knows about them? Who uses them? What power do they have? Probably, nobody really cares, I thought; No governments, no NGOs, no academics, and not the life of one poor woman would be changed by such conclusions. So my inner dialogue paralleled that of the fox in Aesop's fable, who could not reach the grapes hanging above and so consoled itself that they were sour. I told myself that such conclusions are not very significant, unlike Security Council resolutions – which are binding for UN member states – and even those are often ignored. But such are the rituals of the UN. The power of international relations circles around texts and the struggle over words and phrases is the working method of member states to acquire political voice in the big institutional body of the United Nations.

What I learnt: influencing a discourse requires thorough preparation

Influencing a discourse, in this example of the link between trade policies and human development (or the deterioration of women's wellbeing because of free-trade policies – see Elson (2004) and Bakker (2007)), is difficult when no discussion is allowed and consensus-seeking is dominated by diplomatic rituals. Thus, the institutional arrangement of the diplomatic space is defined by majority rule and smaller countries often defer to greater, and more powerful, countries on the international scene.

In order to overcome the limitations set by the institutional arrangements in diplomatic spaces, it is necessary to be well prepared at the discursive level. If I had notes from the panel discussion and quotes from academic writings at hand, I might have been able to persuade or to have stimulated debate and reflection. In the end, good arguments might have won over telephoned orders from the capital. The infusion of academic research into political standpoints – which is intended by the structure of the CSW, in which state-of-the-art knowledge exposed during the first days' panels is meant to provide the basis for agreed conclusions – requires attentiveness, preparation, and the prior identification of critical issues.

Conclusion

In conclusion I want to reflect on the relevance of such texts – Do they matter? For whom? When? How? My initial response was that such texts are irrelevant to 'real life', to poverty, to exploitation and discrimination. But are they really so irrelevant?

In the first, positive example, recommendations were given for gender mainstreaming and placing women in higher positions at EU levels. Under the French presidency, COHOM had prepared Council conclusions for a European security and defence policy. Referring to those conclusions, donors funded development partner governments and women's organizations to formulate national action plans to implement UNSCR 1325. Military and police forces were routinely trained and the gender unit at EULEX, the EU's rule of law mission in Kosovo, received legitimacy, personnel and funding. Also, the accountability of 'duty bearers' towards 'rights holders' is strengthened. I cannot establish a causal link due to the lack of inside information, but the above argument appears, to me, convincing.

What about the significance of the CSW agreed conclusions? Obviously the CSW enjoys high visibility: on 29 May 2010, entering CSW as a Google search term brought up 1,770,000 results. In contrast, entering CSW agreed conclusions achieved only 135,000 results – about 8 per cent of the results returned for CSW as a whole. Can we then infer that agreed conclusions are not very important? In interviews for this chapter, experienced insiders in our bureaucracy, as well as members of feminist NGOs, stressed the importance of the CSW agreed conclusions; they are relevant internally for the UN as they contain directions for thematic actions. If phrases like 'urge' are used, then the UN or member states need to do something. This seems to explain why so much energy goes into the negotiations. Countries from the South – assembled in the G77 – pay special attention to the agreed conclusions, for they are one of their few strong cards at the UN. That is also why the Holy See – a close observer of debates about sexual and reproductive rights – sends several delegates to the CSW to give a speech during the first two days, when governments present their achievements and positions.

Some of my informants think that agreed conclusions have the same strength as the resolutions that are negotiated at the CSW (e.g. about HIV/AIDS or Palestinian women). Others see more relevance in the resolutions themselves, where a shift in discourses can sometimes be detected. For example, the resolution on macroeconomics of 2010 includes an explicit reference to the care economy,[16] which had not been mentioned in earlier resolutions. Delegates brief their ministries on the agreed conclusions so that, once in a while, a message can be used for policy directions or even for changes in law. I could not find evidence as to whether and how paragraphs of the agreed conclusions have been used as a tool of accountability by feminist organizations. Informants from NGOs also doubted whether the agreed conclusions receive attention commensurate with the energy spent in their formulation. In-depth research about the implications of the agreed conclusions has yet to be done. The bureaucracies in state governance structures, together with feminist NGOs, need to publicize the messages of those conclusions so that citizens can claim what was stated about rights, services, and research. But if the agreed conclusions are only a copy–paste, copy–paste recycling exercise without innovation – they are futile.

Maybe the process around the generation of the agreed conclusions is more important than the output. The CSW has become a global event where state representatives – ministers and gender equality bureaucrats and practitioners – and feminist scholars and leaders of the women's movement, meet annually in New York. In 2010, a total of 3,440 NGO representatives from 138 countries attended the CSW's 54th session. They represented 463 NGOs – of which 423 were ECOSOC accredited, and 40 had been accredited to either the Fourth World Conference on Women or to the 23rd Special Session of the General Assembly.[17] In the absence of women's world conferences since 1995, and with no visible initiative for organizing another world conference, the CSW has become the only regular meeting point of state and civil society actors.

The EU does not organize such huge events and conclusions are not embedded in conference settings. Although process matters much as well, as I have tried to show above, there are fewer actors and more communication takes place through email exchange and telephone calls. However, the working groups of the various EU departments meet weekly, and it is there that conclusions are prepared and their general direction is decided. Experts in the bureaucracies of the member states are consulted for inputs, and in this consultation process, European democratic principles are at work through networks among like-minded countries.

The question, Who cares about such texts?, cannot be answered satisfactorily. We would need some empirical research to draw valid conclusions. Most likely, it is committed individuals in the offices of governments, in working parties of the EU, and in departments of the UN organizations and agencies that care about such texts, to advance their agendas and broaden the spectrum of operationalizing human and women's rights. The foundations for this spectrum are CEDAW and the Beijing Platform for Action. We find both in development policy texts worldwide, in national gender action plans, and they are the basis for legal reform, and ammunition for changing discriminatory religious and national laws. CEDAW and Beijing paragraphs are recalled and reiterated in official communications and in conclusions from EU presidencies and from the CSW, which shows that they have not been forgotten, and that they remain a reminder to governments that once, they had agreed to move forward to achieve gender equality and women's rights. However, CSW and European presidency conclusions are less influential than the original texts of Beijing and CEDAW. They do not create storms; only a breeze that blows through a few corridors in which many doors remain shut.

Notes

1 See <www.unfpa.org/public/home/sitemap/icpd/International-Conference-on-Population-and-Development/ICPD-Summary>.
2 'Communications' of the European Commission are not negotiated but distributed by the Commission to the member states for discussion.
3 That both examples are chosen from the period of the Slovenian EU presidency is accidental and has no particular significance.
4 'The Group of 77 is the largest intergovernmental organization of developing states in the United Nations, which provides the means for the countries of the South to articulate and promote their collective economic interests and enhance their joint negotiating capacity on all major international economic issues within the United Nations system, and promote South–South cooperation for development.' <www.g77.org>.
5 <www.eu2008.si/en/News_and_Documents/Press_Releases/April/0404MZZ_ECDPM_Pipan.html> [accessed 19 February 2013].
6 My Austrian colleagues and I assisted Slovenia in the formulation of that paragraph.
7 <www.se2009.eu/en/meetings_news/2009/10/5/working_party_on_human_rights_cohom.html> [accessed 19 February 2013].
8 <www.se2009.eu/en/meetings_news/2009/7/20/working_party_on_development_cooperation_codev.html> [accessed 19 February 2013].
9 <www.consilium.europa.eu/ueDocs/cms_Data/docs/hr/news187.pdf> [accessed 19 February 2013].
10 <www.consilium.europa.eu/uedocs/cms_Data/docs/pressdata/EN/genaff/115157.pdf> [accessed 19 February 2013].

11 Alumni networks are sites of bonding that open doors to jobs and joint activities. With more women in higher education and in international fellowship programmes, this pathway of policymaking will surely be pursued more actively.

12 This observation is self-evident. As in every family, joint meals enable creating and maintaining bonds. Similarly, in the worlds of business and politics, joint meals and cocktails have the same function – to create and maintain 'social capital', as sociologists call it.

13 <www.un.org/womenwatch/daw/csw/index.html#about> [accessed 19 February 2013].

14 <www.un.org/womenwatch/daw/csw/index.html#about> [accessed 19 February 2013].

15 A decision of the United Nations General Assembly on 2 July 2010, which following long discussions on the creation of a UN entity for Gender Equality and the Empowerment of Women, consolidated UNIFEM, DAW, OSAGI, and INSTRAW into a single body called UN Women <http://www. unwomen.org>.

16 '(f) To take and encourage measures, including, where appropriate, the formulation, promotion and implementation of legal and administrative measures, to facilitate the reconciliation of work and personal and/or family life, such as child and dependant care, parental leave and maternity leave and other leave schemes and flexible working schemes for men and women and, where appropriate, shorter working hours, and design, implement and promote family-friendly policies and services, including affordable, accessible and quality care services for children and other dependants, parental and other leave schemes and campaigns to sensitize public opinion and other relevant actors *on equal sharing of employment and family responsibilities between women and men and emphasise men's equal responsibilities with respect to household work'*, (emphasis added) UN DAW (2010), p.22. With thanks to Christa Wichterich who gave me this lead. Available at <http://daccess-dds-ny.un.org/doc/UNDOC/GEN/ N10/305/76/PDF/N1030576.pdf?OpenElement> [accessed 19 February 2013].

17 www.un.org/womenwatch/daw/beijing15/participation.html#ngo [accessed 19 February 2013].

References

Bakker, I. (2007) Financing for Gender Equality. Background Paper. United Nations Division for the Advancement of Women. <www.un.org/ womenwatch/daw/egm/financing_gender_equality/BackgroundPapers/ BP.1%20Bakker.pdf> [accessed 19 February 2013].

Brussels Call to Action (2006) <www.fmreview.org/FMRpdfs/FMR27/55.pdf> [accessed 19 February 2013].

COHOM (Working Party on Human Rights), Comprehensive Approach to the EU Implementation of the United Nations Security Council Resolutions 1325 and 1820 on Women, Peace and Security <www.consilium.europa. eu/ueDocs/cms_Data/docs/hr/news187.pdf> [accessed 19 February 2013].

Elson, D. (2004) 'Social policy and macroeconomic performance: integrating "the economic" and "the social"' in T. Mkandawire (ed) *Social Policy in a Development Context*, pp. 63–79, London: Palgrave.

Couldrey M., and Morris, T. (eds) (2007), 'Issue 27: Sexual violence: Weapon of war, impediment to peace', *Forced Migration Review* <www.fmreview.org/sites/fmr/files/FMRdownloads/en/FMRpdfs/FMR27/full.pdf> [accessed 19 February 2013].

Holzner, B. M., Kollmann, N., and Darwisyah, S. (2002) *East-West Encounters on Reproductive Health Practices & Policies: Indonesian NGO's Meet Dutch Organizations*, Amsterdam: Aksant.

Sherriff, A. (2007) *Enhancing the EU Response to Children and Armed Conflict, with Particular Reference to Development Policy. Study for the Slovenian EU Presidency*, Discussion Paper No. 82, Maastricht: ECDPM <www.ecdpm.org/Web_ECDPM/Web/Content/Download.nsf/0/BDC6B752D6AF3F26C12573D000386342/$FILE/07-82-eSherriff_CAAC%20study_final.pdf> [accessed 15 April 2013].

Sherriff, A., with K. Barnes (2008) *Enhancing the EU Response to Women and Armed Conflict, with Particular Reference to Development Policy. Study for the Slovenian EU Presidency*, Discussion Paper No. 84 Maastricht: ECDPM. <www.ecdpm.org/Web_ECDPM/Web/Content/Download.nsf/0/6292ACBFE8964535C12574420037222C/$FILE/Sherriff_WAC%20study_DP84_April08.pdf> [accessed 15 April 2013].

UN DAW (2010), Commission on the Status of Women: Report on the fifty-fourth session (13 March and 14 October 2009 and 1–12 March 2010).

Wichterich, C. (2010) Frauenrechtskommission: 54. Tagung 2010, Ernüchterung 15 Jahre nach der Weltfrauenkonferenz in Peking, *Zeitschrift Vereinte Nationen* (German Review on the United Nations).

About the author

Brigitte M. Holzner is a psychologist and development sociologist with broad policy-related experience. Her research and teaching in gender studies, mainly at Dutch universities, cover topics of rural development and industrialization, reproductive and sexual health and rights, economic restructuring, legal pluralism, human trafficking, and armed conflict in development and post-socialist transition contexts. Her country experiences include Indonesia, India, Uganda, Ethiopia, Albania, and Kosovo. For several years she was chair of WIDE (Women in Development Europe) – an international advocacy network of non-governmental organizations and women's rights activists. For six years she worked as gender expert at the Austrian Development Agency, a governmental institution of the Ministry of European and International Affairs, before she took up the position of gender adviser in the European Rule of Law Mission in Kosovo.

CHAPTER 6

'It's fundamentally political': renovating the master's house

Patti O'Neill and Rosalind Eyben

Reflecting on her career as a feminist activist and bureaucrat, Patti O'Neill discusses with Rosalind Eyben her strategies at the OECD as the official responsible for supporting the work of the Gender Network of the Development Assistance Committee. She identifies what it is that makes a feminist effective when working inside a bureaucracy and emphasizes the primacy of political skills.

Patti has been a trade union organizer, a senior official in the New Zealand Ministry for Women's Affairs, and has worked for New Zealand Aid. In 2004 she became a senior adviser at the Organisation for Economic Co-operation and Development (OECD) Development Cooperation Directorate – 'the secretariat' that supports the work of the Development Assistance Committee (DAC). The DAC is a forum for all those member states of the OECD that have an official aid programme. Through the work of its subsidiary networks it provides guidance in key areas of development aid. Its members also work together through peer review, whereby two member states assess the aid policies and programmes of a third member state. The DAC is also the definitive source of statistics on official development assistance. In the last decade, the DAC has been the focal point of the 'aid effectiveness' agenda. Patti supports the DAC network for gender equality – GENDERNET – in which gender specialists from bilateral aid ministries and agencies work together to improve official aid performance in relation to gender equality. The World Bank, UNDP, and some other multilateral agencies are also represented as observers at GENDERNET meetings.

Patti and Rosalind first met during the final negotiations over the draft 'Platform for Action' at the Beijing Women's Conference in 1995, when they were both senior officials in their countries' respective delegations. They met again in 2006 when, at Rosalind's request, Patti arranged for her to have a slot at the annual meeting of GENDERNET to introduce the Pathways of Women's Empowerment research programme and to discuss various ways in which members of GENDERNET might wish to be involved.

In the years that followed, Rosalind was invited to be a resource person at a number of GENDERNET events. Meanwhile Patti became a participant in the feminist bureaucrats' project. Parts of this chapter are written

http://dx.doi.org/10.3362/9781780448046.006

by Rosalind – to provide the context to two digitally recorded conversations between Patti and Rosalind. The first took place in Patti's apartment in Paris in 2007 and the second in Rosalind's home in Brighton in May 2010.[1] In these conversations Patti explores and reflects on what she has learnt about the politics of getting women on the agenda of international development policy. The parts of this chapter written in the first person are Rosalind's.

The OECD and GENDERNET

The OECD is the successor to the Organization for European Economic Cooperation, established at the end of the Second World War to administer American and Canadian aid – the Marshall Plan – for assisting Europe's recovery. The OECD has recently moved back to expanded and refurbished buildings that include, at its centre, the Château de la Muette where delegates from member states meet in splendid wood-panelled formal rooms to discuss policy matters of common interest.

In each room is an arrangement of heavy teak tables organized in a hollow square, around which the delegates are seated, behind their country's name plate. To capture the chair's attention, a delegate stands her name plate on its end – one of many OECD customs that the inexperienced delegate learns through observation. Next to the chair – who is usually an official from a member country – sits a staff member from the secretariat who will have drawn up the agenda and will have ensured all the relevant papers have been drafted and distributed. Other interested staff may be present in the room to observe the discussion and if necessary try to influence proceedings in favour of their own department's objectives.

Patti spends a lot of her time at such meetings, which are called to discuss aid policy issues such as environment, conflict, and security, or good governance. She tells me that often, her presence alone is enough to remind her colleagues that gender equality issues should not be forgotten in the subject under discussion. Rather than slide directly into places reserved for the secretariat, she makes herself prominent by walking with a cheerful gait and happy smiles all around the room – just to make sure they will have spotted her.

Patti is one of about 100 professionals in the Directorate for Development Cooperation, which services the work of the DAC. Some of the bureaucrats, like Patti, may have previously worked in bilateral aid ministries or in multilateral organizations such as the World Bank, but others have made their career within the OECD, possibly even previously working in another directorate such as trade and agriculture or economics. I have observed that these long-serving officials are ever alert to the different policy positions of the OECD member states, seeking to secure common ground between them to produce a statement or policy document to which all can agree. When delegates meet, these officials' primary concern is to make things run smoothly – including bringing those delegates who are making waves – rocking the boat of what inevitably becomes conservative consensus – back into line. What role, I wondered, can such a bureaucracy play in supporting the political transformation that is women's empowerment?

I first visited the DAC in 1987, when I took over from a male colleague the job of representing the British aid ministry at the meetings of the DAC Expert Group on Women in Development – the predecessor of GENDERNET. The group had been established in 1979 and had made its major task the drafting and approval in 1983 of the *Guiding Principles to Aid Agencies for Supporting the Role of Women in Development* (Fraser and Skard). In 1987 I found the group working at revising these principles to reflect the internationally agreed 'Forward Looking Strategies' of the Nairobi Women's Conference, which member states should follow to ensure the integration of women in development (WID) in their aid programmes. The group had also been trying to introduce some statistical means of checking how much money and what proportion of their aid programmes OECD countries were devoting to WID. This was through a marking system based on intention at the stage of project approval and was being hotly debated and negotiated at the time I first joined the group. It is now known as the Gender Equality Policy Marker.

In 1987 the chair of the group was the senior WID official in the Netherlands aid ministry and I had been warned by my colleague that she was a very difficult, radical feminist. I did not tell him she was an old friend from when we had both been housewives in Sudan a decade earlier. Not only were she and her like-minded colleagues from the northern European countries struggling with antipathetic delegates such as the previous UK representatives, but she also had to cope with the secretariat that, through its cautious orthodoxy, seemed to constantly seek to undermine what the group had been trying to achieve.

The group was also under threat of its mandate not being renewed, finding little support for its continuation within the secretariat. Two years later the situation had improved. The head of the relevant department in the directorate was now someone more supportive and positive. I recorded in a back-to-office report that the DAC had agreed to a five-year extension because 'the growing recognition of women's critical role in development still has to be translated into systematic action'.[2]

After 1995 the group was once again able to renew its mandate through the requirement yet again to revise the guiding principles, to bring them into line with the gender equality and women's empowerment agenda established at the Beijing Women's Conference. These were published in 1999 as the *DAC Guidelines for Gender Equality and Women's Empowerment in Development Cooperation*. By that time I was no longer directly involved in the work of the group and lost track of what had happened to it. In fact, like the gender equality programmes and policies in many development agencies at the beginning of the new millennium, it was going through a difficult time with a loss of energy and sense of direction. When in 2003 all the DAC working groups were reviewed for their usefulness – and renamed 'networks' – the gender group was rated very low on quality and impact.[3] There was little enthusiasm in most of the secretariat for keeping the group.

In 2004 the advisory post in the secretariat that serviced GENDERNET became vacant. At that time Patti was the New Zealand representative in GENDERNET and also a member of its bureau or steering group. She had to justify travelling to Paris all the way from New Zealand and felt she was able to do that because she took new knowledge and contacts back with her. But she also knew that GENDERNET had the potential to work better. She decided to make herself available as temporary cover for a staff member's maternity leave. She saw the potential for GENDERNET to bring about real change in international aid. 'I thought – I can do this, and would really like to do it. I'd always wanted to do something like this'.

Patti took the job at a low moment for those working for international action for gender equality. An apparent major transformation in global policy for gender equality and women's empowerment, culminating in the 1995 Beijing Women's Conference, had subsequently very rapidly lost momentum. More established ways of thinking about development and societal change retook centre stage; the incoming poverty reduction strategies and the Millennium Development Goals ignored the role of power, culture, and history in shaping individual and societal destinies. Simultaneously, conservative forces – notably the unholy alliance of religious fundamentalists, already active at Beijing, where the Vatican and Iran jointly resisted efforts to advance women's sexual rights – had strengthened during the last decade, as a result of the rise of the evangelical religious right in the United States and elsewhere. Ten years after Beijing the mood among gender equality advocates 'was defensive and low key' (Molyneux and Razavi, 2005: 984).

When I attended, at Patti's invitation, the 2006 annual meeting of GENDERNET, I observed a largely dispirited membership, wondering how to engage with the new 'aid effectiveness' agenda as established by the Paris Declaration of 2005. 'It's not that gender mainstreaming has failed, but that we have failed gender mainstreaming', one participant said gloomily. Subsequently, Patti scolded me for making this observation to the chair of the DAC[4] in her presence. Since her arrival in Paris she had been working very hard to convince the powers that be that GENDERNET was a dynamic and innovative group – which by 2007 it was certainly becoming. I came to learn that being positive and sunny is a very important strategy for Patti. 'I've got a soft outside', she told me, 'with a very hard interior'.

The conversation

Our conversation covered what it means to work for transformative ends within a bureaucracy, including the importance of political analysis and trust-based relationships. In addition to these, Patti identified several other characteristics of an effective feminist bureaucrat.

Renovating the master's house

Rosalind: Patti, you and I are feminists. For me, this means working for the transformation of the social relationships that have sustained gender inequities. Yet, what about the argument that a bureaucracy is quintessentially an organizational form for maintaining the status quo? Is there something contradictory about being a feminist in a bureaucracy? Can a bureaucracy support the transformation a feminist is seeking, and how could we make that happen?

Patti: It's a very interesting question, and obviously one that I've reflected on over the past ten to fifteen years. I often think about that famous idea that 'the master's tools will never dismantle the master's house' (Lorde, 1997: 380).[5] I've thought a lot about this transformation thing, because I think you *can* use the master's tools to *renovate* the master's house, to add rooms to his house, make it *your* house, and certainly to improve the view. I think that is probably the way that I've thought about it, because I think that there are things that can be changed and you have to make it in the bureaucracy's interest to make the improvements. This means making the organization look better, making ministers look good.

But there are lots of hard things to do with that. I think one of the things that we've really got to think hard about as feminists is that we can sometimes look too much like fundamentalists. We can sometimes be too politically correct and miss the opportunity to make at least some steps towards change.

So I think we're talking about two sets of things. We're talking about transforming the lives of women and we're also talking about transforming bureaucracies, so that they become a tool in transforming the lives of women. We've got to be able to unpick these two things and we've also got to know what we're doing at any one point and why.

Because I am feminist, I am thinking constantly about women. I constantly check on whether what I am doing can help make a difference for women. I brought this with me into my work in the OECD. I looked at the core areas of the DAC work – peer reviews, statistics, aid effectiveness – and thought really long and hard about what we could do with these. Let me tell you about what we did with statistics.

I saw the Gender Equality Policy Marker (GEM) had the possibility of being a powerful tool. The marker is used by OECD member states to report the amount of money they are spending in their aid programmes in relation to gender equality objectives. When I first came to the OECD, there were only nine member states fully using it and four partially. Now 23 of the 24 member states are using it, and we are publishing the reports from 20 of these.[6] Of course it looks like a technical gender-mainstreaming tool, but its power lies in it being political. No donor wants to see their aid to gender equality going down. No one wants to see that the member state on the opposite page of the report is spending more money than they are. The GEM's potential is that, within agencies, it opens up political space for discussing what the agency is doing, and draws the attention of senior officials and the minister to the matter. Gender advisers can use the marker to make a real difference to the priority their agency gives to gender. For example, a new donor country decided to adopt the marker and found that their aid for gender equality was very low indeed. Gender advisers used the marker to make the case for legislation and to make gender equality one of the four priority areas in their country's aid programme.

Rosalind: I was involved in the original negotiations for establishing the marker in the late 1980s. I remember the secretariat's approach at that time was very technical. Your predecessors didn't want to understand what some of us knew then – that the marker's potential was its political effect. That was the way then the secretariat saw it had to do its job. It would encourage members to develop procedures, manuals, gender focal points, monitoring instruments. These were seen as what were required to make gender mainstreaming work.

You've changed the way the secretariat works on these issues – you appear to work quite differently, with a political rather than technical agenda. You came in and looked for the political opportunities that gender-mainstreaming tools offered. You are not speaking like a technical bureaucrat.

Patti: Of course, in some instances these tools can help, but we have to be very careful about how we apply them. When staff are required to use checklists, for example, the gender adviser can find herself acting as a policeman. When I first arrived to work in New Zealand Aid I realized that some people didn't want to work with a gender adviser because they thought that all I would ever do would be to criticize their performance and wag my finger at them. You have to be pragmatic with a soft – very soft – outside. But I am as tough as steel inside.

I see gender equality and women's empowerment as profoundly, profoundly political. And when you meet the resistance, it is political. For those of us, like you and me, who have been working on this for thirty years, we know this ... because as feminists we know that the personal is political and we experience this every day of our lives.

This is all hard, but it's worth it. That's why I keep on doing it, because it *is* worth the effort and I see change and I see improvement.

We have a network of amazing people from 23 countries, plus the multilaterals. When the network meets, we try to work together so people have the language and skills to be able to go back and talk to their economists using the language of their economists, or talk to their aid-for-trade people using the language of aid-for-trade, or talk to the conflict and security people using their language.

And those people can really make a difference ... and can really make a difference to donor behaviour. And they can be strengthened by each other … they can learn from each other's experience, they can form informal networks or even more formal networks.

Political effectiveness

Patti works with the long-term goal always in mind. But she is also an excellent tactician, deciding what to do on a day-to-day basis and staying under the radar when she wants to work away at something, without necessarily drawing the attention of senior management or colleagues until it is *fait accompli*, and she invites them to be part of the success.

Patti gave an example of this from the work GENDERNET did with the Paris Declaration on Aid Effectiveness, which had so depressed some of the membership at their annual meeting in 2006. The Paris Declaration of 2005 concerns a set of commitments by donor governments, multilateral agencies, and a group of aid recipient governments, to make international aid more efficient and effective. According to this declaration, effective aid requires recipient government ownership of the policies they are implementing; donors aligning their own policies and resources in relation to these; donors harmonizing their procedures and strategies; a mutual focus on time-bound and measurable results; and donors and recipients being accountable to each other and to their own constituents for the use of resources and for securing results.

The emphasis on bureaucratic efficiency in the Paris Declaration was seen as a setback by those who hope that international aid can be an instrument of social transformation. Yet the most strategic feminist bureaucrats realized that the discourse associated with the declaration provided opportunities to create discursive shifts in the rules of the game. For example, the emphasis on results, broad-based ownership, and accountability, could be a chance to probe 'results for whom?' and 'accountability to whom?'.

Patti: Many of us felt that gender equality and women had been left out of the Paris Declaration. We started to set about thinking, 'well, how can we change that?' There was this amazing opportunity to use the principles of the Paris Declaration – alignment, harmonization, managing for results, accountability, and ownership – to actually advance the situation of women in partner countries. GENDERNET has always applied these principles to gender equality work. Always, always, always. There was nothing new from our point of view. But suddenly these became also the principles that were driving all international aid. So, given our experience, why couldn't we think of ways that those principles could be used to actually advance the situation of women?

Several networks of the OECD decided that we'd hold a major conference on this very topic, and that we would try and shift the whole 'efficient delivery of aid' scenario to one that is much more about development effectiveness and achieving the MDGs.

Now there were a lot of people who thought that our agenda – particularly the human rights and gender equality interests – was totally irrelevant to the efficient delivery of aid. And sure, from their point of view they could argue that really effectively. But we thought it was a battle worth fighting. Even though put under a lot of pressure to ensure that our political leaders knew all about the conference we were planning, I said no, no, let's organize everything first and then tell them. If we had gone public too early, those who thought our agenda an irrelevance would have started to organize against us and they would have started to form much more powerful coalitions of countries which would have said 'no, Paris is about efficient aid delivery – these issues are irrelevant to what we're trying to achieve'.

So we thought further about this and we saw what we could do. We could involve them in the conference – have them come to the conference, have them play a really active role in the conference, and have them end up owning the conference and owning the conference's success, if indeed it was a success … which of course it was! And so afterwards, those that would have stopped the conference happening, if they had known about it too early, ended up being active contributors to it.

Political effectiveness requires being able to scan your own organization's culture within the context of the broader political landscape, to recognize where are the emerging political opportunities. When you see shifts in the development agenda – as we saw with aid effectiveness … we needed to be positioned well to take advantage of that whole different way of working that seemed to be emerging and which the donors and the partners were buying into – this is the groundwork to identifying the action you need to take, including the individuals you need to focus on.

Trust-based relationships

Some gender specialists in development bureaucracies focus on getting the technicalities of mainstreaming right, and perhaps not enough on looking at the political relationships that they have to form or indeed sometimes have to challenge.

Rosalind: What, in your opinion, is the single most important thing you need to do to work effectively as a feminist bureaucrat?

Patti: I think I'm probably one of those people who think that development is all about relationships. You asked me earlier, do my managers know what I do some of the time? I think one of the most powerful things we can do is form alliances that sometimes people characterize as inside–outside. We can create pressure from the outside on us, by working with non-governmental organizations, but we have to make that a really mutual relationship. The pressure from the outside is really good. It can sometimes be really uncomfortable for us and it can even be irritating sometimes. It's quite important that we don't become defensive when it is uncomfortable. At the same time we also need to demonstrate to our allies, and be really clear that we are listening really hard and that we are taking on board their criticism, and what they are saying ... and we also need to give information back.

One of the things that I worked really hard at, together with AWID,[7] is this whole issue of how much money is actually going into women's organizations.

I talked about gender equality policy markers earlier, but we now also have a specific statistical code for how much money is going into women's NGOs – both at local and international levels – and into women's ministries. That achievement came about through GENDERNET working with AWID and women's funding organizations, so that we could find out how much money donors were putting into funding women's organizations.

When building alliances we need to avoid jumping to conclusions about each other. Both you and I were involved in the preparation for Beijing. I was in the Ministry for Women's Affairs and worked easily with the more progressive NGOs in preparing our government's negotiating position. Many of us, including myself, were very supportive of actually trying to make Beijing the place where we could get the word 'lesbian' in a document, and certainly a place to talk about sexual rights. At the same time we wanted to keep the Catholic Women's League of New Zealand with us, because on most things they were quite progressive and supportive. I learnt that it's too easy to make judgements that are just wrong, such as 'progressive equals good', 'Catholic equals bad' and things like that. Because on most things there was a high level of agreement, and not a watery kind of agreement, but quite a progressive level of agreement around women and what we should be doing. It's a matter of finding that level of agreement.

Rosalind: Some feminist bureaucrats find all this very difficult. One person told me how when her organization was not performing very well on gender and was subjected to external criticism, her management would put her up in front of the critics. She got very confused. On the one hand she had a sense of loyalty to her employers and felt she had to defend her organization's track record. On the other hand she was looking for this external criticism to help bring about the change the organization needed. She found it very challenging to manage the situation so that the blame for failure wasn't passed on to her, while taking advantage of the sometimes rough criticism for internal political advantage. Have you any advice to people who find themselves in that situation?

Patti: I've probably been in that situation myself, thinking back to my time in the women's ministry when the NGOs were obviously criticizing us. Building relationships of trust with some key individuals is absolutely critical and I've never had the trust broken. There is someone at the moment with whom I sometimes openly share information, but she never puts it out publicly unless I say it's okay to do so. If I say nothing, she knows then that it's okay to circulate papers and information more broadly and that's a totally trusting relationship going on. We've worked now together for several years like that, and I've worked like this before with other people. It's a two-way relationship – she provides me with information in a timely way too!

Also, being honest with NGOs works. Saying to them, even in politically difficult, situations, 'we haven't got the answer, we know we're not doing this right', and being open about it rather than defensive, works. It's really hard not to be defensive, and sometimes we all fall into that trap of wanting to answer on behalf of our organization and we sound inevitably defensive and weak. It's okay to say that you haven't got the answer.

We have to be very careful that everything we do is complementary – to see that an international NGO can move forward in a way that we can't, and we can also move forward in a way that they can't. Having honest conversations about this is very important for alliances. If I see a new and emerging issue, such as I do at the moment on conflict and security issues – which our network hasn't worked on well but where there's now a critical mass of members who want to work on it – that's really important, and we have some specialized areas where we can really contribute – like knowing how much has been spent on conflict and security. That means I write to UNIFEM[8] and I will say to them, 'where do we fit in that picture? What's the thing that we can do over here in this network to support what you're doing, or that is sufficiently different to complement what you're doing?'

One thing I don't like seeing – and this happens in all kinds of sectors, not just in gender equality – is we see something being successful and then people go and copy it. That's fine between bilateral agencies, but working on the global scene it's important that we're complementing, not just copying each other, while also learning from each other. I think these relationships between individuals can be remarkably helpful.

Let me be specific. In the lead-up to the Accra High-Level Forum on Aid Effectiveness,[9] I was challenged by someone from an international organization (actually, she was challenging herself and her own organization as much as challenging me) to identify the three key things we wanted to get into the Accra Agenda for Action. She wanted to work with GENDERNET so we could get these in at an early stage, so that they would then become non-negotiable. Neither of us wanted the horror of someone coming out of the room at the last minute saying, 'there's nothing about women and children in the document'. And then – God forbid – ending up with a paragraph or sentence about the 'vulnerability of women and children'. That challenge from her, coming months before Accra, was incredibly helpful to me.

Rosalind: So, a trusting relationship involves at certain times not telling others about the relationship. It's also about challenging each other constructively. It's about recognizing and building on complementary roles. It's about mutual respect.

But some feminist bureaucrats get very nervous about being in contact with people outside the bureaucracy – particularly when in government bureaucracies, civil servants are not meant to have a political position on anything. So sometimes when we do this, don't we sail very close to the wind?

Patti: Absolutely! I've always been very interested in this, and it goes back to working in the New Zealand Ministry of Women's Affairs where I worked for a conservative government and for a conservative minister. But even in working for that conservative minister, I found that she knew I was well connected to the opposition party but she was also secure enough in herself to even ask me (and others) to stay in touch with or work with members of the opposition party.

That's the most politically risky thing that a senior public servant can do. They don't come more risky than that. That's probably why I have called it 'a political high-wire act'. If I had gotten anything wrong in doing some of those things, I would have lost my job. There's no question about that. The public servant is the one that's sacrificed in those circumstances.

We need to be courageous about these things, because the worst doesn't usually happen all that often. You can think of the worst, and you can know what the worst is going to be, but it rarely happens.

Rosalind: In all this alliance building, do you need to be prepared to have lots of informal conversations?

Patti: Of course, and that's how you build the trust. Being honest in those informal conversations, and sometimes sharing with your allies the very real difficulties. If you share with them the very real difficulties you get some empathy happening. They start to understand the complexities of the political environment within which you're working, and you understand better what they need and are pressing for. In building that trust, people mostly don't disclose what you're saying if they trust you – and if they know you're being honest, it's worth the risk.

Rosalind: This reminds me – at the beginning of this conversation you mentioned DAC peer reviews. When I was in GENDERNET, the gender specialist in the aid agency being reviewed would pass informally to her counterparts in the reviewing countries a list of really difficult questions for the reviewers to ask. This was all done under the radar and I thought it was always pretty risky but worth doing. And then I discovered that the men did this as well! I learnt that my own permanent secretary had paid a discreet visit to his counterpart in one of the aid agencies reviewing our aid programme, providing him with inside information and a list of questions for that agency to ask the permanent secretary later in the formal process – because he wanted to get the minister to be put on the spot. Then I realized that often gender specialists working as bureaucrats in ministries are being more risk-averse and less aware of the political games that everybody else is playing.

What makes an effective feminist bureaucrat?

Establishing and nurturing *trust-based relationships* within and outside the organization is clearly essential. But I wondered what else Patti identified as important – for a feminist bureaucrat to be effective.

Creating win–win situations

We need to avoid being 'the finger-wagging gender police', she says. That is why Patti attends DAC meetings with a friendly smile on her face. She works hard at being useful to her colleagues. This does not mean that she expects to convert all of them to committed feminists but that 'we need all the friends we can get', while bearing in mind that 'some friends are going to be better than others as allies and influencers and at pushing the right buttons'.

Win–win situations involve meeting people halfway, by helping them do their job better through integrating gender equality concerns in their own work. However, on our part, this means keeping our language simple and providing clear messages. Patti stressed how all her working life she has tried to avoid gender jargon because 'people's eyes glaze over' and potential allies are lost.

Choosing your battles

Bureaucratic politics tends to draw on language and metaphors commonly associated with warfare: strategy, tactics, engagement, outflanking, alliances, adversaries, and so on. For a long time, I have struggled to describe my own understanding of political action without using such language but, to my own regret as a would-be pacifist, I still find it the most illuminating way of describing my own experience. Patti seems to think along the same lines, but her key point here is the need for focus – particularly if resources are limited. Clarity on what one is trying to achieve and how to get there – strategy – must be combined with constant scanning of the environment and readiness to shift tactics in response to emerging opportunities.

Role playing

Patti told me that when she worked at the New Zealand Ministry of Women's Affairs she used to keep a jacket with big shoulder pads on the back of her office door, along with a pair of high heels in the corner. She would pop these on whenever she was called to see the Minister – 'putting on my armour', she said. This reminded me of my own royal blue 'Mrs Thatcher' suit that I used to own when I was a civil servant, and would wear on days when I knew I would have to be very assertive.

We are more effective when we speak, look, and behave like those we are seeking to influence. Of course, there is a risk with such role play. We might forget it is just an act and let the role take us over, particularly in an organizational environment where certain ways of behaving and thinking are encouraged and alternatives are disapproved of. This is why Patti stressed how important it is to be conscious always of what we are doing and why.

Being positive and optimistic

This is one of Patti's great strengths but 'also a weakness', she commented. Her enthusiasm for creating win–win situations can lead to her giving away too much, too soon – through being too prepared to compromise. We spoke of the advantages of working in tandem with a trusted ally, so if Patti is the 'soft cop', she tries to identify an ally as a 'tough cop' working alongside her.

Reflective practice

Rosalind: So is it important to consciously reflect on and learn from your mistakes or are you just acting intuitively all the time?

Patti: Partially intuitively, since you've asked and since I'm an honest person. But I don't really think it is just intuition, is it? I think because of the determined way in which I've been working, you are constantly creating, recreating and changing the political conditions in which you work to make the outcomes more inevitable and more positive. And I think I've done that in a number of fields, so it isn't just intuition.

I do have 'dark nights of the soul' as I've always called them, throughout my life, where I wonder if I am doing the right thing. I used to feel like I solved the world's problems as I walked to work, because if I had a 'dark night of the soul', I'd think, 'well, what is it that I'm going to fix today and what is it that I'm going to shift?'

Having a political vision can help you quite a lot to think, 'what did I do well? What did I do less well? What would I do differently next time?' It's not threatening to yourself or organizationally ... Those are a good set of questions to be constantly asking yourself.

Postscript: reflections from a workshop of gender specialists

I showed a video of my conversation with Patti at a workshop in a Scandinavian country for gender specialists working in international development agencies. Afterwards they commented on what had impressed or challenged them.

In their own country, gender inequality is perceived as something of the past, something that is no longer a problem – even though they themselves believed that it still is. It may seem a very good place to be a gender adviser compared with other countries, but there is a sense that you are sending your messages into swirling fog. While there is no resistance, there is also no clarity and no support. It is hard to stimulate enthusiasm for gender inequality in their own organizations. Staff pay lip service to it, but one ends up with fatigue.

Hence they were particularly struck by Patti's enthusiasm and positive outlook, including her emphasis on making her colleagues look good. However, there might be drawbacks to this approach. Thanks to the support of the gender specialist, colleagues might be recognized by the organization for their good 'gender' performance while her own efforts in supporting these colleagues might pass unnoticed and thus unappreciated. It also requires careful thought about how to create and respond to the demand from others to work alongside them. It relates to Patti's emphasis on picking and choosing opportunities as they emerge, rather than sticking to a pre-conceived plan.

Above all, they were impressed by how much Patti emphasized that an effective gender specialist must be a conscious political actor, aware of and analyzing the power relations that shape opportunities for change.

'Why have we neglected power?' the workshop asked. 'And is renovating the master's house sufficient? Or should we at the same time be digging away at its foundations?'

Notes

1 The conversation in Brighton is available at <www.youtube.com/watch?v=VfrcuVXDzIY>.
2 Quoted in my back-to-office report from the draft of an OECD document *Aid in the 90s*.
3 From a conversation in 2007 between the author and Richard Manning, chair of the DAC.
4 The chair of the DAC is always a very senior official from a member country who has oversight of the work of the director and his or her staff in the development cooperation directorate, and who chairs the high-level (ministerial) meetings of the DAC.
5 This is a reference to Audre Lorde's essay 'The master's tools will never dismantle the master's house' first published in *Sister Outsider* (1984), The Crossing Press.
6 OECD (2010).
7 The Association for Women's Rights in Development (AWID) is 'an international, multi-generational, feminist, creative, future-orientated membership organization committed to achieving gender equality, sustainable development and women's human rights' <http://www.awid.org>. Where is the Money for Women's Rights? (WITM) is a multi-year action-research initiative founded in 2004 to gain a better understanding of funding trends for women's rights work and how best to expand the resource base for feminist movements and women's rights organizations <http://www.awid.org/Our-Initiatives/Where-is-the-Money-for-Women-s-Rights>.
8 Now UN Women.
9 Held in 2008 to review progress in implementing the Paris Declaration. The resulting document – agreed to by donors, recipient governments, and multilateral organizations – is known as the Accra Agenda for Action.

References

Creditor Reporting System database <www.oecd.org/dataoecd/9/34/47335126. pdf>.

Fraser, A. (2004) 'Seizing opportunities: USAID, WID and CEDAW' in A. Fraser and I. Tinker (eds) (2004) *Developing Power: How Women Transformed International Development*, New York: Feminist Press.

Lorde, A. (1997) 'Age, race, sex and class: women redefining difference' in A. McClintock, A. Mufti, E. Shohat (eds) *Dangerous Liaisons: Gender, Nation, and Postcolonial Perspectives*, Minneapolis: University of Minnesota.

Molyneux, M. and Razavi, S. (2005) 'Beijing plus ten: an ambivalent record on gender justice', *Development and Change*, 36: 984 <http://dx.doi. org/10.1111%2Fj.0012-155X.2005.00446.x>.

OECD (2011) *Aid in Support of Gender Equality and Women's Empowerment. Statistics based on DAC Members' Reporting on the Gender Equality Policy Marker, 2008–2009.*

About the authors

Patti O'Neill has been coordinator of the OECD's Development Assistance Committee's Network on Gender Equality since 2004. Before joining the OECD, she worked as a senior adviser on women's rights for the New Zealand Agency for International Development. Throughout the 1990s she held senior positions at the New Zealand Ministry of Women's Affairs. Earlier in her career she was a librarian and trade unionist. She was also an activist in New Zealand's anti-Springbok tour movement. She is an active and committed member of the Association of Women's Rights in Development (AWID) and has always been a proud (and sometimes, loud) feminist.

Rosalind Eyben is a Professorial Research Fellow at the Institute of Development Studies, University of Sussex. She is a social anthropologist with a professional background in development policy and practice, and a committed teacher in the IDS doctoral and master's programmes, including on gender and development. She has designed and facilitated numerous workshops for international development practitioners all over the world. Her research interests focus on power and relations in international aid. From 2006–11 she convened the global policy programme of the International Research Consortium on Pathways of Women's Empowerment and is currently developing a new area of work exploring the knowledge/power practices of donors that sustain the invisibility of unpaid care as a development policy issue. In 2010 she launched the Big Push Forward that has created an international network challenging the current audit culture in development. She was awarded a CBE in 2000 and is a board member of UNRISD and ActionAid UK.

CHAPTER 7

Who is the better feminist?
Negotiating the middle ground

Laura Turquet

In this chapter, Laura Turquet draws on her experience working as a gender adviser at the international non-governmental organization (INGO) ActionAid UK. By describing a series of events, she explores the successes and challenges of lobbying the UK government's Department for International Development (DFID), while struggling to avoid marginalization within her own organization. She tries hard to make alliances for change, and for personal support, with feminists working within DFID, as well as other civil society organizations, but finds herself stuck in the middle – regarded as neither a proper donor nor a proper feminist. She concludes that strong alliances built on mutual understanding are needed between feminists working on the inside of bureaucracies, and those working on the outside, in order to bring about change in favour of gender equality and women's rights.

This chapter is about the challenges and opportunities that presented them-selves to me as a women's rights adviser at ActionAid UK. It highlights how feminists working in international development bureaucracies – like me – can work together to advance a women's rights agenda within their organizations. But it also underscores the point that in order to be effective in doing so, it is essential to understand how I and others are positioned and to recognize the room for manoeuvre that exists. It is also important for those in the women's movement to trust feminists working from 'the inside'. While of course that trust has to be earned, doubting the intentions of those who are politically committed but choose to work within large international development organ-izations, or treating us as somehow less authentic as feminists, is frustrating – on a personal level, and because it closes down the many strategic opportu-nities to work together for a shared goal.

I grew up under the Thatcher government in the 1980s, in a family where politics was a constant source of conversation around the dinner table. My mother brought me up to be a feminist, although I didn't actually study gender until I did my master's degree, when I was encouraged to apply a femi-nist critique to mainstream international relations theory. After I left univer-sity, I worked for nearly two years at the Fawcett Society – a small feminist campaigning organization named after Millicent Fawcett, one of the UK's early 20th-century suffragist campaigners – lobbying the three main political

http://dx.doi.org/10.3362/9781780448046.007

parties to take steps to increase women's representation in parliament. I would have stayed longer, but the funding for my post – always precarious because the work was 'political', meaning that most charitable trusts could not support it – ran out.

After a stint at the Institute of Development Studies (IDS), I joined ActionAid. As a women's rights adviser, my task was to raise women's rights up the agenda of the UK government, through lobbying DFID. When DFID was founded in 1997, the Labour government made a conscious effort to engage with the INGOs headquartered in the UK, recognizing that they were a gateway to large numbers of the general public who cared about overseas aid. The unprecedented 2005 public campaign 'Make Poverty History' further raised the profile of international development and engaged the public, not only in giving money to charity but in campaigning for rich-country governments to do more to tackle global poverty. Hence, lobbying DFID became a full-time job for many people in INGOs and a whole infrastructure of networks and joint lobbying meetings, letters, and public campaign actions developed as a result.

During this time, gender equality had fallen off the agenda of most of the INGOs, if not in their programming, certainly in their lobbying and campaigning in the North. The gender mainstreaming approach had made the issue 'everyone's business, but no one's concern'. For most lobbyists, the message they got about gender was that whatever issue they were working on, the situation was probably even worse for women. So gender was simply tacked onto whatever issue they were campaigning on, often by the addition of the statement 'especially women and girls', but without much thought about what it actually meant.

ActionAid

In 2005, ActionAid International was one of the first INGOs to move its headquarters to the global South – to Johannesburg. At the same time it adopted a new strategy, 'Rights to End Poverty', and together these two steps marked a new phase for the organization. The strategy was rights-based, with six thematic priorities, of which women's rights was one. The international head of the women's rights theme made a very conscious move away from a gender-mainstreaming strategy, towards a more political women's rights approach. Although the headquarters of ActionAid International had moved to the South, ActionAid UK in London retained the biggest policy-and-campaigns capacity, as well as raising the majority of funds for the organization.

The director of policy and campaigns in the UK at the time, a feminist, decided that having women's rights capacity in her team was very important and she set in motion the internal discussions needed to put that capacity in place. She made two strategic decisions: Firstly, since there was money available for only one post, she decided to recruit two part-time women's rights officers rather than one full-time officer who might end up isolated and ghettoized. She also calculated – correctly – that once in place, the part-timers could probably have their hours increased, whereas it would be difficult to make the case for a whole new post. It also fitted with her commitment to create high quality part-time posts within the department, making these jobs more accessible to those with family responsibilities. Secondly, she decided that the two women's rights officers would report to the head of policy, rather than be in their own small team, again vulnerable to marginalization. Being in this position also meant, in theory, that no policy product would leave the organization without being approved by the head of policy, who was also the person in charge of managing the women's rights work.

In addition, some of the responsibility for mainstreaming and carrying out the watchdog role lay with the head of policy and not with the women's rights officers themselves. In so many cases, gender officers in INGOs become demoralized by constantly having to insert themselves into others' work, usually once important decisions have been made, and usually without the budget or influence to make a real impact. The mainstreaming role also positions these gender officers as the 'gender nag', or the gender police, wearily having to 'gender proof' documents, rather than spending their time energetically making a positive case for a women's rights approach.

I joined ActionAid UK in August 2006 as one of the two women's rights policy officers. I had wanted to work for ActionAid for a while; the organization was very well regarded by colleagues at IDS, whose opinions I trusted, as it was seen as the INGO that led the field when it came to supporting social movements – including the women's movement. My job at IDS was a communications role and although elements of it enabled me to pursue my own particular interests, what I really wanted was a political campaigning and lobbying role on women's rights. I looked for positions in some of the smaller NGOs, but they rarely came up; and when they did, they asked for five years' experience working on the issues, which I didn't have at that point. I suppose, unconsciously, I also chose an organization that was relatively better resourced than Fawcett and therefore offered better job security. When I was offered the job at ActionAid, I did not perceive the organization as a bureaucracy and did not think I was becoming a bureaucrat. I thought I was simply continuing my career as a women's rights activist.

So I set about my job, both integrating women's rights into the existing work of the policy and campaigns department, and also developing 'stand-alone' women's rights work. The work was essentially about advocacy and lobbying – mainly targeted at DFID and other UK government departments, as well as corporate targets for our women workers campaign – and public campaigning, whereby we mobilized ActionAid supporters to lobby their MPs by writing letters and taking other campaign actions.

Just before I started, DFID had received a critical peer review of its gender policy from the OECD Development Assistance Committee (DAC). It said that while DFID had once been a leader on gender equality work, it had 'taken its eye off the ball'. This finding was also backed up by an internal review of

DFID's gender work, which came to similar conclusions. Around this time, a new gender adviser was appointed to DFID, and she set about exploiting this opportunity to develop a new internal strategy called the Gender Equality Action Plan, as well as a glossy booklet to make the case for gender equality. This booklet was aimed mainly at an internal DFID audience, and the drafting process gave the gender adviser a chance to engage the minister and get him to buy into the new plan.

Working together across organizations and networks

In this context, I write about four separate but linked events, which illustrate how feminists working from different locations – in women's organizations and networks, in large INGOs, and in donor organizations – can work together to mutually reinforce each other's work, and advance women's rights agendas within large bureaucracies. The stories are about a public event, a lobbying opportunity, a letter, and a women's rights strategy meeting. Together they show that when these relationships work well, it is possible to open up opportunities for change. But they also show that this is only possible when there is a clear understanding of one another's positions and the particular opportunities and restraints that each individual operates under. Sometimes, a lack of understanding and a sense of moral one-upwomanship from those working in women's rights organizations, closes the door to strategic partnerships that could be very fruitful.

The public event: putting words in the minister's mouth

The first story is about a big public event that we planned for International Women's Day 2007. Before I joined ActionAid UK, the director of policy and campaigns had asked a feminist consultant to advise on how to strengthen the organization's work on women's rights. Aside from recommending the women's rights officer posts, the consultant also suggested that once they were on board, ActionAid UK should work across teams on a big project: to make the work more visible, internally as well as externally; to build confidence within the organization; and to create some buzz and enthusiasm about women's rights.

We decided to organize a large public event on International Women's Day. We wanted, not only to create a buzz internally, but also to demonstrate publicly that many people cared about women's rights and wanted the UK government to do more to support them around the world. We organized the event in partnership with a small women's rights NGO in recognition of the fact that, while ActionAid had recently discovered its interest in women's rights, this smaller organization had been consistently working away at this issue the whole time. So we thought we should share this opportunity with them, along with our greater resources to back it. We hoped that it would also make clear our feminist credentials and our commitment to working with the women's movement. To some extent, this strategy mirrored the approach taken by the head of the international women's rights team, which was to bring several established women's rights activists into ActionAid International, and to partner with women's organizations to build trust and credibility.

The rationale for our event in the UK was also bolstered by the fact that our colleagues in the women's rights team in ActionAid International had been putting together a new coalition focused on violence against women and HIV, and had produced a report to launch it. The report analysed spending on women's rights, HIV, and violence against women, and criticized donors for not placing high enough priority on these issues. They also wanted to launch the coalition and the report on International Women's Day. While ActionAid UK did not always align its work with ActionAid International, as a new women's rights team we wanted to support our international colleagues, especially given that one of the donors they focused on in their new report was DFID.

I knew that the gender adviser at DFID was also working on the new Gender Equality Action Plan, aimed at reinvigorating the ministry's work in this area. It seemed to me that by inviting the development minister to speak at our public event, we could achieve a number of different aims: It would give the minister his first major platform on women's rights since taking up the job several years before. It would give DFID's gender adviser the opportunity to write a speech for the minister and get his buy-in for the new Gender Equality Action Plan. It would create opportunities for ActionAid's new advocacy work on women's rights, because once the minister had publicly stated his commitment to these issues, the door was then open to us to hold him accountable for his promises. And finally, if the event was successful, it would also generate energy for women's rights work within ActionAid UK – demonstrating that there was an exciting and positive agenda in this area. So, I started talking with the gender adviser at DFID, to discuss this opportunity and work out how we could make the most of it to advance our shared goals.

Of course, the minister received invitations to speak at NGO events on a weekly basis, so we had to think about how to make our event stand out. The fact that DFID had been criticized, both by the OECD-DAC and in an internal review of its work on gender equality, provided one impetus: here was a chance for the minister to demonstrate publicly his commitment to women's rights. But, we had another factor in our favour. About a year before, ActionAid UK had published a report which was very critical of DFID and it had become a surprise media hit – on the front page of the *Guardian* and as the top item on BBC's influential *Newsnight* programme. DFID was furious with ActionAid UK for – in its view – undermining the case for aid before an already sceptical UK general public.

With a new ActionAid report due to be launched on International Women's Day, the gender adviser was able to suggest to the minister and his team that another potentially critical report was coming out, and the best way to mitigate the risk that this presented was to be on the panel for the launch – to acknowledge that DFID had fallen behind in this area and to highlight the new Gender Equality Action Plan as a sign that the ministry was ready to 'up its game' on gender issues once more.

In fact, the gender adviser knew full well that the report was not particularly critical. The director of my department, a much more experienced lobbyist than me, recognized the gender adviser as an ally, and suggested we share an advance copy of the report with her. Having the report enabled the gender adviser to tailor the minister's speech accordingly, to support the key messages of the report, and to open up space for our future lobbying efforts.

So the minister came to the event, which had attracted an audience of more than 500 people. It had quite an uplifting celebratory feel, despite the serious subject matter. The minister gave the impression of having enjoyed it – he eventually had to be dragged off by his officials – but he had stayed long enough to hear all the other speakers and to take questions. He came with a positive approach and went away feeling good about gender equality issues.

The next day at DFID, the event had apparently created a buzz. It showed that the minister was interested and serious about addressing this area, and it created ongoing momentum for the Gender Equality Action Plan. Meanwhile at ActionAid UK too, people felt good about this very successful event and we had a strong basis for the work going forward.

Through working together, we managed to achieve all of our aims. It worked well because both the gender adviser and I recognized that we were 'on the same side'. It was clear that I didn't have to persuade her to support women's rights – she already did; the task was to get the minister on board. We both understood our respective positions very well and saw that we had different things to bring to the table, in pursuit of our shared goals. I couldn't have persuaded the minister to speak at our event on my own, or have drafted a speech for him supportive of our lobbying aims, but neither could the gender adviser have organized a public event, or launched a new civil society report. Our professional relationship – built on mutual trust, respect, and political understanding – enabled us to work together very effectively.

The lobbying meeting: one step forward, two steps back

Later we would have a chance to capitalize on our success in influencing the minister, but in this case we were much less successful. To accompany the launch of the Gender Equality Action Plan, DFID's gender adviser decided to invite the Gender and Development Network (GADN) to discuss the plan and input ideas at an afternoon meeting at the department. The gender adviser had even managed to persuade the minister to attend the last half hour of the meeting, to hear our deliberations and proposals for strengthening DFID's work on women's rights.

The GAD Network was one of the first, but similar networks focusing on different aspects of development – aid, trade, climate change – had proliferated, bringing mainly INGO staff together to agree joint lobbying and campaigning positions. Many of these networks were well resourced by the INGOs and members had plenty of time to devote to joint working. Increasingly, DFID said that it didn't want to have multiple meetings with individual NGOs, but preferred to hear one civil society message. So, these networks were an important channel for influence.

However, my experiences with the GAD Network up to that point had not been that positive. I observed a rather flagging network with little money, and a steering group made up of very good, but overworked and demoralized women who were working on gender and development in different places: big INGO mainstreamers, policy and programme people from small women's rights organizations, and a couple of individual academics and consultants.

Steering group meetings tended to be poorly attended and low energy. A lot of the discussion was around the trials and tribulations of gender mainstreaming in an INGO that sidelined and marginalized gender issues, despite ambitious public proclamations, or of working and overworking in small, underfunded women's rights organizations, whose staff were sick of repeating their gender messages to an uninterested DFID. Aside from regular meetings with various people at DFID, and information sharing about our work, we didn't really have much of a plan to influence the gender agenda.

So here was our opportunity to deliver some sharp, well-thought-out lobbying messages to the minister – and we even had a couple of hours together to prepare ourselves in advance. But, the meeting was a disaster and as a lobby we totally blew it. The hours of preparation were mainly devoted to people taking it in turns to express scepticism and doubt that the new Gender Equality Action Plan would make much of a difference – why would it, when so many previous plans had failed?

There was little engagement in how to gain traction – just exasperation at why DFID couldn't just get on with the job it was committed to do. For some of the more experienced advocates there was a real sense that they'd been here before, and weariness of having to repeat the same old arguments. I had encountered this before at another meeting of women's rights people from NGOs and universities – one of my first meetings at ActionAid – where I arrived full of enthusiasm and hope only to be greeted with heavy cynicism: the view that ActionAid had discovered 'gender' again, but it wouldn't be long before the cycle turned and it was out of vogue once more.

On reflection, one of the problems with lobbying DFID on the Gender Equality Action Plan was that it mainly focused on DFID's internal arrangements, its capacity to 'do gender', and so it was quite hard to get fired up about what were, essentially, the mechanisms for gender mainstreaming. Nevertheless, it was important for us to perform in this space; to demonstrate to the minister that this well organized lobby was holding DFID accountable for its commitments on gender equality, and to enable the gender adviser to follow up and continue to build support for the agenda internally.

But when the minister came in to hear our thoughts on DFID's efforts to strengthen its work on gender equality, he was greeted with an incoherent mix of complaints and grumbles; a few big sweeping statements and nothing very concrete. The only thing that got picked up was a proposal that the new UK gender equality duty, which requires public bodies to promote equality between women and men, be applied to DFID's overseas work, as a lever to generate more consistent commitments and focus. The idea never stuck, but it was the only concrete proposal that anyone made.

The gender adviser was shocked and later reflected that she should have done more to prepare the external lobby. Maybe so, but it was also very clear that we had to get our act together. The view from other DFID staff who were in the meeting was apparently summed up by the statement: 'well you can't trust the NGOs on this issue; they'll just come up with a shopping list of demands'. The contrast between the feel-good optimism that the minister had got from his experience of the public event and the negative atmosphere at the lobbying meeting was stark – even though he had been tasked with making a speech on a difficult issue that was beyond his comfort zone and had faced some critical questions from the audience.

Another problem we had at this meeting, and also more generally – both within the network and in our work at ActionAid – was the frequent accusation that we didn't have strong enough 'asks'. These 'asks' are the things that you go into lobbying meetings with: concrete, deliverable, policy proposals that are aimed at achieving the outcome you want. According to various people in ActionAid, women's rights 'asks' were too 'fluffy'.

I was told that the idea that aid should be used to support countries in meeting human rights commitments – including women's rights – was 'motherhood and apple pie'; no one could disagree with it, but it wasn't meaty enough to put in a briefing. It certainly wasn't adequate to counter the accusation that we couldn't advocate for aid to be used for gender equality because it would constitute conditionality – not much different from donors demanding that recipient countries spend money on Northern consultants or arms. Instead, we needed 'asks' that were the equivalent of 'reduce the proportion of aid spent on technical assistance by x per cent by y date'. The ability to engage with DFID on this kind of technical level was seen as essential for an NGO lobbyist. It was ironic that the demand that aid be spent in ways that supports women's rights was seen as fluffy, compared to the much more conservative demand of tweaking the amount that donors spend on consultants.

This was curious, since it seemed to me that as part of a broader, radical, civil society agenda NGOs should be engaging on the political level much more, rather than on this detailed, technical one. In recent years, the advocacy departments of big INGOs have become increasingly detached from their programming activities; without the political legitimacy of their programming, perhaps technical engagement is all that's left. If DFID is able to keep INGOs occupied with thinking through the technical details of their aid programme or their gender-mainstreaming arrangements, a great deal of the political space that enables lobbyists to argue 'this is a matter of justice – I don't care exactly how you do it – just find a way' is lost. This is not to say that lobbyists shouldn't have a robust political analysis of what is and isn't possible and base their strategies around this, but it's also essential not to lose the political ground that constitutes civil society's legitimacy.

Indeed, the gender adviser at DFID commented that ActionAid's more political stance on women's rights, as opposed to the blander gender equality agenda, was helpful to her because it was this political ground that those feminists working *within* donor organizations often could not occupy. This makes it all the more important that those on the outside do, thereby creating more political space for allies on the inside to make their case.

The letter: marginalized in our own organizations

The third incident shows that even if women's rights advisers had better 'asks', we would struggle to get them heard or accepted by our own colleagues. While my colleagues and I had been beavering away at organizing the International Women's Day event, little did we know that our manager, the head of policy, was working on a joint agency letter to DFID outlining the development lobby's priorities for the next G8 meeting. He had negotiated a letter that was (true to form, if you believe the DFID staffer) a long laundry list of 'asks' that we wanted to see taken forward – as these joint agency letters often are.

It covered aid, trade, HIV, water, governance, climate change, and more; and it included not one single mention of gender equality or women's rights. I did not see the letter before it was sent, but it was signed off by the head of policy and had also been seen by the executive director of ActionAid UK. Because the joint agency letter was drafted by ActionAid, and, alphabetically, ActionAid was the agency at the top, it became very closely associated with us. Coming after our big public display of commitment to women's rights at the event the day before, it looked rather ridiculous.

The letter landed on DFID's gender adviser's desk and she was tasked to respond to some of the points it raised as part of her broader brief on equity and rights. She was profoundly disappointed to discover that the letter offered no opportunity for her to respond on gender equality (although she did in fact manage to get some references to it into the response). The point was that the letter gave her no opportunity to say to the minister: 'look there's a big vociferous external lobby on this issue and we need to respond' – to reinforce what the public event had achieved.

The gender adviser sent the letter to a number of people, including the chair of the GAD Network, and the adviser also called me to let me know what had happened. She recognized that the letter had gone out while I was embroiled in organizing the event and she knew that had I seen it, I would have tried my hardest to get some gender language into it. She recognized that I was as disappointed as she was, as well as a bit embarrassed. The gender adviser was careful to make sure I understood that in making a fuss about the letter, she wasn't trying to undermine me or make me look incompetent. She sympathized with my position and together we recognized the opportunity to use this incident as a way to open up space for me and the women's rights agenda within ActionAid. The gender adviser sent an email flagging the issue to ActionAid UK's chief executive and when questioned in turn, the head of policy had to concede that the episode was, at the very least, highly inconsistent. The gender adviser also asked the chief executive for a meeting, which gave me the opportunity to brief him and to get further buy-in and profile for women's rights at a senior level.

By contrast, the reaction from other members of the GAD Network was very different. The chair sent an email to the steering group, of which I was a member, flagging the letter and notifying the group of her intention to write to all the signatories – most of whom were chief executives of organizations that were members of the network – in protest. While I thought this was a good idea, and right that my organization was being held accountable for its commitments, there was no recognition or concession that clearly, even on a personal level, the women's rights advisers at ActionAid would not have been happy about what had happened, and that it had obviously been beyond our control. While I had felt solidarity and trust with the DFID gender adviser, I felt much less understanding from my own fellow women's rights activists: there seemed a slight feeling of *schadenfreude* – that the day after our flashy event we had come unstuck, and entirely unsurprisingly for those who had lost faith that the big INGOs would ever really take women's rights seriously. Again, there was a slightly weary sense of 'we told you so'.

As well as being disappointing, it was also a missed opportunity. We could have had a useful discussion within the steering group – which included ActionAid, Oxfam, and Christian Aid, three of the most powerful development INGOs in the UK – about the best way to capitalize on what had happened. Given that it was members of our own steering group who would be drafting responses to the network on behalf of their chief executives, we could have advised on the best approach to get maximum impact. It could have been a moment to leverage more money out of the big INGOs for the cash-strapped network, or we could have tried to get a discussion among the chief executives of the biggest agencies about gender equality and how they intended to integrate it into their broader work leading up to the G8.

The GAD Network letter was useful to the extent that ActionAid International's head of women's rights was on the mailing list, and so had heard about the incident. She asked questions of both ActionAid UK and the international head of policy about our approach to the G8, and why we were not taking strong women's rights messages to the summit, resulting in more integration than there otherwise might have been.

What this incident demonstrates is that as women's rights officers in ActionAid, we had to navigate the territory of intermediaries to some extent. Because of where we were situated within an INGO, we had potentially more power to influence than the women's organizations, as well as more resources, access and credibility with DFID. But on the other hand, we sometimes struggled to exercise influence over our own organizations. What we needed from the women's rights organizations within the GAD Network were two things: we needed them to help us to hold our organizations to account for their promises (and in this sense, the GAD Network reaction to the letter was the right one), but we also needed them to understand that we were their allies in this effort, and that if we worked together we could do this more effectively. And on a personal level – because we worked hard, sometimes in quite hostile and difficult organizations, for the same goal – we wanted them to see us as allies.

By contrast, there was much greater understanding between me and the gender adviser at DFID – and it worked both ways. On one occasion, for example, I was aware that a colleague of mine at ActionAid was privy to DFID discussions about some important delivery targets. I realized that there were no targets in this framework on gender equality. Recognizing that the gender adviser at DFID was either in the dark (as we had been about the letter) or struggling to make the case, I rang her to find out what we could do together. It turned out that she had no idea these targets were being negotiated, but armed with the information I shared with her, she inserted herself into the discussions and DFID subsequently adopted a high-level target on delivering on gender equality.

Straddling the middle ground

Another incident further demonstrates how tricky this middle ground can be. With the High-Level Forum on Aid Effectiveness coming up in Accra in 2008, INGOs had been lobbying for more and better aid. This forum was organized to discuss the implementation of the Paris Declaration – intended to be a technocratic agenda on aid delivery – which had been seized upon by civil society, as well as some feminist bureaucrats, as a way to broaden debate on aid quantity and quality.

Colleagues in my department at ActionAid UK were quite involved in these lobbying efforts, and we had tried to persuade them to incorporate women's rights messaging into their campaign. But despite our best efforts, we were told either that our 'fluffy' asks were not concrete enough, or (completely the opposite) that pushing for aid to be spent on gender equality was imposing on developing-country governments a form of conditionality that was undemocratic and couldn't be supported. We spent a lot of time trying to improve our analysis, in order to come up with 'asks' that were more acceptable to our colleagues, but on reflection I'm not sure anything would have passed the test.

Since we weren't gaining any traction in our own organization, we were excited when the international women's rights network AWID became engaged in the issue, and we thought we could support the efforts through this route. AWID saw the aid effectiveness debate as a way of focusing attention on long-standing demands for better funding for women's organizations and more scrutiny of what proportion of aid budgets went to programmes to advance women's rights. When a European women's rights network organized a conference in Spain, AWID decided to hold a meeting directly afterwards, to bring women's rights organizations together to strategize on the 'road to Accra'.

My colleague and I were going to the conference and asked to attend the strategy meeting afterwards. We hadn't received confirmation, but assumed no news was good news and made arrangements to stay on. When we got there, however, we were told that we weren't welcome at the meeting because the women's organizations wanted to strategize 'without donors in the room'. It was the first time I had been labelled a 'donor' and I was quite surprised.

I think this situation probably reflects a broader concern among women's organizations about INGOs. To some extent, for many small women's organizations in the South, ActionAid *does* operate as a donor, and for them INGOs have become part of the problem, as they are squeezing the small organizations out of the picture. There is a feeling that INGOs like ActionAid are increasingly bidding for – and winning – big pots of bilateral donor money aimed at civil society, because the smaller NGOs lack the capacity to go through the procurement processes that these require. In this situation, ActionAid does act as an intermediary donor, channelling money into the smaller organizations that cannot access the money directly.

However, as a colleague in ActionAid pointed out to me, it is increasingly the case that these pots of money are being won either by big INGOs like ActionAid or Oxfam, or by the large consultancy companies like KPMG. It seems obvious which is preferable; but, I suppose under these circumstances, ActionAid has to accept that we *are* seen as donors and that our input in the strategy meeting was not welcome. However, it was frustrating to find ourselves marginalized in the work on aid effectiveness from within our own organization – by colleagues who said our messages on women's rights and aid were 'motherhood and apple pie' – and excluded from involvement in the issue by women's rights organizations too. It felt strange and a little uncomfortable to be straddling this middle ground.

I had hoped that by linking up with AWID, we women's rights officers would be in a better position to influence our colleagues within ActionAid UK. Since ActionAid was recognized as one of the key INGOs in the aid debate, I thought that if we could 'engender' their lobbying, we could play our part in supporting the women's movement's aid agenda. While our colleagues rejected our analysis as too 'fluffy', it would have been harder for them to reject the case made by AWID. This was particularly true given ActionAid's commitment to working with and being informed by social movements and women's rights organizations.

In the end, it wasn't to be. I think AWID was a bit confused about what to do with us in ActionAid: in their eyes we weren't proper donors, with all the influence that brings, but we weren't proper women's rights activists either. Perhaps I should have made my own intentions and strategy clearer to them.

Or maybe it was clear – but AWID made a calculation that they didn't need to influence the mainstream INGOs to have the impact they wanted. They formed a very effective alliance with the OECD gender adviser (see O'Neill and Eyben, 2013), so it was evident that they recognized the value of working with feminist bureaucrats; perhaps a calculation was made that my position inside an INGO was not central to their chosen strategy. By contrast, the OECD gender adviser's position was much more powerful, with much more direct access to where the key decisions were being taken, making an alliance with her much more strategic. It is also possible that AWID had had its fingers burned working with INGOs, the majority of which 'talked the talk' on women's rights but rarely delivered, and which tended to dominate the political space to the exclusion of women's organizations.

However, at times it felt like there was an element of one-upwomanship: a certain moral grandstanding, that feminists in women's organizations were somehow more authentic and committed than those in big bureaucracies like ActionAid. It is true that we didn't have the same struggles associated with working in small under-resourced organizations, including the very long hours and poor pay, but we had our own battles. In some respects, working for a small women's organization can be more empowering, because you're surrounded by people who agree with you on the basic premise of the importance of women's rights, something heavily contested within bureaucracies. When you have to deal with this kind of resistance every day on the inside, and then find a lack of understanding from your fellow feminists on the outside, it can be disappointing. I'm sure it was never personal, but because working for women's rights felt, and still feels, like a very personal commitment and pursuit – definitely more than just a job – it was at times difficult and frustrating.

Conclusion and a further reflection

I have told four stories based on my experiences as a women's rights officer working for ActionAid UK. Each of these stories shows the challenges of negotiating the middle ground of being a feminist working from an INGO location. They demonstrate how much of a feminist bureaucrat's skill rests on the effective use of inside–outside strategies – a challenge, not least because as feminists within INGOs, our identities as insiders and outsiders are constantly shifting.

The first story – the only unqualified success out of the four – was about a public event that worked well, precisely because DFID's gender adviser and I developed a very effective inside–outside strategy. Both of us recognized, from our different positions, what was possible, and we worked together in a relationship of mutual trust and respect. We recognized that our different positions – she on the inside of DFID, me as the civil society outsider – gave us different strengths and opportunities. By mapping and aligning these different opportunities, we were able to identify the mutual benefits in organizing the event, in sharing information at important moments, and in leveraging key resources (a large crowd on my part, a positive speech by the minister on hers). Neither of us could have done it without the other, and together we created spaces within our own organizations to influence colleagues and move our agendas forward.

While the other stories highlight examples of where my work was less obviously successful, each incident either opened up unexpected opportunities, or taught me something new about being a more effective feminist bureaucrat. In the failed lobbying meeting, the gender adviser at DFID cursed herself for not preparing the gender lobby better; I blamed my GAD Network colleagues for not presenting more coherent and compelling messages to the minister. It was an example of where neither the DFID gender adviser on the inside, nor the GAD Network (me included) on the outside, activated the kind of inside–outside strategy that had worked so well at the public event. The gender adviser should have given us more information on what the minister needed to hear and we should have tested our arguments on the gender adviser in advance – to hone them for better delivery and a greater likelihood of success. The lesson for us all was that these strategies need a lot of preparation and careful choreography to make them effective; they can never be taken for granted.

The case of the lobbying letter that failed to mention gender equality, highlights the extent to which feminist bureaucrats are often marginalized – or seen as outsiders – within their own organizations. Despite all the buzz created by the public event, ActionAid UK missed its first opportunity to demonstrate some commitment to integrating gender equality into its lobbying work. In this instance, while my ally at DFID completely understood my position, fellow feminists in the GAD Network were much less sympathetic. Both made a fuss: but while the former did so in consultation with me, so that we could work out the best way to capitalize on a bad situation, the latter did so without recognizing the difficult and personally demoralizing position I found myself in. The trust and respect I was afforded by one, was absent in the other.

Finally, my unsuccessful attempt to play a strategic role in the aid effectiveness campaign by using my position – this time as an insider – in a powerful INGO, demonstrates the need for greater understanding by those in women's organizations of the potential role that feminist bureaucrats can play in advancing the gender equality agenda. In this instance, I felt that the opportunity for an inside–outside strategy was missed because they did not recognize in me a potential trusted ally, assuming instead that because I was based in a Northern INGO, I was a donor, and therefore not useful. However, the OECD gender adviser did manage to work very effectively with AWID in exactly the way that I did not. It may be that with her much greater experience she was simply more effective at implementing an effective insider–outsider strategy than I was, or perhaps AWID made a calculation that working with me to change ActionAid's policy messages on aid was not a priority in terms of achieving their aims, instead choosing, perfectly reasonably, to focus on influencing the OECD more directly. However, if we had communicated more effectively – if I had had the confidence to be explicit about the opportunities I saw, and had not felt marginalized, as though in some way not a proper part of the women's movement – the result would perhaps have been different.

Several participants in the collaborative project that inspired this book, including Patti O'Neill, Joanne Sandler, and Everjoice Win, have moved into bureaucracies after years in social movements and women's organizations, and see this experience as key to their legitimacy with external allies. But for those less well known within the movement, especially those from the North, more proof is sometimes needed. I remember when I first met my ActionAid colleague in Malawi: she was extremely sceptical about me and my role – 'who did I think I was, "doing" women's rights in developing countries?' It was only when I mentioned that I had previously worked on women's rights in the UK context that I was given grudging approval – that I'd passed the feminist legitimacy test. It was the start of our friendship.

This story also illustrates the fluidity of our identities as insiders and/or outsiders. To my colleague, even though we worked in the same international development bureaucracy, I was an outsider – a feminist from the North working on women's rights in the South. To the gender adviser at DFID, I was the outsider, but for the women's organizations I worked with in the Gender and Development Network, I was on the inside, located within an INGO. For those of us working in UN Women, as I am now, we are seen as insiders by the women's movement, but as outsiders by many of our colleagues in the UN system. The fact that our positionalities are not fixed, but are shifting constantly, highlights the need to avoid the moral grandstanding of some in the women's movement which implies, 'I'm a better feminist than you'.

One of the purposes of this book is to help others to understand the everyday realities of being a 'gender mainstreamer' by shining a light on the work that feminist gender advisers do. For me, being part of the original project was an invaluable opportunity to reflect on my own work and to learn from others. In a job that was constantly 'one step forward, two steps back', it was particularly important in enabling me to distance myself from feelings of disappointment and frustration when things were not going well.

It can feel relentless and baffling. In 2009, I moved to a new job at UNIFEM where I represented the organization in an interagency group on the Millennium Development Goals. I went to meetings for about nine months and faithfully flagged gender equality at every one. I tried to be creative and interesting in my comments so that I wasn't seen as the boring 'gender police officer', banging on about 'my' issue. And I was heartened that in line with their own responsibilities to promote this agenda, I was supported by others in the room. Tied up by other work, I wasn't able to attend the final meeting at which an outcome document was agreed. 'Oh well,' I thought, 'someone is bound to ensure that gender equality is mentioned.' A few weeks later, a colleague saw the outcome document and queried why gender equality was only weakly mentioned in it. I was amazed – that after all that work, I turned my back for one meeting and the whole issue had been lost. I explained to my boss what had happened. She reminded me that we can't be expected to take responsibility for the failures of gender mainstreaming: the fault lay, not with me, but with all the others in the room; and she was right. I've seen newcomers to the role of gender mainstreamer – most recently a friend in the World Bank – absolutely baffled at how difficult it can be to do this job, even when you have the evidence, the arguments, and the high-level support lined up.

Realizing that 'my' failures are not actually my fault, but an intrinsic part of the job, has enabled me to analyse and understand what is happening, to see the blockages as a manifestation of patriarchal power resisting change, and to think creatively and strategically about how to circumvent it in future.

Reference

O'Neill, P. and Eyben, R. (2013) '"It's fundamentally political": renovating the master's house', in R. Eyben and L. Turquet (eds), *Feminists in Development Organizations: Change from the Margins*, pp. 85–100, Rugby, UK: Practical Action Publishing.

About the author

Laura Turquet has worked as an advocate and researcher on gender equality and women's rights for the past decade, with experience in diverse settings – from a small feminist campaigning organization to the newly established United Nations Entity for Gender Equality and the Empowerment of Women (UN Women), where she manages the organization's flagship publication, *Progress of the World's Women*. She has published many reports on gender equality issues including violence against women, access to justice, and the Millennium Development Goals. Laura has master's degrees in history and international relations from the Universities of Edinburgh and Sussex.

CHAPTER 8

Finding our organizational way

Rosalind Eyben

Meeting at a weekend-long retreat, the five women discuss what 'success' is for a feminist bureaucrat, and the challenges of gender mainstreaming. They agree on the importance of analysing and understanding the organizations they work for, and of finding opportunities to influence by 'working with the grain'. However, this carries its own risk – of becoming over-institutionalized and no longer being able to see where change is possible. This is the continuation of a series of fictionalized conversations begun in Chapter 4, in which the author is a participant observer.

After New York (Eyben, 2013) we have decided to next meet in our own time – rather than that of our organizations. We are going to a house in the country – but located conveniently close to an airport – that Marianne has borrowed from a friend. Ratna emails us the week before we meet. *Despite what is shaping up to be a crazy few months as we hurtle towards the end of the year, I certainly plan to be there to fill up the tanks! Too often we do this work running on empty!*

We meet over a weekend – because of our very busy schedules, but also the doubt in some minds as to whether our employers would have agreed to us participating in such a meeting, if organized during working hours. Ratna and Gillian are able to charge travel costs to their organizational budgets, but the others have to pay from their own pockets.

Two whole days together provides the luxury of getting to grips with the challenge of transforming our organizations. We start by looking at our definitions of success – answering the question Ratna posed in New York. *Is success about effective gender mainstreaming? What do we think about gender mainstreaming?* We agree there has been some slow progress over the last ten years or so, and we consider how this has come about. It is about what Marianne calls 'working with the grain': taking advantage of an organization's instruments, discourses, and procedures, and being able to assess when the opportunities are available to use them.

So what is success?

After breakfast, we gather in a large, light-filled room that looks out onto a forest glade. We sit quietly for a few minutes, appreciating the stillness. Ratna breaks the silence.

http://dx.doi.org/10.3362/9781780448046.008

'It's very easy to write a radical document' she says. 'You can look at it and think – doesn't that show how radical I am? But actually, it can be entirely ineffectual. Because if you're not carrying anybody with you, it will just sit on a shelf. And yes, you might get brownie points from all the people who are judging your feminist credentials, and it will look great. But in terms of what it achieves in total – it achieves very little. And actually, something that is more pragmatic, but has got a much wider kind of acceptance and understanding, is likely to go much further. Even if it looks a lot less radical in terms of what it's trying to achieve.'

'I wonder whether our successes in producing radical documents are just self-referential games', Marianne says. 'Are we perhaps just providing a progressive veneer for the fundamentally conservative aims of our organizations? I agree with Ratna. We need to be pragmatic. However, if anyone looked at what someone like me or you does behind enemy lines, takes it out of its context and examines it, then they could easily think this is just unacceptable. These people have sold out. They've been co-opted.'

Not everyone shares Marianne's fondness for conflictive metaphors, but we all agree that what might look like success from the inside, seems pretty pathetic from the outside. Karin is the most positive about what we can do. She argues that, cumulatively, our small wins may achieve more sustainable change than something more radical that we might try to introduce – only then to fail completely.

Claudia worries about working for a global policy organization. 'Everything is so intangible and remote. What do I have to do with *real* life? What *difference* am I making in the lives of rural women in Bangladesh? While I do think it worth trying to make the organization take gender seriously, how would I know if we had been successful? Because non-gender specialists would *know* what questions to ask – and when – in order to integrate gender concerns into their work. Monitoring and evaluation systems would include sex-disaggregated data routinely and consistently. The demand for gender equality expertise would be resourced and provided in a timely way. Corporate reporting mechanisms would hold staff accountable for commitments on gender equality. Business plans would include meaningful and measurable gender equality indicators, which would be monitored.'

'Oh, I've had to develop those', Karin says, looking gloomy.

'Well, apparently I feel more positive about these than you do', Claudia says. 'Success is when our publications celebrate achievements in promoting gender equality. And when independent evaluations of delivery against gender commitments *show* that lessons are learned and improvements are made, year on year. This is not exhaustive – but it *is* based on the learning journey that I've undertaken since taking on this role'.

'You can get caught up in organizational politics,' Ratna says with a frown, 'spending all day just answering emails and reading stuff. And six months will have gone by and you won't ever have changed. Or you'll have even forgotten what it's like – the reality, on the ground, for women.'

'The real sign of success is getting money to the women who need it,' says Gillian.

'Aha! But *who* gets the money also matters,' Marianne says. 'More money for women's organizations is not necessarily the same as more money for women. In many aid-dependent countries, NGOs are a donor invention, and money going to middle-class advocacy organizations in the capital might not make the slightest difference in poor women's lives.'

Gillian looks at her. She appears about to say something, but stays silent. Karin tells us she is still thinking about what Claudia has said. Her big success has been to get gender equality into the ministry's corporate performance framework, which means that country programme directors have to put something about gender into their delivery plans. 'I found somebody to come and talk to our team about how this process is being put together,' she says. 'What's the corporate performance framework, what does it look like, how does it work, who's responsible? To demystify it, effectively. Because it was – like many things in the ministry – there was this big thing going on and nobody quite knew who was responsible for doing it and how you engaged with it.'

'That was very brave of you', Marianne says, 'because I guess a lot of the people pretend they know how it's all going on, and don't have the courage to say, "actually, I don't understand, I'm an ignoramus, please tell me".'

'*Well*, I suppose because I was new ...' Karin reflects.

'So you took advantage?' Marianne gives a warm laugh.

'Yes. I'd say, "I've been in the job for two months – tell me how this works." Since then I've been learning all about what the ministry calls monitorable indicators and tangible results ... what Claudia was talking about'.

'Oh, my God!' says Marianne, 'This terrible language. But success is also getting people to say things that you didn't think they were going to say. I love getting my director-general to say things ... and then we repeat them ever after.'

'It's trying to get the key policy moments and the key political people within the organization to back you up. To say things and commit themselves. And then you can use that ... to shift the discourse and shift the priorities,' Claudia says. 'But this can seem very sterile when it's things like changing the placement of a paragraph, or a comma. You have no idea what impact that can have ... The institutional incentives drive you to focus a vast amount of energy on the placement of a comma.'

'The problem', Karin sighs, 'is that *necessarily* some of our successes never get publicized, because we are resorting to subterfuge. Much of what I do will never be appreciated by anyone except myself – and some close allies.'

Marianne quickly concurs. She recounts a story of the last meeting she had with the ministry's director-general, shortly before his retirement. He told her that if he had realized earlier on all the things she had been getting up to, he would have stopped her. We like this story. We talk about how our views on success differ from those of our managers and peers. We have to perform well according to *their* criteria as well as our own. Ratna says that to make things even more difficult for ourselves, we try to apply our feminist principles of working in a non-hierarchical and inclusive manner when doing what management requires of us. Claudia talks about a colleague who was a model of persistence, diplomacy, and inclusiveness in seeking to secure organizational agreement for a regional gender equality strategy, but who was criticized by management for it having taken so long. She had then gone on maternity leave, and her successor – who had benefited from all the preparatory ground work Claudia's colleague had done – unfairly claimed it as her own, and got the credit once the strategy was agreed. On this rather depressing note, we break for lunch.

Before reconvening, we put on our boots and coats and go for a walk through the forest that surrounds the house. We are so busy talking we lose our way. We start arguing about which of two paths is the right way home; and then laugh at ourselves over our disagreement. Eventually, the house appears in front of us, and soon we are back in our meeting room, warm and snug.

Talking about gender mainstreaming

Karin starts us off. 'I am thinking about what I felt like, when I first started at the ministry, and I remember not having a clue what was going on. I understand gender reasonably well, but I just didn't understand what was going on. I didn't understand the acronyms, I didn't understand the processes, I didn't know I was being asked for opinions on things where I didn't even know … I just didn't understand it. And I found it quite difficult.'

'Yes, indeed,' Ratna says. 'And once we've learnt what's going on, how do we change things? Over the last ten years there has been a shift in effort. We used to spend a lot of time doing gender analysis … We were trying to get the information, trying to get some sort of analytical information base. But there was very little emphasis on what you actually *did* with that information.'

'It's not that we've got the gender analysis stuff right,' says Marianne, 'but we're better at recognizing that it needs to be backed up with policies, actions, budgets. And that there needs to be a focus on the organization itself – its kind, its culture, its mechanisms of accountability.'

'Hang on!' Karin exclaims. 'There's still a debate about whether you focus on changing the organization or putting your efforts into getting part of the organization, and its resources, to do useful things for women out there in the real world. I know ideally one does both – what used to be called a 'twin track' approach. But is this really feasible?'

No one answers this question directly. Instead, Claudia talks about what she has been doing. 'We've finally got our gender equality strategy approved and it's quite a huge thing – that *everybody* will be responsible for gender mainstreaming. And this is for the next strategic plan. So I think we've managed to go from having a section being responsible and leading, to still leading but saying that everybody's accountable – every project will have either a policy marker or all the frameworks will have to show outputs in terms of gender.' She tells us, however, that she caused some considerable controversy in the process, when her organization was drafting its new strategic plan.

'I obtained everyone's programme statements – all the other divisions – and, sort of, put gender in ... engendered all their outputs and indicators. And I insisted on attending all the meetings. They didn't call us to the meetings. Then I said, "You can't have this document go out if you're talking about gender mainstreaming in your vision but when it comes to your strategy you don't talk about it. That's not good enough."'

Claudia explains she is still unsure whether the success she hoped for has been achieved. She is worried that she has not seen the final version of the strategic plan and that, possibly, what she thought had been agreed in earlier drafts, has been watered down. At a strategic planning workshop she had encountered considerable resistance. 'By chance the workshop was on 14 February – St Valentine's Day – and some of the men present started trivializing the whole thing, saying they "weren't in love" with what was being proposed.'

Gillian disagrees with Claudia's approach. Gillian has focused on getting her organization to fund projects on specific themes, such as women's land rights, rather than trying to make sure that all the programmes and projects incorporate gender issues. 'One of the things I made clear when I came in was to say, "Look – I don't do gender mainstreaming. If that is the mandate, I am not your mainstreamer." I want to make sure I have this space carved out, with money, and that has been my consistent line from the beginning. I don't do gender mainstreaming and I don't speak that particular language. Useful as it may be, I'm just not that kind of person.'

Claudia, surprised, asks why Gillian has taken this line. She replies, 'I was coming from a region where this gender-mainstreaming language was all over the place. Donors were picking it up, everyone was picking it up, and the politics had disappeared ... The feminist politics had disappeared. At a very personal level, people like me were being seen as the bad people, because we were talking the feminist "rights" language while the nice women were doing "gender". Another problem with gender mainstreaming is that it makes the staff working on gender issues very internally focused.'

'Yes,' says Marianne thoughtfully, 'it can become all about the internal politics, which the focus on gender mainstreaming always tends to produce ... Because you become caught up in how to make sure you're in the right meeting at the right moment, how you can get involved in the strategy at a particular moment, and so on.'

'An important part of how we established the work,' Gillian says, 'was to say, "No, we are not going to obsess about the internal stuff, we're going to look external. We will help you with the internal stuff, but it is not going to consume us." I still feel that this is the one bit where we haven't had enough of a political strategic focus – and I'm deliberately calling it political.'

'So even for you, Gillian, the twin track challenge remains,' Karin points out.

'And the problem with *your* approach, Claudia', says Ratna, 'is that as soon as you've got the commitment on paper, everybody says, "Oh, we've done our bit." And they don't do anything more.'

'That's it,' says Marianne. 'A successful strategy is one that has explicit targets of how much gets spent on gender equality.'

Karin tells us she is proud of successfully introducing gender budgeting into her ministry – and this despite resistance from senior bureaucrats because of the procedural complications, and from the minister because of his worry that this might lead to the setting of quantitative targets against which he would be held accountable. 'I succeeded', she says, 'in introducing a new chapter in the budget proposal that sets out explicitly how much money is allocated – new funds – how much can be tracked down for gender equality as a main target, as a subsidiary target, and exactly which budget lines. I think it is important for transparency and accountability – because if it's not explicit in the budget proposition, nobody will be able to say, "Where did that 100 million go? What did we spend it on?" Now it has to be accounted for.' It was difficult to implement technically, she tells us. She is not aiming to achieve a specific target – only to have a system in place, to monitor whether there are year-on-year increases.

Marianne agrees that the technicalities of gender budgeting have to be overcome. Although she has been successful in getting it introduced as a requirement of the NGOs her agency is funding, she is finding it impossible to convince her colleagues to use it in the official aid programme, because of these difficulties.

'Well,' Ratna says, 'technical reasons can be given for not doing something, when in fact the resistance is political. From my own experience working in a ministry, politicians find gender mainstreaming tedious. It is difficult to draft an interesting press release announcing a success in changing the assessment criteria for reviewing project proposals!'

'You are right', Karin says. 'The minister was looking to make a splash in the real world out there, and did not want to be bothered with approving changes to procedures. Yet we need that support from the top, as our bureaucracies can be very resistant to procedural change.'

There is more to be said but it is time to break for the day. Over supper and a log fire, we talk about our lovers, our children, good films we have seen, and holidays we are looking forward to. The next morning, talk about mainstreaming continues.

Working with the grain

Despite our different views on mainstreaming, we agree that we share a sense of slow progress.

'It's like a carpenter,' says Marianne, 'who creates something new from the material available, by working with – rather than against – the grain of the wood.'

We think about this for a moment, as we look out at the trees, their shapes skeletal in the mist, as their last leaves drift to the ground. But the mood inside the room is far from autumnal.

'You know,' Ratna says, 'we have definitely been helped by a change in the normative climate.'

She gives an example of how she influenced an all-male committee, tasked to establish the funding criteria and then review and select projects proposed by NGOs to her organization. 'There were some background documents that already had a stated commitment to gender – but this is common in the UN system, as you know. But once you point out these commitments, the board – even an all-male one – has to take notice.'

And yet Gillian queries whether an improved normative climate is always so helpful. Her NGO says all the right things but … 'I wonder whether it is sometimes easier when people openly disagree or resist. Then you know what you are dealing with. On the other hand, when people say "Oh yes, gender is really important" and write it into things without any intention of really doing it, it's harder. Because you don't know who or what it is your fighting against.'

'Oh, I agree', Ratna says. 'People *do* just pay lip service. But in my case, because I was noticing what was going on, I could hold the board to account.'

Always inventive with metaphors, Marianne suggests the trick may be to not worry too much about the discourse, but rather to imitate the strategy of a virus. To get, unobtrusively, into the structure and then to replicate. 'Like a virus,' she says, 'you start with the cells that are least resistant to attack.' She describes how she took this approach when seeking agreement to a new gender action plan, following a negative independent evaluation of the implementation of the organization's previous plan. She opted for those parts of the organism with low levels of resistance or – to mix metaphors – what she describes as the 'low-hanging fruit'.

'We asked ourselves: "What's within our reach? What are the easiest things that we, a very limited group of people, can do?" I drafted the plan so that it fitted in unobtrusively, a bit like a Trojan horse,' she laughs. 'I suppose the tactic I've always used is to play the corporate line as strongly as possible in everything that we do. When we put our gender equality plan in front of them, people were saying, "This is a really smart plan." And they weren't talking about the content at all! They liked its presentation and they could see how it just fitted into the work that they have been doing right then. And so that immediately put us in a strong position, because departments had been thinking in these ways already. It meant they were being reassured that what we were asking them to do was not new, but merely additional – and it was additional within processes and tracks that they had begun.'

The conversation ebbs and flows as we explore our fascination with the organizations we work for. Ratna picks up a thread from earlier in the morning. She talks about trying to make change happen by working with standardized institutional artefacts, such as policy brochures, ministerial speeches, etc. 'I volunteered to take over from someone who was obviously overworked, to write the deputy director's speech on health policy. This meant I could make sure the speech included the right messages.'

Karin tells a story of how she once failed to get the messages she wanted into a policy document. When drafting the ministry's policy on abortion, she learnt that her political masters were keen to appease a well-organized network of faith-based women's organizations that strongly objected to legal abortion. 'So then we decided to change the text – from supporting "legal abortion" to go for "safe, self-determined abortion".'

'Working with the grain is OK, Marianne,' says Claudia. 'But it can stop you sticking your neck out, and it can make you back-pedal – like Karin just told us she did. I start asking myself, "Am I an obstacle to the change that I'm seeking to make? Or an obstacle to the change that others are seeking?" Yes, I think there are times I have been overly conservative and concerned about institutions, that I should and could take more risks.'

We break for lunch and a further exploration of the forest. This time, we quickly find our way back, and once in our meeting room, we continue a thread of conversation we had started on our walk.

Assessing and seizing opportunities for influence

Ratna says, 'You've got a small number of people within the organization, particularly in a bureaucracy, who are completely on your side and understand the issues. But they are often quite few, and in quite a weak position. So how do you create space around them, so they've got a bit more leverage? There is a lot of, just general inertia and frantic busyness in people, who have got a million and one other things they need to think about … and gender equality is yet another thing they're being asked to bear in mind. So I think a lot of it's about trying to do what you can, to make sure somebody isn't a blockage, and allowing the people who *are* enthusiastic about it, and who have got capacity, room for manoeuvre.'

'Are you talking about working with people in your organization?' asks Karin.

'It's sometimes an internal thing and sometimes an external thing,' Marianne replies, 'trying to get people from civil society, for example, to talk to the kind of people they need to talk to internally. And I think that kind of strategizing and tactic is completely context specific, and it's to do with who you're trying to influence in that context.'

'What about all the effort people put into trying to influence some policy document,' Gillian chips in, 'as if the documents mean something when they mean absolutely nothing? Does this kind of advocacy actually make any difference? There can have been some mammoth great lobby, and really coordinated civil society, women's ministry, gender focal points, networking together sometimes quite successfully. And the sum total of their lobbying results in one sentence.'

'But actually,' Marianne says, 'it's better having sentences there than not having them.'

'Well, I'm of the view,' Ratna says, 'that sometimes, it's probably not that important to have that sentence; that maybe the consequences of all that lobbying are *themselves* important in terms of the energy created. I think that you can't read off from the process, from the product. I think the process has its own consequences.'

'Yes, exactly,' Marianne agrees, 'and influences people along the way. And it might be ... even if the document does have any impact, if in any way it is an instrument of accountability ... it could be that that sentence is actually quite a coup! But, there's a wider question in my mind, about what I think about all this advocacy, and I'm really unsure about it.'

'But on the other hand,' Ratna says, still fretting about success. 'If we were all busy, actually working at grassroots, would that actually – in terms of time, money, and resources – be more effective? I don't know.'

None of us know the answer to her question. Instead, we talk about how there are years and decades when much is achieved, and other times when hunkering down and keeping the flame burning is the most that can be hoped for. There are also moments, Marianne points out, when we may argue among ourselves whether a situation is one which requires encouraging external allies to vociferously oppose something, or one where what may appear a threat can be turned usefully into an opportunity. Claudia tells us that she thinks the recent emphasis on adolescent girls, and the support being given them by private sector foundations like Nike, is a real opportunity for influencing development agendas.

Gillian disagrees. 'What many of these foundations are doing is profoundly anti-rights.'

'This can be tough,' Marianne says. 'I agree with Claudia that we should seize opportunities – particularly in difficult climates. But we can be under pressure from our external networks to shift the discourse more decisively. They may think we've betrayed them if we stop using rights language. It just shows again the importance of making friends with them, so they understand and support what we're doing.'

'Claudia was talking yesterday about instrumental change,' says Karin. 'This uses tools and techniques that fit within the status quo to promote greater attention to gender equality and better outcomes for individual women and girls. That's what foundations like Nike are doing – and to be honest, quite a lot of what I am doing as well. It's not the same as transformational change, which questions the status quo and alters the underlying power dynamics that perpetuate gender inequality in the first place.'

The afternoon draws to a close and we pack our bags to go our separate ways. Claudia emails us from the airport. *I am really struck by our need for mutual understanding and sharing. The amount of energy in the room was amazing: the sympathy, support, and advice. Why don't people do this more often?*

Conclusion

It is not easy to work inside organizations where the support for feminist transformative agendas may be largely absent, even in those where rights language is common discourse. Working with the grain may mean having to avoid the appearance of seeking to change things, while looking for room to manoeuvre within the limited space available.

That limited space can be a problem if it constrains the feminist bureaucrat's imagination. And yet she risks failure when seeking to introduce a change that is too alien to the way the organization works – one that goes against *its* grain. By working too closely with the grain, we risk over-institutionalization and the loss of capacity to think outside of the box. Over-institutionalization can prevent being alert to opportunities that may arise independently of one's own efforts, and these may be opportunities that can be used craftily in support of the feminist bureaucrat's objectives – without being co-opted by someone else's agenda. All this requires political judgement, and the courage to act on it.

Reference

Eyben, R. (2013) 'Feminist identities', in R. Eyben and L. Turquet (eds), *Feminists in Development Organizations: Change from the Margins*, pp. 55–66, Rugby, UK: Practical Action Publishing.

About the author

Rosalind Eyben is a Professorial Research Fellow at the Institute of Development Studies, University of Sussex. She is a social anthropologist with a professional background in development policy and practice, and a committed teacher in the IDS doctoral and master's programmes, including on gender and development. She has designed and facilitated numerous workshops for international development practitioners all over the world. Her research interests focus on power and relations in international aid. From 2006–11 she convened the global policy programme of the International Research Consortium on Pathways of Women's Empowerment and is currently developing a new area of work exploring the knowledge/power practices of donors that sustain the invisibility of unpaid care as a development policy issue. In 2010 she launched the Big Push Forward that has created an international network challenging the current audit culture in development. She was awarded a CBE in 2000 and is a board member of UNRISD and ActionAid UK.

CHAPTER 9

Values and systems: gender equality work in different organizational settings

Ines Smyth

Ines Smyth works for Oxfam and spent a year as the leading gender specialist at the Asian Development Bank (ADB) – an institution with a very different ethos and priorities. She explores how the characters of the two organizations shape their commitments and approaches to promoting gender equality in their programmes. Her experience at ADB helps her to look at the world of international NGOs in a new light. She concludes that feminist bureaucrats must persist in tackling obstacles and areas of resistance – even within NGOs – where too often, simple solutions are expected for social problems of intractable complexity.

> We seem to be overcoming our fear of power, and have embraced it like a lover.
>
> Batliwala (2009: 140)

This chapter is about moving, for a period of just over a year, from a large international NGO (Oxfam Great Britain, hereafter referred to as Oxfam) to the Asian Development Bank (ADB) – institutions with different ethoses and priorities, as well as different geographical locations.

My reflections are professional and personal, as I make explicit my positionality as a feminist, middle-aged female, 'gender advocate', and activist. I use these latter two terms to reflect on one of the themes of this collection: that there is a difference between feminist activists on one hand, and bureaucrats who happen to work on 'gender issues' on the other. I define myself as a gender advocate and activist because my concern for women's rights spans my private and work lives, and because I do not perceive my organization, however large and formally structured, as a bureaucracy where individuals are driven by self-interest, as I shall show later.

The focus of this chapter is on how I perceived the differences between the two institutions – and their respective advantages and disadvantages – through the many filters of my experience; and on how I tried to make use of different opportunities available to pursue my long-term aim: promoting women's rights in the context of development work. I did have additional and related purposes in spending time at ADB, and they are explored in the next section of the chapter.

http://dx.doi.org/10.3362/9781780448046.009

It should be noted that this chapter does not attempt to evaluate the achievements of either of the organizations in terms of gender equality. Certainly, this is not about 'which of the two is better at women's rights work'. Also, by way of clarification, I should add that my comments are shaped mainly (though not uniquely) by perceptions and conditions at the respective headquarters, in Oxford and Manila. Both are large and complex institutions, and so focusing mostly on headquarters is a limited but more realistic endeavour. Finally, I should say that my knowledge of Oxfam is considerably more extensive, given the many years (more than a decade) I have spent there, when compared with my limited time at ADB. A year is certainly not long enough to fully understand such a complex institution.

Structure of the chapter

First, I explore my motivations in accepting the post of leading gender specialist at ADB, and the range of emotions associated with this. I then use the framework employed by Miller (1998) to identify three elements that influence organizational responses to gender equality work: the organization's openness to external influences, the fit between the gender equality project and the organization's mandate, and the presence and capacity of gender advocates within it. Second, I look more specifically at the comparative strength of ADB in embedding gender mainstreaming in organizational systems, versus the emphasis Oxfam puts on 'hearts and minds'. Third, I look particularly at ADB's relationships with women's organizations and networks compared with the situation in Oxfam.

Finally, I reflect on the experience of 'going back'. Following my period at ADB, I returned to Oxfam where I still work as senior gender adviser. The exercise of reflecting on the experience, at a distance of a few years, and comparing the two organizations for the purpose of writing this chapter, clarified the sources of the many ambiguities I feel in continuing to operate in this large, development NGO. However, the exercise also confirmed that, despite or because of those, I consider it a privilege and a worthwhile career being a gender advocate within this organization, both because I continue to share its overall values and because I am conscious of the positive influence it can have in the lives of women, especially in developing countries.

The move: emotions and motivations

Rarely do the decisions we take have simple and single motivations. This applies to my decision to join ADB as leading gender specialist. I believe it was (to use a migration terminology) the result of push and pull factors.

Such factors came together in my desire to reflect and learn more – and better – outside the boundaries that the pressures of daily tasks create. NGOs give great emphasis to knowledge and learning, and have adopted from the private sector the language of 'learning organizations' (Britton, 1998). They often see themselves as the bridge between abstract and theoretical knowledge generated in academic contexts, and the realities experienced by men and women living in poverty. This combination of abstract knowledge and practical experience is considered essential for effective policymaking. Working on gender issues often means taking on some of this bridging role, and also mediating between feminist theory and epistemology – often seen as esoteric and not a little alien – on the one hand, and concepts or methodologies that are accessible, acceptable, and applicable to development practice on the other. This role also entails translations and compromises that often prevent practitioners – including gender advocates – from exploring and debating relevant issues more openly and fully, and in their true complexity.

Thus the strongest of the motivations behind my decision to leave one organization for another was the desire to learn and interrogate in greater depth, and from novel perspectives, the issues and approaches I had been working with for so many years. As a gender adviser in Oxfam I had not been operating according to a master [sic!] plan, but developing strategies (with others) according to external and internal influences, and adapting them to opportunities and results as they evolved. And while familiarity may not necessarily breed contempt, it does dim ingenuity and initiative.

In other words, reflective practice – a notion central to this collection – is a useful tool that can be sharpened by changing one's environment. Batliwala (2009: 140), with reference to feminists, puts it well: 'We have been exploring how to reach out, rather than bringing people in – going into spaces where we are not in command, where we must learn, and become the apprentices'. In leaving Oxfam and joining ADB for a while, I reached out and became an apprentice, and this opportunity to learn was much appreciated.[1]

I had spent many years in Oxfam, mostly as a gender adviser, and what was encouraging me to leave was the weariness that inevitably accompanies work where – despite progress – steps forward must be jealously guarded from the backward slippages that accompany organizational restructurings and personnel changes; where fundamental social transformation is supposed to happen with few resources, and within the timespan of discrete 'projects' and the boxes of logical frameworks; where one's beliefs and values must often be adjusted and translated, so that they can be accepted by others with different values and priorities (Britton, 1998). This is not a categorical and negative appraisal of Oxfam's work in this field; rather, the necessary acknowledgment that what we are trying to change – in terms of gender relations and norms – is too large to be contained or achieved by the efforts of a single individual, a single project, or a single organization – however large.

One more factor that pulled me towards ADB and the more senior position I was to occupy, was the desire to move my career upwards, as gender posts in NGOs are rarely distinguished by their seniority or the power they hold. While the notion of power is amply debated in the feminist literature – in fact, power is central to it – personal dealings with its reality reveal layers of ambiguity and discomfort. Privately, some of us may suspect that the male political discourse is correct, and that as women we are not suited to hold positions of authority (Naciri, 1998). And while relatively little power was associated with my new position at ADB, the change in status came with a sense that there was something intrinsically improper about my desire to achieve a higher rank. Even the prospect of earning more was somewhat touched by a sense of guilt; as an activist, should I be enticed by selfish considerations such as earnings?

At the time, the phrase 'sleeping with the enemy' (or rather, napping, since my union was to be of relatively short duration) kept coming to mind. Its definition made sense, as it 'is used to describe a situation involving a non-adversarial relationship between two individuals or entities that would normally be unfriendly or adversarial ... Often, this type of cooperation is met with suspicion from supporters of both parties'.[2]

This may all have had to do with my lack of confidence as an individual, my working-class background, or simply the trepidation that comes with any change, but no doubt it was also influenced by certain feminist debates. In fact, as a white, Western, middle-aged woman, these dilemmas had additional connotations. Mohanty (1988) argued that the Western gender and development tradition (and more specifically its scholarship) had contributed to reproducing a monolithic notion of women in the Third World – a view detrimental to the promotion of the rights of women in developing countries. Despite the criticisms levelled against it, Mohanty has been influential, including in making many Western feminists in the 1980s and 1990s much more aware of the role they play through their engagement as either scholars or development practitioners. I was not exempt from this, and as I considered the move from Oxfam to ADB, these considerations were foremost in my mind, bringing a sense of apprehension and vague guilt at my own motivations.

Strong systems versus hearts and minds

I expected that the two organizations would be very different: Oxfam being an international non-governmental organization (INGO) and ADB an international financial institution (IFI). While the literature (spanning decades) highlights how the term NGO includes a 'huge diversity of institutions' (Edwards and Hulme, 1992: 14), they are still distinguishable from IFIs. IFIs are bodies with government members, while NGOs are defined by their being non-governmental. This difference is also reflected in their sources of funding – with IFIs supported financially by member states, and NGOs by a variety of sources (the public, foundations, and the private sector, as well as donor nations) – which determine to whom they are mainly and formally accountable, or at least should be.

Despite these differences, NGOs and IFIs have gradually acquired similar characteristics in the last decades, for example an increasing role in development and global governance, and some convergence in language (of participation, good governance, empowerment, etc.). The failures of adjustment programmes (and to some extent the pressure from NGOs) have led IFIs to embrace poverty reduction as a stated purpose, and thus have come closer to development NGOs' defining concern. Nevertheless, the two types of organizations still have very different mandates and agendas: repeated crises and various paradigm shifts have not displaced economic growth and the market from the centre of the IFIs' pantheon, while the needs and perspectives of individual men and women, and of communities living in poverty and experiencing disasters and marginalization, remain without doubt the central reference points for the thinking and action of NGOs, whatever their size.

I became aware that there are other differences between ADB and Oxfam, notably the much greater financial resources and the much more hierarchical structure of ADB. The latter was particularly tangible; office space and furnishings in ADB reflect a strict hierarchy, with administrative staff (of whom the great majority, it should be stressed, are Filipino nationals) occupying desks in open areas, and mostly expatriate staff ('professional' staff) housed in offices that become larger and better appointed as their occupants' seniority increases. In contrast, Oxfam's offices are entirely open plan, and this includes spaces for those in the most senior positions. In Oxfam hierarchies are rather flat and this also means that, at least at headquarters, it is possible to interact freely across all areas of work and levels of seniority. I am able, for example, to contact Oxfam's executive director directly when necessary. In ADB this would be unthinkable and to communicate upwards a strict protocol is followed. An interesting ritual is observed at Christmas, when all staff are given strict instructions on how and when to await the general director's 'walkabout', and whether and where to stand in the official photograph.

It also appeared to me that what Duncan Green (2008) concludes in relation to the World Bank is true for ADB as well: despite many internal differences of opinion, the overall liberal ideology and economic orthodoxy is still dominant among its staff (excepting, as a rule, social development and gender advisers). Staff members in Oxfam, in comparison, seem more diverse in terms of background and qualifications (few are economists), and tend to espouse a very different ideology. In my many years in Oxfam I have often been on staff recruitment panels, for positions that have varied considerably in seniority and technical fields. Very frequently, candidates seemed to be genuinely attracted by the values of the organization, and were often prepared to accept positions below (in pay and rank) what their qualifications may have allowed them to achieve, in order to be able to contribute to social development and poverty reduction. This appeared more often the case for female candidates, for whom a frequent route to 'development work' (dealing directly with communities or doing advocacy and campaigning) seems to be that of taking up administrative positions. In 2009, 67 per cent of Oxfam's HQ staff were women, though this fell to 48 per cent at the two highest levels of seniority. Despite a widespread tendency to work long hours, it is possible for staff to seek arrangements that facilitate childcare or other family responsibilities through flexible or part-time work (20 per cent of HQ staff are part-time, and of this 85 per cent are women).

Fairly soon after joining ADB it became clear to me that concerning gender work, the differences from Oxfam were considerable. The sharpest difference between the two was that ADB had succeeded in embedding its gender work in robust systems. Such systems were and remain relatively weak and inconsistent in Oxfam. On the other hand, Oxfam is generally characterized by an environment where people's behaviour, values, and language reflect the relevance and importance of gender equality and women's rights, in other words where 'hearts and minds' are mostly (although not totally) committed.

ADB's commitment to the promotion of gender equality is enshrined in its Bank policy on gender and development in ADB operations which requires 'addressing gender considerations in ADB's macroeconomic, sector, strategy, and programming work, including studies on the impact of economic reform programs on women; undertaking gender analysis in projects; and ensuring the consideration of gender issues at all stages of the project cycle, including identification, preparation, appraisal, implementation, operation and maintenance, and monitoring and evaluation' (ADB, 2006). ADB's 'Operational procedures on gender and development in ADB operations' sets the procedures to be followed. The main element is the classification of bank projects in four gender categories (ADB, 2010):

Category I: gender equality as a theme (GEN), applied where there is an explicit aim to promote gender equality;

Category II: effective gender mainstreaming (EGM), applied where the design of the loan includes women's participation and related features;

Category III: some gender benefits (SGB), where there are only some gender features on loan designs;

Category IV: no gender elements, which is self-explanatory.

The processes and decisions that surround such classification represent the cornerstone of ADB's gender systems (other elements are the country gender assessments (CGAs) and a number of capacity development initiatives) on which other activities rest. For this reason, I limit my observations to these.

The system clearly has problems. First comes its complexity (my biggest challenge in the first months at ADB was to understand it): different categories (namely the first versus the rest) belong to different bank systems; the sheer number of the elements that define each category, as the ADB 2010 Report states; and the fact that categories I and II are combined into an additional category known as 'projects with significant gender mainstreaming'. The system changed in 2008, thus making it harder to track progress. Finally, and perhaps more seriously, the classifications are assigned at and are limited to the approval phase of projects. They do not apply to their implementation or results.

Despite these weaknesses, the system provides a *mandatory*, open door for gender considerations to be included in loans and other projects, and thus it is regularly followed. Another interesting aspect of the ADB system is that for the projects in the first two categories, a detailed gender action plan (GAP) is required. This is perhaps one of the most promising tools to ensure that gender concerns are taken into consideration beyond the approval stage of loans: that they are implemented and monitored, and their results assessed – at least for projects that include such a plan.

By contrast, the impression during my stay was that ADB was far from having achieved the same level of concern for gender issues in its own internal environment. Gender composition of staffing could be considered a tangible demonstration of this. During my time there, I observed that while women made up less than a third of professional international staff, they were around three quarters of local (usually much more junior) staff. Various attempts were being made to improve the gender balance in the professional ranks, but it was unclear to me what practical steps were being taken or what they were achieving. This was because this 'internal' matter was considered outside the scope of work of the leading gender specialist.

More striking, and more difficult to document, was the quality of daily practices and interactions. For example, staff members at ADB would use a form of English peppered with gendered terminology (more junior female colleagues may be referred to as 'girls') and pronouns ('he' for both 'he' and 'she'). It was not unusual to hear comments on the appearance, dress, or age of female colleagues, whether derogatory or complimentary. The bank seemed to have limited concern for a work–life balance that would accommodate gendered family obligations. Formally and publicly I was told several times that 10 per cent of overtime was obligatory for all. Travel schedules for those with very young children were not less intense than those of others. In private conversations with female colleagues with young children it was clear that they found this as challenging as other professional women in their situation, but that this was made worse by the intransigence of their senior managers.

In a particularly memorable event – ironically, a lunch arranged by the Professional Women Committee – speakers insisted that at ADB, women who wished to advance their careers must simply 'play the game' – just like their male colleagues – rather than try to change the game itself. Anything else was seen as seeking unfair advantages. One of the speakers then compared granting any concession (in terms of flexible time, working hours, travel regimes) to 'women who choose to have children' to doing the same for someone who may 'choose to spend their evenings drinking and taking drugs', i.e. ADB should not be deemed responsible for personal choices of lifestyle. Understandably the statement shocked those present, however with one exception, they felt unable to challenge it.

What could be the reason behind this situation where workable systems had been developed and had taken hold to support gender work, but where values of gender equality received such little space and recognition? One possibility is that this was the result of explicitly thought-out strategies of 'institutional gender entrepreneurs' who, fully cognizant of the hierarchical nature of the organization, reached the conclusion that focusing efforts on systems rather than attitudes and values would achieve better results. The steep hierarchy would indeed make questioning or resisting organizational systems extremely difficult. I occasionally found myself wondering whether this was also a situation where, as Green (2008: 303) says, 'staff concern for career and salary leads to a high level of conformity and conservatism'. This would not be inconceivable for ADB, because of the significant 'career and salary' when compared to employment in NGOs. In what way did such a situation influence my work in ADB? The systems represented a challenge at the beginning, as understanding the classification and other procedures was no simple matter. For the remainder of my stay at ADB I was content with using and promoting such systems to the best of my ability, to ensure that loans and other projects had as many relevant and realistic gender components as possible, or at a minimum, a gender analysis.

I felt more confident in trying to induce change in the culture of the organization within my limited sphere of influence. At the very basic level I instituted less rigid and authoritarian relationships with staff and others, these being in my opinion more congenial to gender debate, and in the hope of modelling less hierarchical values and practices for broader adoption. I also brought from the NGO sector participatory techniques for training and planning. Those are not unknown at ADB, but the preference is still for formal events where adult learning is passive and participation is limited. For example, at social development training with staff and at a large meeting with government representatives, I promoted methodologies (case studies, videos, role play, group work) that are in standard use in NGOs, and that opened the possibility for a more questioning attitude to the matters at hand, and hopefully, also for the future.

The situation in Oxfam is in some sense the reverse. Oxfam has made only limited attempts to classify projects, programmes, or initiatives from the perspective of whether or how they address gender equality issues. The existing system requires information on the percentage of any given project that focuses on one of the five 'aims' of the organization (in the fields of livelihoods, basic services, humanitarian response, governance, and gender equality). But there does not seem to be a clear definition of what this refers to and thus it is subject to many different interpretations. The consequence is that, while projects that address women's disadvantage as their primary purpose (what can be called 'stand-alone projects') can be identified and counted, the same is certainly not true for the mainstreamed elements of other projects and programmes (where the main focus may be livelihoods, education, or other more generic aspects of poverty). More recently (at the end of 2010), attempts were being made to introduce quantifiable elements (percentage of projects with a 'gender objective') to our work, but it is too early to assess their potential.

Beyond this, there is no mandatory system that requires separate plans for gender aspects of other areas of work, in other words for mainstreaming. While projects and programmes are obviously monitored and assessed (including those focusing on aspects of women's rights), and occasional gender reviews are carried out, there is no requirement in the organization for a regular and systematic analysis of the directions and achievements of gender equality work. Perhaps the much less hierarchical relations and informal structures may mean that existing gender requirements are agreed to but can be ignored without much fear of sanction (or expectation of rewards).

My experience of working in Oxfam for over ten years is that great emphasis is put on establishing that the values it holds are clear and shared across the organization. Oxfam says on its internal website: 'We truly believe that a world without poverty is possible. That everyone has a right to a life worth living. And that with the right support people can take control, solve their own problems, and become self-reliant and independent'. Oxfam has long realized that the values it espouses must apply both to its external mandate of fighting poverty and suffering, and to its internal practices. Moser and Moser (2005) quote Oxfam comments that it could not realistically expect to achieve at the programme level what it could not achieve in our own workspace.

The in-depth study of Oxfam's organizational culture carried out by Pialek (2008) concludes that the discourse of the organization indicates a shared consciousness of gender issues: 'Formally sexist language and concepts have been exorcised, equality language is incorporated within all human resources literature and policy, job descriptions explicitly highlight gender awareness as a key quality, policies and analysis incorporate gender terms' (Pialek, 2008: 173). Despite this, according to Pialek, progress has been achieved at the cost of persisting problems: a degree of hidden and passive resistance to the 'project' of gender equality, ambiguities about whose responsibility gender-mainstreaming work should be, and the sanitization of gender issues away from their feminist roots.

Pialek's analysis continues to be valid to this day. There are 'persisting problems' in whether all hearts and minds have been conquered. For example, Let's Talk, an initiative recently implemented to create innovative spaces where personal concerns or questions on gender equality could be raised openly led to constructive and open debates in several countries, but failed to take off at headquarters. Informal enquiries indicate that this may be due to the inevitable turnover of personnel who may not have been previously exposed to such notions; to a sense among some staff members that inequality between men and women has been overcome in the UK; and that some of the issues raised in this context are considered 'private matters'. This is neither a surprise nor an indication that Oxfam failed in its efforts, rather a reminder that gender equality work – like women's work more broadly – is never done, and that we need to remain alert to all difficulties and opportunities as they emerge.

Nonetheless, Pialek's overall conclusion is positive, since it recognizes that staff at Oxfam generally recognize the existence of gender inequalities and the importance of addressing them. In my opinion there are various reasons for this relatively favourable environment: one is simply the fact that gender concerns, issues, and debates have a long history in Oxfam. The history of gender equality work goes back at least 20 years, sufficiently long enough to penetrate the language, thinking, and overall culture of the organization. The embedding of such concerns in Oxfam has been helped by other factors besides longevity: its skills and commitment to communicate its values effectively, both internally and externally (the in-house journal *Gender and Development* has much to be thanked for this); the persistence of several generations of 'gender entrepreneurs'; and perhaps most importantly, and mentioned earlier, the fact that Oxfam attracts staff who often already share core values, including a degree of commitment to gender equality.

It is hard to describe whether and how in my capacity of gender adviser I have been contributing to this environment and encouraging progress, as my approach has changed over time and to suit conditions. A recent noteworthy aspect of this has been the collaboration with other gender advocates on changing the organization's language – which is an essential aspect of the culture – from 'gender' to 'women's rights'. There are several reasons behind this, including the need to make explicit the purpose of our work (the promotion of women's rights) and to overcome the professed confusion (be it genuine or not) around the 'gender' words that seemed to be preventing action. Accompanied by some interesting debates,[3] the current slogan of the organization is: 'Putting women's rights at the heart of all we do'.

Openness and networking

How different development agencies have included gender equality and women's rights in their priorities has been subject to much analysis, especially in evaluations of gender mainstreaming as the strategy endorsed by the Beijing Platform for Action in 2005 (see, for example Hafner-Burton and Pollack, 2002; Porter and Sweetman, 2005). There seem to be two main channels through which organizations open up to gender considerations: through external influence and through the work of 'internal advocates'. Here I am focusing on the former, as the role of the latter has been mentioned in several instances above.

I agree with Hafner-Burton and Pollack (2002) that international organizations with a neo-liberal agenda – among which I include ADB – are less likely to adopt gender-mainstreaming concerns as compared with more 'interventionist ones'. I would add to this that both a cause and a consequence of this tendency is the nature of their relationship with, and their permeability to, the influence of women's rights and feminist organizations.

Without embarking on a long exploration of terms, I am making a distinction here between those diverse groups (mixed or 'women's only' groups) that embrace an ideology and undertake activities to promote women's rights (whether they adopt a language of feminism or not), versus groups that are not concerned with equality between men and women, but still may bring women together as women.

ADB has a long tradition of interacting with civil society. Since 1998 it has formalized this relationship through policy, and later through instituting the NGO and Civil Society Centre. The latter has the purpose of engaging in dialogue with civil society organizations, integrating their knowledge into the bank's operations and promoting possible collaboration. However, its relationship with women's organizations is restricted to a certain type of actor, in terms of the organizations with which it interacts on gender equality matters, and who, within the bank, does the interacting; and by being carried out under institutionalized terms. My experience from the time spent at ADB was that there is a history of connections and collaborations on gender with the World Bank, and with representatives of bilateral institutions. This is especially through the OECD-DAC Network on Gender Equality (GENDERNET), and the links to representatives of those (mostly Nordic) governments that have contributed to the Gender and Development Cooperation Fund (GDCF) since 2003. Such connections were restricted to a small number of individuals within ADB (for example those who attended the annual GENDERNET meeting in Paris) and regulated by institutional parameters that left little room for open discussion of substantial issues.

A clearer example of an institutionalized relationship is the existence of the External Forum on Gender (EFG), similar to the World Bank Consultative Group on Gender. This is a group of eminent and committed individuals with considerable gender expertise. The group was formed to 'promote and facilitate dialogue between ADB and external experts and advocates on gender and development issues'.[4] My experience was that the annual meeting at headquarters in Manila, while useful to a degree, was too carefully choreographed in terms of invitees, conduct, and topics, for discussions to lead to a genuine and possibly challenging dialogue. Attempts at extending the types of interaction beyond the annual meeting and at moving the meetings to a resident mission where the members of EFG could visit ADB programmes did not succeed (apparently due mostly to financial considerations). In addition, the dissemination of and responses to the annual recommendations of the EFG had to go through such slow and elaborate processes that by the time they happened, they appeared to have lost poignancy and relevance.

Other connections with the 'gender community' were through the many consultants that ADB recruits for different tasks (both in countries and at headquarters), and especially the gender specialists (as well as the permanent local staff) the bank has in some of its resident missions. Many such individuals (as well as some staff at headquarters) consider themselves feminists or have connections with feminist and women's rights organizations in their countries and beyond, and are at times able to bring into the bank evidence, ideas, and actions of a progressive nature. On the other hand, they experience all the challenges familiar to 'internal advocates': their voices and messages are more muted when compared, for example, to those coming from other 'development partners', i.e. the multilateral and bilateral institutions mentioned above. In some cases this really meant, as Razavi says, that the positions of such internal advocates became watered down, for example by the adoption of an instrumentalist (rather than rights-based) stance that left little room for bringing into the bank more challenging notions inspired by a feminist tradition (Miller and Razavi, 1998). This does not mean that the work of consultants (especially those engaged on a long-term basis and at the resident missions) is ineffectual. On the contrary, where progress is made on including elements in loan agreements that are beneficial to women or that aspire to promote gender equality, this is often thanks to the technical and tactical skills of the individuals concerned, their knowledge of government institutions, and their commitment to their chosen field.

Despite these positive examples, formal and strong links with women's rights and feminist organizations appeared limited, including contacts with key networks through which women's organizations exchange experiences. This applies especially to international networks such as AWID (Association for Women's Rights in Development), DAWN (Development Alternatives with Women for a New Era), ISIS International (an NGO promoting women's rights mostly through information and communication), and the Women's Global Network for Reproductive Rights (WGNRR). For example, ADB does not participate in AWID's regular Forum as it is not seen as relevant. It is also worth noting that both ISIS and WGNRR are based in Manila (ISIS since 1991), while DAWN has a strong representation in the country. Given the proximity, opportunities for dialogue could be better cultivated. An introductory meeting I arranged between DAWN representatives and ADB staff was cordial but did not lead to longer-term relationships.

Seen from the other side, many feminist organizations and individuals have been simply unwilling to engage with an agency they see as embodying an ideology and practices that have contributed to increasing and feminizing poverty (Dennis and Zuckerman, 2006). My understanding from discussions with friends and colleagues is that this is also the outcome of past experiences in attempting to influence and possibly collaborate with ADB, which have left such organizations unconvinced of the usefulness of investing their scarce human and financial resources for very limited results, because of the impenetrability of the banks.

This particular aspect of the relationship between ADB and external bodies has been analysed at the country level in Thailand. Pantana et al. (2005) confirm what I found to be the case at headquarters and conclude that there is reluctance on the part of many NGOs in Thailand to engage with the bank, which is perceived, despite its professed support for an anti-poverty and pro-rights agenda, as still prescribing the same neo-liberal economic growth model that has historically led to negative social and environmental consequences.

As mentioned, some of the reasons for this situation have to do with the institutionalized nature of many of ADB's external relationships. It can also be explained by the fact that some of the criticisms, for example by Gender Action, are perceived by the IFIs as unduly strident and irrelevant, and unhelpful in bringing about internal reforms. Nonetheless, ADB itself recognizes that there are weaknesses in the way it relates to relevant external actors. A 2009 evaluation report emphasizes ADB's need to make more efforts to identify potential development partners for gender and development work and to document the joint experience (ADB, 2009). It will be interesting to see what kinds of changes this recommendation may bring about, and whether these lead to a broader dialogue with women's organizations locally or regionally.

Joint practical work – for example towards the regular country gender assessments (CGAs) that ADB produces – seemed to provide better opportunities for linking ADB to other and diverse institutions. The planned preparation of the latest CGA for the Philippines – during my stay at ADB – was a good opportunity for collaboration across institutions and individuals with very diverse approaches to gender work, including those who define themselves as feminists. This was made possible by several factors: the crucial one was the existing capacity and reach of feminists and women's organizations in the Philippines that made them indispensable partners in such an undertaking. Feminists and their organizations in that country have the maturity and confidence to have already established their own relationships (for example as consultants) with ADB without feeling either threatened or compromised by such temporary liaisons. The presence in ADB of colleagues – more 'gender entrepreneurs' – with the necessary interest in gender equality matters and knowledge of local civil society, guaranteed the resources and space for such an undertaking. Finally, my own contacts with feminists – and I like to think mutual trust – and my position in ADB gave legitimacy to the undertaking from both perspectives.

The result was that the CGA report could cover issues – such as reproductive rights – that were of timely concern to the women's movement in the country, as well as representing the outcome of genuine consultations with men and women in communities in different parts of the country. This practical collaboration seemed to reassure some of the local activists who had initially been suspicious of my joining ADB (perhaps I was being perceived as 'sleeping with the enemy'), and led to more frequent interactions outside ADB's concerns and activities, such as participation in seminars and other events. It is interesting to speculate how much similar practical engagements in other countries are inspired by the priorities of the organization or by those of the women's movement.

I tried in other ways to establish links with women's organizations and their representatives. Inviting Noeleen Heyzer, then executive director of UNIFEM, to speak at a 'high-level seminar' offered the opportunity to debate relevant issues publicly and formally, in the rare presence of someone able to bridge the gap between the institution and the women's movement. The event was extremely well attended and thought-provoking, both because of its theme (trafficking of women) and because of the genuine affection demonstrated in the interaction between speaker and audience, markedly different from the detached tone typical of such debates. I similarly invited other women's organizations (including the steering committee of DAWN) to events at ADB for informal exchanges of ideas.

How does this kind of external collaboration compare with the situation in Oxfam? Its main partners are national and local NGOs, as well as development networks with which it forms alliances for advocacy and campaigning purposes. A 2009 review found that only a small percentage of women's organizations are formally in a partnership with Oxfam (i.e. in a funding relationship, with official agreements). Since then a large programme on women's political leadership and participation (Raising Her Voice) is being implemented in partnership with dozens of women's rights organizations in 17 countries, including networks that operate at regional level (for example in Africa for work on the African Women's Protocol).

The imperfect classification system used in Oxfam, mentioned earlier, still does not capture the many additional relationships that it has with women's rights organizations. While Oxfam's Global Campaigns[5] have not always included a sufficiently large, active, and fair presence of women's rights networks, or an adequate consideration for their policy positions, dialogues with a variety of feminist alliances engaged in campaigning are progressing well. 'We Can', the campaign to end violence against women to which Oxfam has contributed in many countries of South Asia and beyond, is in a network of innumerable organizations, most of them focusing on women's rights and violence against women. Feminists representing a variety of institutions are members of the advisory board of Oxfam's journal *Gender and Development*. As in the case of ADB, consultants with expertise on gender – as well as volunteers and interns – are frequently employed to carry out project assessments and other research. Oxfam has long been linked to AWID, and is an active member of the UK Gender and Development Network (GADN) – the medium through which development organizations, academics, and others come together to exchange information and jointly advocate for women's rights. Similar interactions, if in different degrees and configurations, characterize the relationships between the women's movement and Oxfam in the various countries in which it works.

Cultivating relationships with the women's movement has been a key part of my work, because I believe this is one of the ways in which women living in poverty can be truly heard. My ideas are nurtured and my activism realized through membership of various international networks and by representing Oxfam at events such as the AWID Forum, the activities of the UK GAD Network and the annual meetings of the UN Commission on the Status of Women. Another strategy is encouraging Oxfam to enter into collaborations on specific themes with specialized networks, for example on environmental and climate change matters with Women's Environment & Development Organization (WEDO) or on issues pertaining to agriculture with Women Organizing for Change in Agriculture and Natural Resource Management (WOCAN). Such relationships are also important because they allow us to hold up the more progressive views and practices in gender and women's rights issues for emulation by our own. Writing and publishing on relevant matters have a role to play too, as they influence overall debates that, in due course and at times subliminally, reach Oxfam's thinking and practice.

Strengthening Oxfam's links to the women's movement has been an agreed strategy not only within Oxfam GB, but also among the gender experts and advocates from the various affiliates (14 as I write) of the Oxfam International Federation. In fact, cultivating, developing, and agreeing on collaboration regarding gender equality work *within* the federation has been a growing component of my work. This reflects both the general trend in the federation and the effectiveness of such cooperation in gender equality work. The personal relationships developed in this context are also among the most valuable sources of support and inspiration.

Going back

My decision to return to Oxfam was in part dictated by wanting to be closer to my family and by other personal considerations, and in part by what I perceived to be a more familiar and more congenial professional environment, with the possibility of interacting more frequently and directly with a community of like-minded people (Oxfam's hearts and minds).

The time spent as an apprentice at ADB was challenging. I had to learn new and intricate language, systems, and procedures and to get acquainted with many new people and some new places; an invaluable opportunity for renewal that made the experience itself extremely worthwhile. The opportunity to compare the two organizations was instructive. It led me to reach the perhaps obvious conclusion that robust systems, strong values and convictions, and open channels of communication and influence with organizations supporting women's rights are all essential to effective work towards gender equality.

The comparison also encouraged me, on my return, to use Oxfam's more congenial environment to pursue an approach based on the conviction that it is not sufficient to only make use of positive opportunities but that we must openly confront persisting obstacles and areas of resistance. In my experience this is not a popular approach in NGOs, where problems are always 'challenges' and where social problems of intractable complexity are expected to have immediate and simple solutions. Criticisms – however constructive – from gender advocates are frequently taken to be confirmation of their 'negative attitudes', linked perhaps to the fact that feminist-inspired analysis is associated with struggle and contestation, and the demonization of feminists is still pervasive (Smyth, 1999). Challenging these attitudes needs to become part of our efforts toward convincing 'hearts and minds'.

I went back determined to continue, not only deepening the transformation of 'hearts and minds', but also renewing efforts to influence Oxfam to adhere more strictly to existing gender systems and to establish stronger ones, since in Oxfam the apparent consensus on the importance of women's rights remains hostage, both to individual interpretations and limited capacities for translating conviction into action, and to inevitable structural changes. This is a healthy reminder that despite the fundamental differences in mandate and priorities between the two organizations, both remain 'master's houses' (Staudt, 2002) where many rules and structures are male-dominated, albeit to differing extents. Because of this, we gender advocates must always remain vigilant and continue to renew our strategies, even in contexts, such as that of Oxfam, where the environment is more agreeable and receptive.

A very liberating personal legacy of my experience in ADB converges around less rigid notions of power, and overcoming what Barriteau (2003) calls 'moralism', defined as 'the pursuit and pronouncement of singular, essentialist, righteous truth claims about women's lives intended to convey the rightness of our positions and prescriptions' (2003: 132). In my case, I believe I may have indulged in a form of moralism with regard to personal and professional choices and their coherence with one's values. When applied to others this may have made me suspicious of strategies that bring feminists closer to 'shaping the use of power', especially in organizations (such as IFIs) where much power seems to reside. When applied to myself, this appeared to be at the root of the moral discomfort I experienced before joining ADB.

Being in ADB gave me the opportunity to appreciate more the gender advocates who continue to work in such a challenging environment, and to respect more their personal commitment and the effectiveness of the strategies they adopt. It also made me kinder towards my own decision and motives for wanting to 'sleep with the enemy', both as a legitimate strategy and as the source of renewed confidence, appreciation, and resilience to continue my work in Oxfam.

Notes

1   Though they are not named here, I want to thank the ADB colleagues who became my guides and mentors during this time.
2   <http://www.wisegeek.com/what-does-sleeping-with-the-enemy-mean.htm>.
3   For example, whether Oxfam should focus only on the rights of 'poor women'.
4   ADB (2009) 10th Meeting of the External Forum on Gender and Development (EFG), Auditorium Zone D, ADB Headquarters, Manila 14–17 July 2009.
5   Global campaigns are always undertaken by all affiliates of the Oxfam International confederation, rather than by the individual organizations such as Oxfam Great Britain.

References

Asian Development Bank (2006) 'Gender and Development in ADB Operations', OM Section C2/BP, Manila: ADB.

Asian Development Bank (2009) 'The Asian Development Bank's support to gender and development phase I: relevance, responsiveness, and results to date', Special Evaluation Study, Manila: ADB.

Asian Development Bank (2010) 'Gender mainstreaming in ADB projects', Report of the Technical Working Group, Manila: ADB.

Barriteau, V. (2003) 'Confronting power and politics: a feminist theorizing of gender in Commonwealth Caribbean societies', *Meridians: Feminism, Race, Transnationalism* 3: 57–92.

Batliwala, S. (2009) 'Feminism is coming of age: celebrating diversity and power' *Development* 52: 140–3 <http://dx.doi.org/10.1057%2Fdev.2009.3>.

Britton, B. (1998) 'The learning NGO', *Occasional Paper No.17*, Oxford: INTRAC.

Dennis, E. and Zuckerman, E. (2006) *Gender Guide to World Bank and IMF Policy-Based Lending*, <www.genderaction.org/images/GA%20Gender%20 Guide%20to%20World%20Bank%20and%20IMF%20FINAL.pdf>.

Edwards, M. and Hulme, D. (eds) (1992) *Making a Difference: NGOs and Development in a Changing World*, London: Earthscan Publications.

Green D. (2008) *From Poverty to Power: How Active Citizens and Effective States Can Change the World*, Oxford: Oxfam International.

Hafner-Burton, E. and Pollack, M. (2002) 'Gender mainstreaming and global governance', *Feminist Legal Studies* 10: 285–98 <http://dx.doi.org/10.1023 %2FA%3A1021232031081>.

Miller, C. (1998) 'Gender advocates and multilateral development organizations: promoting change from within' in C. Miller and S. Razavi (eds), *Missionaries and Mandarins: Feminist Engagement with Development Institutions*, pp. 138–71, Rugby, UK: Practical Action Publishing.

Miller, C. and Razavi, S. (eds) (1998) *Missionaries and Mandarins: Feminist Engagement with Development Institutions*, Rugby, UK: Practical Action Publishing.

Mohanty, C. (1988) 'Under Western eyes: feminist scholarship and colonial discourses', *Feminist Review*, 30: 61–88 <http://dx.doi. org/10.2307%2F1395054>.

Moser, C. and Moser, A. (2005), 'Gender mainstreaming since Beijing: a review of success and limitations in international institutions', *Gender and Development*, 13: 11–22 <http://dx.doi.org/10.1080%2F13552070512331332283>.

Naciri, R. (1998) 'Engaging the state: the women's movement and political discourse in Morocco', in C. Miller and S. Razavi (eds) *Missionaries and Mandarins: Feminist Engagement with Development Institutions*, pp. 87–111, rugby, UK: Practical Action Publishing.

Pantana, P., Real, M. J., and Resurreccion, B. P. (2005) 'Officializing strategies: participatory processes and gender in ADB's capacity building in Thailand's water resources sector', *Development in Practice*, 14: 521–33.

Pialek, N. (2008) *Gender Mainstreaming in Development Organizations: Policy, Practice and Institutional Change*, PhD thesis, Department of International Development, Queen Elizabeth House – St Cross College, Oxford University.

Porter, F. and Sweetman, C. (eds) (2005) 'Editorial', *Gender and Development*, 13: 2–10 <http://dx.doi.org/10.1080%2F13552070512331332282>.

Smyth, I. (1999) 'NGOs in a post feminist era' in M. Porter and H. Judd (eds), *Feminists Doing Development: A Practical Critique*, pp. 17–28, London: Zed Press.

Staudt, K. (2002) 'Dismantling the master's house with the master's tools? Gender work in and with powerful bureaucracies', in K. Saunders (ed.) *Feminist Post-Development Thought: Rethinking Modernity, Post-Colonialism, and Representation*, pp. 57–68, New York: Zed Books.

About the author

Dr Ines Smyth is a women's rights in development practitioner. For more than a decade she has worked for Oxfam, promoting the rights of women in the development, humanitarian, and policy work of the organization. Before joining the NGO community she pursued an academic career at the Institute of Social Studies in The Hague, at the Department of Applied Social Studies at Oxford University, and at the Development Studies Institute at the London School of Economics. Her main interests, illustrated by several publications, are those of gender in development theories, women's work, reproductive rights, and gender and disasters. She remains a feminist activist.

CHAPTER 10

Re-gendering the United Nations: old challenges and new opportunities

Joanne Sandler

This chapter portrays the experiences of feminists confronting institutionalized discrimination within the UN bureaucratic machine. It documents how over four years of difficult negotiations, feminist advocates inside and outside the bureaucracy contributed to the successful merger of four UN organizations into a new UN entity: UN Women. The chapter vividly portrays the conundrum that femocrats committed to transforming institutions face in balancing the dual aspirations of advancing women's rights worldwide, while transforming the patriarchal and bureaucratic cultures of the organizations in which they work.

Interrogating the architecture to promote gender equality and women's empowerment

If institutions are gendered, the potential exists for them to be 'regendered' – including in ways that could transform their internal cultures and their external support for gender equality (Mackay and Krook, 2011). The potential for transformation of mainstream institutions to support cultures of equality – from justice systems to large international non-governmental organizations to United Nations bureaucracies – is what underpins the decision of many feminist and social justice activists to work from the inside. Since the first UN World Conference for Women in Mexico City in 1975, large national and multilateral bureaucracies have created spaces for gender specialist and gender advisory units and organizations within their structures, creating a gender 'architecture' that could not have been imagined 40 years ago.

I remember vividly the day in 2004 when I uttered the phrase 'gender architecture' for the first time. I had attended a UN inter-agency meeting to hear a colleague from the OECD-DAC brief us about something called 'aid effectiveness'.[1] His briefing carried a strong warning to the UN: either get on this train or get left behind. He kept referring, messianically, to the critical necessity of recognizing that the 'aid architecture' was irrevocably changing.

I zoomed upstairs to UNIFEM and burst into the office of then executive director Noeleen Heyzer, parroting the doomsday message of my OECD-DAC colleague: 'Noeleen', I gasped. 'The aid architecture is changing. And the gender architecture is unprepared, inadequate. What are we going to do?'

http://dx.doi.org/10.3362/9781780448046.010

Noeleen understood immediately. A review of UNIFEM, recently undertaken by an independent advisory committee (UN 2004), had pointed out in stark terms how inadequate UNIFEM's structure and positioning in the UN system were for the ambitious mandate that had been assigned by member states of the United Nations. This review – requested by UNIFEM's consultative committee, chaired by Jordan's ambassador to the UN and overseen by an external advisory committee headed by former executive director of UNFPA Nafis Sadik – pointed out how UNIFEM's lack of high-level leadership, autonomy and authority, and resources, and its fragmentation from the three other UN gender-specific organizations[2] were systemic obstacles to its ability to fulfil its mandate. The underlying question that the committee overseeing the assessment posed was, how can UNIFEM engage in high-level policy advocacy, when the low hierarchic level of its leadership means that it cannot even enter the rooms where high-level policymaking is taking place?

Many reviews of gender mainstreaming in multilateral and bilateral organizations had revealed similar patterns: gender units are established without adequate human resources or budgets; gender theme groups that bring so-called gender experts from various organizations together are composed of junior staff with little access to or influence on decisions; and gender advisers are marginalized from mainstream decision-making, and their advice is not taken into account. UNIFEM was an autonomous organization – not a 'unit' or an 'adviser' – but it was part and parcel of this highly undervalued landscape.

Perhaps it was not surprising that despite valiant efforts by those who commissioned the assessment, it was largely ignored by the UN leadership. But the impediments now had a name, and naming is the first step. The reluctance to take any action was the wake-up call that inspired UNIFEM to advocate for systemic and structural changes in the gender architecture of the UN.

On 2 July 2010, almost six years after the UNIFEM assessment was met with a deafening silence, the General Assembly passed resolution 64/289, establishing the UN Entity for Gender Equality and the Empowerment of Women or UN Women. The resolution merged the four parts of the UN system that had been established over the past 60 years as 'specialist' gender equality organizations/departments:

- The UN Division for the Advancement of Women or DAW was established in 1948 and was the Secretariat for the UN World Conferences on Women.
- UNIFEM and the International Research and Training Institute for the Advancement of Women or INSTRAW – the former a fund and the latter a research and training centre – were both established in 1976 in response to calls from women's organizations and gender equality experts.
- The Office of the Special Adviser on Gender Issues or OSAGI was called for at the Fourth UN World Conference on Women at Beijing in 1995 and was the gender equality 'specialist' with the highest position in the UN hierarchy.

The merger created an organization headed by an under-secretary-general who reports directly to the UN secretary-general, a giant step forward. It is intended to address the gaps of fragmentation, authority, and inadequate leadership, voice, and resources that have plagued work on gender equality for decades. In September 2010, Michelle Bachelet, former president of Chile, accepted the position of executive director of UN Women. Having a former head of state with such a distinguished record of accomplishment lead a more unified structure in the UN presented at the time an unparalleled opportunity to put women's rights on many more critical policy agendas and to elicit a more effective and robust response to gender discrimination from the UN system in the countries in which it is present.[3]

It will be some years before we know if the results that emanate from the shifts in the UN gender architecture will live up to expectations. Women's and development organizations and networks around the world – from the Gender Equality Architecture (GEAR) Campaign to the UN Women Godmothers in the UK – as well as member states, other UN organizations, and influential individuals have all articulated what they expect from UN Women.[4]

Will UN Women be able to meet the huge expectations generated by its creation? Certainly this depends on member states and others significantly scaling up the financial and human resources required to advance women's rights. But this chapter focuses on the internal political dimensions; it posits that organizations or units tasked with promoting gender equality in mainstream organizations face pervasive institutional discrimination, which has a complex impact on the individuals that work there – particularly those who join because of their commitment to feminist organizing and women's human rights. It shows why UN Women must insist on *institutional* equality as a pre-condition to fostering change on the ground, space for women's rights advocates, and transformation of the UN system based on gender justice. It describes the organizational roadblocks and propellers that UNIFEM discovered, as an illustration of what UN Women might watch out for. But it goes beyond UNIFEM because the experience is familiar to any organization or unit tasked with promoting gender equality in the multilateral and bilateral system, and in large government and non-governmental bureaucracies.

The gender architecture encompasses ministries of women's affairs, gender units, equal opportunity offices, and women's organizations and networks. While they are often underfunded and inadequately staffed, the best of them figure out ways to build alliances and establish valued technical and political credentials that place them in high demand. However technical excellence is not sufficient: in their daily work, each of these must confront the systemic institutional discrimination and the structures that seek to sabotage their success. Each must undertake a political analysis that acknowledges the corrosive effects when power, elitism, patriarchy, politics, and gender discrimination join together to hold back progress on women's rights. Confronting this is rarely explicit in their mandates, work plans, or job descriptions, but if left unattended, it is almost certainly the path to irrelevance and extinction.

Toward re-structuring gender equality in the UN system

The establishment of UN Women is a victory for women's rights advocates. It also represents a step forward for UN reform; a long-standing effort to reorganize the UN to become more coordinated and coherent. It is probably true that never in the history of the UN did an organization volunteer to be dissolved in the interests of its constituency, organizational effectiveness, and UN reform. But the gender equality organizations did.

An unusual confluence of events enabled the creation of UN Women. In 2006, the UN secretary-general convened a high-level panel on system-wide coherence (a term that covers all things related to streamlining the UN and making it more coherent), but there was no mention of gender equality in the panel's original terms of reference (UN, 2006a). Women's rights advocates, including UNIFEM and many civil society groups, used all of our networks in New York and in countries visited by panel members to lobby for its attention: Noeleen Heyzer appealed to one of the co-chairs during the panel's first meeting in New York;[5] women's groups organized when panel members travelled to Egypt and Pakistan; and Bandana Rana of SAATHI (Nepal) gathered a million signatures to present to the panel's Pakistani co-chair, demanding that it pay attention to gender equality. Finally, the GEAR civil society campaign – started with initial UNIFEM support – reached out to UN delegates and women's and social justice organizations worldwide. Ultimately, the panel's terms of reference were changed to incorporate gender equality.

The panel issued a set of findings about reforming the entire UN system, with a 'merged' gender equality architecture as part of this package. The report made a specific recommendation that the UNIFEM assessment could not have made: to merge four entities into one, with an under-secretary-general as its leader (UN 2006b).

While women's rights advocates greeted the merger recommendation of November 2006 with jubilation, it was met with a combination of shock and consternation in parts of the UN bureaucracy. These reactions mirrored typical and inherent blockages to advancing gender equality – or other issues that challenge the power of elites – in bureaucratic institutions.

At the political level, many member states – especially the G77[6] – rejected the entire coherence panel report. We heard from many delegations that they did not have substantive issues with the gender equality components, but they rejected the recommendation as an indication of their dissatisfaction with the entire high-level panel process. So gender equality became a political 'hostage' to other issues, including the failure of the coherence panel report to push the boundaries of Security Council reform.

Some of the units and specialists that work on gender equality in the UN system formed another blockage. A number of them were roundly dismayed by the recommendations, seeing them as contrary to the gender-mainstreaming approach that had been the centrepiece of the UN's overall gender equality strategy, as well as (for some) the death knell for their own units or jobs.

At the highest levels of the UN system, some heads of agencies were extremely supportive while others proclaimed that this was no time to start a 'new' UN organization. The secretary-general's support was unswerving, and he noted publicly that 'The United Nations is investing in women because it is the right thing to do and because it is a smart thing to do – possibly one of the smartest things we can ever do. I will support UN Women in every way I can with every ounce of my energy and commitment'.[7] At the same time, however, one head of agency proclaimed, during a briefing from staff on the status of inter-governmental debates on the entity prior to its establishment, 'Don't think for one minute that I want to compete with *another* UN organization for funds'.

With multiple sources of opposition, political manoeuvring, and misunderstanding, it is no wonder that a reform that could have happened immediately took four years. The four entities are now merged and the promise is significant. But at the end of the day, we must remember that while the structure of the organization was changed by merging four existing institutions, and the level of leadership changed – a huge step forward in a bureaucracy – the patriarchal and elitist structure in which the new organization is embedded remains the same. This is part of the work that must now be taken up by UN Women, with close vigilance by women's networks worldwide.

UNIFEM: a primer on structuring organizational inequality

UNIFEM's first director Margaret Snyder has catalogued some of the early strategies for confronting institutional roadblocks to the fund's work on gender equality (Snyder, 1995). UNIFEM colleagues and their partners on the ground regularly demonstrated courage and creativity in confronting rules and organizational cultures that too often run counter to advancing women's human rights:

- Where gender equality was relegated to a 'cross-cutting' issue that did not receive funds commensurate with other issues, they worked with national partners and donors to develop grant-making 'basket funds' at country level – where multiple donors contribute funds for a particular gender equality objective – thereby increasing the resources for women's rights organizations and issues and creating new, locally owned knowledge on effective strategies.
- Where UN colleagues were frustrated because they could not get technical support from gender equality experts in the UN system, UNIFEM staff brought gender focal points and UN resident coordinators together to develop annual gender equality 'contracts' in specific sub-regions, so that the heads of UN country teams in a particular geographic area could identify ahead of time the kinds of technical support that they needed, giving gender experts in the system the time to source this from the UN and its national partners.

- Where fragmentation and missed opportunities for creative partnerships impeded progress, they promoted innovative approaches that expanded space for other UN organizations to join in, whether through UN Action Against Sexual Violence in Conflict[8] or through forging cross-regional and cross-national partnerships to promote and protect the rights of women migrant workers.

These achievements do not come easily, however. Documenting the types of systemic institutional sabotage that UNIFEM faced throughout its life is a hedge against history repeating itself with UN Women. What follows is a subjective, partial, but hopefully revealing story.

It shows, firstly, how structural decisions, made on the basis of a combination of reason and the political climate of the UN inter-governmental process, have a far-reaching impact. There is no doubt that General Assembly delegates had the best of intentions when, in 1976 for the UN Decade for Women, they established the UN Voluntary Fund, which became UNIFEM in 1984.[9]

UNIFEM's founding resolution was formulated in close consultation with and the approval of the UN's legal experts. How it was interpreted is a dramatic manifestation of the preservationist power of patriarchy.

Other UN organizations that started off small – such as UNFPA – were also set up to be initially 'administered' by UNDP, but as they grew, they consistently became more autonomous. UNIFEM was following the same trajectory, but a combination of factors – from internal strategy to global politics to resources and UN reform – made the pace slower than it should have been. The UN Department for Economic and Social Affairs (UN DESA, which was home to the Voluntary Fund) and UNDP – which are no more and no less gender-blind or gender-discriminatory than most other multilateral organizations – had to play the unwitting roles of gatekeepers for the patriarchy. This offers important lessons for UN Women.

There were three strategies for structuring this inequality. The first was silencing or at least reducing UNIFEM's voice and its ability to manage its own business. Until the late 1990s, UNIFEM did not have full authority to sign its own cheques or approve recruitment of all of its staff. It often had to lobby for the opportunity to represent itself or speak out for gender equality and women's rights in key policy venues, and it was often excluded, with the response given that its leadership was not at a high enough level to be included on the podium or at the meeting. In many venues, the administrator of UNDP 'spoke' for UNIFEM; according to UNIFEM's founding resolution, the administrator was 'accountable' for it (Snyder, 1995: 62 and 80).

When we raised – with our governing and advisory bodies (both the UNDP/UNFPA executive board and the UNIFEM consultative committee) – the ways in which our inability to make staffing decisions or to represent ourselves was impeding our effectiveness, we were repeatedly told that this was done in the interest of efficiency. Why did we need our own systems when UNDP could run them for us? Like many marriages that hinge on inequality, UNIFEM had the lion's share of responsibility, but insufficient authority to manage itself. The arrangement worked fine when there was an administrator or a head of finance or a resident representative who was supportive – but there were too many instances where this was not the case.

I remember that when I was working at the International Women's Tribune Centre in the 1980s, we received a phone call from UNIFEM – located around the corner. Staff had come to work on a Monday morning to find that over the weekend, UN DESA (its host at the time) had unilaterally decided to take over the space and move UNIFEM to a different building. No one had informed UNIFEM, whose director was on mission in Japan; they simply left a note instructing staff to go to the new address where they found their furniture and belongings piled chaotically. The space taken from UNIFEM remained vacant for many months.

Ten years later when I joined UNIFEM as a consultant, many facets of the situation were similar, and relate to the second strategy for structuring inequality: constantly questioning UNIFEM's right to exist – which meant huge amounts of time invested in digging up precedents just to prove why we were present. This included 'jabs' like publicly questioning why UNIFEM field staff were participating in heads of agency meetings of UN country teams or questioning UNIFEM's right to have its logo alongside other UN organizations in a jointly-funded publication or web application. It also encompassed more serious threats, such as more powerful UN colleagues agreeing to absorb UNIFEM into their own organizations at the behest of a donor agency.

The third tactic was strategic public and private demonstration of 'power over'. The administrative arrangements between UNDP and UNIFEM left many opportunities for the larger, more powerful organization to show the weaker one who was boss. For instance, UNIFEM was dependent on UNDP to make payments; if UNDP decided to withhold payment requests or put them at the back of the line, UNIFEM had few options. Similarly, UNIFEM recruitments had to go to a UNDP approvals board; when UNDP – who set the board's agenda – 'ran out of time' and failed to deal with UNIFEM's requests at three sessions in a row, UNIFEM had no recourse. Power holders can do this with their 'property'.

One might ask why we didn't assert our rights and protest to the UN's leadership or governing bodies. We did; and when we did, we paid an even higher price: we were labelled 'poor team players', we were 'whiners', we were 'radical feminists', or – the worst label of all – we were 'behaving like NGOs'.

Patriarchy was most effective at limiting UNIFEM's reach and influence by failing to address the level of UNIFEM's leadership. In UN terms, UNIFEM's executive director was at level D-2, raised from D-1 in 1989 at the request of the outgoing founding director Margaret Snyder, but still lower than many department heads in UNDP, lower than the deputy directors of UNICEF and UNFPA, and lower than the heads of the New York liaison offices of some Geneva-based UN organizations. Thus the head of a liaison office with a relatively small budget and a staff of less than 30 in just one location, was at a higher level than the head of UNIFEM who had a $200 million budget and nearly 900 staff and consultants in 80 offices worldwide.

The level of the executive directors remained the same from 1989, despite the fact that UNIFEM's budget, staff, and consultants increased by more than 10 times, and successive General Assembly resolutions gave it an increasingly broadened role, both geographically and thematically. Four UNDP administrators and two secretary-generals missed the opportunity to raise UNIFEM's leadership to assistant secretary-general (ASG) level, despite letters, justifications, and lobbying by well-respected experts, friendly member states, and UN colleagues. The reasons changed with each lobbying effort: 'We had an ASG for you but we had to give it to someone else' or 'We agree that UNIFEM leadership should have a higher level but if we raise yours, we'll have to raise that of other associated funds', and so on. The consequences were significant: keeping the unit or organization responsible for gender equality at a lower and hence disadvantaged level is another pathway for restricting its influence and effectiveness in a hierarchy where organizational access is determined by the level of leadership.

UNIFEM's lower leadership level suppressed all other post levels, so UNIFEM directors in the field were often one or two ranks below their counterparts. To those who say, 'so what?' – you have never worked in a bureaucracy. You've never been told to move from your seat at the table (even when there are seats free) because your rank is not equal to others. This really happens. You've never had to sit through meetings where, because of your rank, the legitimacy of your presence is debated. You've never been the only one asked to leave the room when a peer review of other directors is taking place because your rank is too low. Some will say that these are all trappings – and that is partly true. But it means that continuously and systematically you and others are reminded that you are unequal, lesser, disadvantaged. It means that your voice is restricted and the issues you try to put on the table are easily dismissed. And as 'the women's fund', it's a constant reminder of how women are treated in the wider world, made manifest at decision-making tables within the UN.

From its establishment, UNIFEM fought this marginalization without pause, and was joined at times by women's rights networks at country, regional, or global level. In the 12 years prior to its merger into UN Women – and often in partnership with supportive UNDP leadership and colleagues – UNIFEM secured the right to sign its own cheques, appoint its own staff, and have representational status on the ground. These were small but significant victories.

It is important to document the catalogue of strategies that UNIFEM's leadership teams – from founding director Margaret Snyder to its last executive director, Ines Alberdi[10] – formulated to enable it to survive and thrive, as each responded to the politics, challenges, and opportunities of their time (Snyder, 1995). For the majority of the 15 years that I consulted with or worked inside UNIFEM, I was privileged to be part of an organization led by Noeleen Heyzer.

UNIFEM not only survived, but also grew exponentially in both presence and resources. This did not happen by chance; it was part of a strategy.

UNIFEM leadership understood three things: first, it had to build relevance within the UN by embracing UN reform and seizing the opportunities that it offered – opportunities like the high-level panel or the pilots of 'Delivering as One' (UN 2006b). Second, it had to expand resources and presence, because having staff on the ground and budgets to enable full participation in UN country teams were the only roads to expanding women's access and voice, to influence the system where it mattered most – at the country level. Like other bureaucracies, the UN is too often a 'pay to play' system, and if your organizational resources are inadequate, so too is your organizational voice. Last – but most important – was partnership with a constituency. The importance of this cannot be overstated. I will never forget when a very irritated high-level UN official warned us, after yet another failed effort to dissolve UNIFEM, 'The only reason we can't absorb you is because you have a constituency. That is what is saving you'.

Over the past few years, the UN secretary-general and heads of agencies have been making an all-out effort to raise the numbers of women in the leadership of the UN. The leadership often understands their commitment to gender equality as a struggle to achieve greater gender balance, e.g. to get more women into higher-level positions. There have been significant advances; more women are seated around the UN's highest decision-making tables now than ever before, with 30.9 per cent of the highest level posts (under-secretary-general and assistant secretary-generals) held by women in 2009 (UN 2009). Keep in mind too, that the UN did not have a woman under-secretary-general until Dame Margaret Anstee's appointment to that rank in 1987.

This change in percentages is important, but it is only a part of the picture. The dynamics of structured inequality can only be understood through an analysis of the 'deep structures' of organizations (Rao et al., 1999). Much of the work on transforming the deep structures that perpetuate gender discrimination in institutions is focused on making organizational life more conducive to the different realities of women and men at the individual level: e.g. having more flexible hours, day care, providing employment to male spouses who follow their wives overseas, mentoring programmes, and positive action.

But while the UN is taking some steps to address structural gender inequality at the individual level and retain more women in leadership, recognition of *institutional inequality* – that is positioning an entire organization or unit and the people in it at a structural disadvantage because they work on gender equality – is far less obvious; and that is the trap that UN Women must avoid.

A battering effect on staff

There are an increasing number of women – and men as well – who are passionately committed to women's empowerment and rights in the organizations and units that work on gender equality in large multilateral or bilateral organizations. Some have been working in feminist NGOs and have joined these organizations to work on change from the inside. Despite legitimate complaints from women's organizations that better paid jobs in international NGOs and multilateral or bilateral organizations are reducing the talent pool accessible to them, it is absolutely essential for women's rights activists to be located in these bureaucracies. It is one of the ways that change happens.

I too now meet an increasing number of 'career' civil servants, from within the UN system or from government or academia, who join UN Women or gender units of other UN organizations to advance their careers. But after feeling the full weight of institutional gender discrimination and after seeing the enormous demand for support from governments, the UN, and civil society, their consciousness and ire get raised.

This is systemic. I have seen it happen equally to men and women who worked at UNIFEM and other organizations or units that advance gender equality. The men that I've met who work on gender equality issues in multilateral organizations have told me about the snickers and the teasing that they encounter from other men: from relatively innocuous comments like, 'What does the gender man have to say about that?' to far more sexist and misogynistic remarks. Recently, I was at an international conference on gender-responsive budgeting (GRB), with robust participation from many male and female colleagues working in ministries of finance. One of the African men – who is the GRB champion in his country's finance ministry – told me that he had recently met with a European donor representative. When the ministry colleague informally told the donor representative about the way that GRB was strengthening internal systems of accountability and transparency, the donor representative laughed and said, 'Why would a smart and capable guy like you want to spend time working on gender issues?' Depressingly, these comments are not uncommon. But, in most cases, they strengthen the resolve of my male colleagues to make a difference for women's rights.

After twelve years at UNIFEM and reflecting on its effect on individuals – and on my own entry to feminism through organizations and centres addressing violence against women – I see the parallels between what happens to some staff of these organizations and battered women's syndrome – with four stages of response: denial, guilt, recognition/awareness, and empowerment. The problem is that many individuals stop after the first two stages, and never reach stages three and four. This is how it works:

Denial

Like the singer Rihanna, who was beaten up by her boyfriend Chris Brown, but then publicly excused his behaviour,[11] there are a surprising number of apologists for institutional sexism amongst those who work on gender equality. Gender units in large development organizations – that have to write reports to governing bodies on the progress their organization is making on gender equality – regularly hyperbolize, hide, or tweak information in their reports, at the oft-unspoken behest of their supervisors or colleagues. Rarely can an 'employed' gender expert or gender unit unveil the sexism inherent in their organization without facing the consequences of being designated a poor 'team player'. More powerful colleagues will turn the blame around and pin the inadequacy on the gender unit, for failing to provide good capacity development or technical support.[12]

For instance, it is denial when we affirm statements of UN resident coor-dinators, both male and female, who come to open or close a meeting on gender equality and then observe (often saying, 'let me be provocative') that there are too few male participants and that the women in the room have to try harder to 'attract' men to this work. We nod our heads, rather than ask if they raised the question of women's absence when they were in a room full of predominantly male heads of agencies, or to what extent they are using their power to change the incentive systems so that men will want to work on gender equality.

We rarely talked publicly about the similarities between UNIFEM's organi-zational arrangements and its relationship with UNDP – or the relationship of a directorate of women's affairs to the ministry of social welfare or of the gender unit to its overarching policy unit – and the situation of disenfran-chised women worldwide, who are subjugated by the state, their male family members, and more powerful women 'agents' of men in the family. And when we did point out the structural inequalities to those who could have easily done something about them, more often than not the response was silence or embarrassed guffaws or supportive oh-they're-just-pulling-your-chains or recrimination … but very little action. You soon learned to stop raising it, except in the safest spaces.

Guilt

When we deny that the structure is irrepressibly and unapologetically discriminatory, we have only ourselves to blame. When we cannot get our colleagues to implement agreed guidelines for promoting and protecting the rights of women and girls in refugee camps, we think we did not strategize properly. When an evaluation of a mainstream programme or unit shows gross inadequacies in their work on gender equality, we feel that we did not produce the right technical support. When we try to mainstream gender equality into a poverty reduction strategy or large-scale programme and are asked to produce a clear evidence base for strengthening commitments to women, we feel inadequate that we could not present the magic piece of evidence that would convince our colleagues to include a result and a budget to advance women's rights. We fail to realize that no such evidence would do so. We fail to assign accountability where it actually belongs.

I recently attended the final workshop of a two-year action-learning process for three UN country teams to reflect and document, based on their own experiences, what actions can support effective joint programming on gender equality (see Rao, 2013). I was quite struck by the initial reflection provided by one of the teams. By all accounts they had managed to build on the comparative advantage of UN organizations in that country to produce stunning results in a short period of time, successfully supporting national efforts to get more women into political positions and to extend the country's first network of shelters for women into the provinces. National decision-makers were extremely satisfied and it was widely known that the UN's accomplishments on gender equality had positive spin-off effects on the overall reputation of the UN country team.

Yet in the presentation on their learning process, the four women who made up the team pointed out that they had 'failed' when it came to gender mainstreaming and therefore other programmes supported by the UN country team were not sufficiently gender-responsive. The irony was inescapable. Here was a relatively small inter-agency team consisting of only five or six people that had helped to deliver quantifiable, tangible benefits to the country, was deeply appreciated by national partners, and had improved the reputation of the entire UN country team. But their sense of success was marred by their feeling that they had not spent a sufficient amount of time 'helping' their other UN colleagues to incorporate gender equality into their work.

This should be a warning to UN Women. Many supporters still talk about UN Women as the panacea for the UN system's shortcomings regarding gender equality and 'holding the system accountable'. But it must be made crystal clear that while UN Women can play a specific role, each UN organization remains accountable for its own performance on gender equality. Clarifying lines of responsibility and accountability is essential.[13]

The sexual division of labour that so blithely accepts women's dual productive and reproductive roles is alive and well in international organizations, justified in the name of 'gender mainstreaming'. And the dynamic that perpetuates the mentality of 'blaming the victim' continues as well. Staff in gender units – like others who feel powerless and turn their frustration inward rather than strategizing to overturn what is oppressing them – are much more likely to publicly criticize each other than to say anything about those in power who fail to change inequitable gender arrangements.

Recognition/awareness

It's a liberating moment when you realize that it's the institution itself – and not your inadequacy – that is the greatest impediment; and an even more liberating moment when you realize that it is possible to make creative use of any political space that the institution provides for advancing women's human rights. For me, this moment came when we were trying to organize a global videoconference on ending violence against women in the UN General Assembly in 1999.[14] The resistance to using the General

Assembly for a global advocacy initiative on violence against women was monumental and came from many different directions. We were challenged by our peers and decision-makers in other parts of the UN: what if descriptions of violence against women were so graphic that they embarrassed the delegates? How would we avoid stigmatizing specific countries? What if the technology did not work properly and we embarrassed the secretary-general? The excuses were never-ending; the concerns were all for the institution, rather than for women and girls.

It made me realize how closely patriarchy guards its sacred policy spaces in the United Nations; and it affirmed what I knew as a feminist, but what is so easy to forget in bureaucracies: logic, evidence, and common sense have only a limited influence – when the going gets tough, only a well-orchestrated inside–outside political strategy will work.

The advocacy and expectations of women's movements and networks were critical to our argument for holding the videoconference in the first place. But to secure the General Assembly, we needed powerful inside champions: in this case the deputy director of UNICEF, a woman from the staff council, and several other colleagues made the difference. They guided us behind the scenes and made crucial phone calls when they were needed; they told us which levers to pull and prepped us for meetings. And we got the General Assembly. Women from Kenya and Mexico and India spoke directly about their experiences of violence. The secretary-general said he would come for 20 minutes and he stayed for 90 – visibly moved. Ten years later, almost every UN organization works on ending violence against women and, in 2008, a different secretary-general launched his global campaign – including his male leaders network – to speak out against this violence.

The struggle to bring testimonies about violence against women – from women and men – to the General Assembly in 1999 made us realize that the Security Council – another hallowed policy space – needed to be the next point of policy advocacy. We joined with a vast network of women's peace and security advocates, and one year later, Security Council Resolution 1325 was agreed.

Do not mistake the shorthand way I have presented the changes above as indicating that they happened quickly; they all resulted from years of advocacy and the efforts of countless women and men. The struggles represent what happens when one recognizes that patriarchy is not immutable and that your role as an inside feminist change agent is to challenge the institutions of patriarchy and exclusion, whether in the Security Council, the justice system, or in macroeconomic policymaking. That change is only possible, however, when one stops making excuses for those in power, stops apologizing for being oppositional, and stops taking the blame for others. It is only possible when you use your position in the institution to bring in the voices of those who are most affected, to speak directly to power-holders.

Empowerment

Empowerment comes when recognition and awareness become part of your DNA. You become entrepreneurial at using the unique opportunities that an international organization offers to stimulate reverberating changes for women's human rights, whether that means using your 'position' to create space for HIV-positive women to secure a place at the policymaking table in a country that is deciding its national HIV and AIDS strategy, or invoking Security Council Resolution 1325 to pressure your UN colleagues to include women's rights activists as part of mediation teams. You figure out how to use the rules on which bureaucracies run to support – rather than work against – gender equality. You use your power to press for incentives for positive action to advance women's rights, and consequences for failing to adhere to hard-won policy guidelines. You figure out how to stimulate internal and external changes without being dragged down into the routine of gender-mainstreaming checklists. You identify others within the organization who are similarly committed to transformation and with whom you can build alliances. And ultimately, you are far more effective – for women's human rights, for development, and for the organization that employs you, even as it tries to stop you.

Institutions like the UN can be an engine of positive change in support of gender equality. Despite all of the grousing and hand-wringing about whether or not we should give up on international institutions as sites of potential change for women's rights, there is a definite link between agreements made in the General Assembly, follow-up to human rights conventions and treaties ratified, and concrete changes on the ground – whether these are more women in positions of power in municipal councils, more funds to repair obstetric fistula, or more girls in school. There is a definite link between the *increasing number* of resolutions that the Security Council has agreed which recognize women as agents of peace-building or condemn rape as a tactic of war, and increased protection of women from sexual violence.

Those in international institutions who are tasked with promoting women's rights must understand that they are in privileged spaces and should use their power and position to continue pushing for better policies and bigger budgets, and to call for unswerving commitment to their implementation. They must speak truth to power. They will be lampooned and called names – from 'gender police' to 'radical feminists'. They will wonder if they might lose their jobs or pensions. Sometimes they will be isolated. My colleagues at the former UNIFEM knew all too well the punishing marginalization that can come from UN colleagues – most of whom had more power and status than they did – when they spoke out for larger budget allocations for women's empowerment in Afghanistan, insisted that women's rights advocates from Sudan should have a place at the table at donor conferences, or that the resources of UN Women should be equal to those of other UN organizations. It is uncomfortable. But it goes with the territory.

The promise of UN Women

UN Women is cause for optimism. There is a rightful expectation that the visionary leadership and political courage of an under-secretary-general heading an autonomous UN organization focused on women's rights and gender equality – in partnership with the significantly increased number of women heads of agencies that the secretary-general has appointed over the past couple of years and a growing number of supportive and articulate male leaders – will melt the most egregious forms of obstruction and create a newly-paved pathway for the UN's work on gender equality. There is rightful hope that having a place for UN Women at the UN's highest decision-making tables will build the leadership's understanding and its commitment to put real muscle behind the piles of policy guidance and gender equality strategies that, to a great extent, have remained paper tigers.

The creation of UN Women is happening at a time when there is greater acknowledgement – at least in discourse and analysis – that social and economic justice depends on the involvement of both men and women. It happens at a time when mainstream institutions – from the World Bank to *The Economist* – are proclaiming that women are critical engines of economic development. It is happening at a time when we see women standing side by side with men to bring down entrenched authoritarian leaders, when record numbers of girls are going to school, and when new technologies are making possible an unprecedented level of connection and activism for women of all ages, races, and classes.

Nevertheless, the gestation period has shown quite clearly that change may not happen in the time period envisioned. On the positive side, UN Women's core resources increased by 60 per cent in 2011, reaching $125 million.[15] However, despite the projection in the secretary-general's comprehensive proposal on UN Women[16] that $500 million was required for start-up, the total 2011 budget reached only $227.2 million, and 2012 projections are that the total budget will still fall far short of even $300 million. Though not impossible, change without additional resources will be challenging.

But I would contend that three years after its establishment, UN Women is still in its early days. The radical potential of UN Women is in being more than the sum of its parts, and about more than just the UN system. The conundrum for UN Women is to become equal in power with other UN organizations that are inherently bureaucratic and patriarchal, while at the same time triggering a transformation of the system of which it is a part. This has mundane aspects to it, like challenging everyday procedures for procurement and contracting that impede partnerships with women's organizations, and it involves taking on more entrenched power structures, like those that grant impunity to UN leaders who fail to protect women from sexual harassment and violence or who perpetrate it themselves.

UN Women's power will come from its ability to challenge and change the system and, as a result, vastly strengthen its backbone. For this, it needs people on the inside who are empowered, entrepreneurial, and able to take calculated risks; people who have a support system within UN Women that enables them to push back when the patriarchy tries to silence their voice, make them invisible, or abuses its power – as it most definitely will. And it needs broad-based alliances and partnerships, both within and outside the UN.

It will be crucial to have partnerships with the women's rights networks that played such a fundamental role in calling for its creation. The fact that UN Women has a global and articulate constituency is one of its primary sources of strength and influence. These networks cannot disengage now that UN Women is established: That was just the first step. We must hold UN Women to account, but more importantly, we must work with UN Women to use our collective voice to hold the UN system to account – its member states, agencies, and leadership – and to demand change. Even with a powerful leader and access to higher-level decision-making venues, UN Women is still one of the smallest UN organizations and it is compelled to follow procedures that are not of its making. At the same time, doors that open for UN Women have the potential to open other doors for more and more women, from grass-roots groups working at village level to women's caucuses in parliaments.

Conclusion

What has happened in the Arab spring of 2011 should inspire us, but also make us alert. The men and women – young and old, rich and poor, Christian and Muslim – who stood shoulder to shoulder in Tahrir Square, secured a breathtaking result. But as power has consolidated itself, as norms and standards for governance are shaped, the presence and influence of women have dropped precipitously. This has happened in numerous liberation struggles worldwide and in many local and institutional transformation processes. What can organizations like UN Women, in partnership with and in support of others, do to change the predictable march of history?

This brings me back to the conundrum I began with. We cannot underestimate the complexity of UN Women's task, since it depends on and must be an effective member of a development assistance system that operates, all too often, antithetically to many of the values and goals that UN Women espouses. UN Women's ability to be an effective champion of women's rights at country level, and within the UN itself, will be proportional to its ability to engage and grow the considerable constituency that called for its existence in the first place.

I shared a draft of this chapter with a number of colleagues within UN Women. One colleague challenged me to disentangle which of the obstacles to UNIFEM's and the gender architecture's effectiveness were linked to patriarchy and which were linked to the power of elites in the UN and elsewhere to prevent any changes to the status quo. A handful urged me to be more solution-oriented and to put more emphasis on the institutional progress we have witnessed, including better performance by UNDP and other UN organizations. They acknowledged the importance of speaking 'gender truths', as one observed, but also wanted more on what UN Women can do to turn the situation around. They noted that we cannot wait decades; we need to see change at a much faster pace, and UN Women has to lead this process.

In addition to thanking my colleagues for their very insightful comments, I would say that I am not aspiring to offer prescriptions or solutions – I only highlight some of the potholes on the road to gender equality in bureaucracies, in the hope that UN Women might recognize and swerve to avoid them or confront them head on. And I offer a further hope: that the constituency that struggled so valiantly to advocate for creating UN Women can look back a decade from now and feel gratified that they had put in place something that made a real difference.

Notes

1   The original version of this paper was finalized in 2011, during the early days of UN Women before it had completed its first full year of operation, and before its governance and leadership structure were firmly in place. I have since included some recent developments but have not updated the chapter to reflect all of the structures and changes that have been put into place. For those interested in a recent update on UN Women's progress, see 'Progress Made on the UN Entity on Gender Equality and the Empowerment of Women Strategic Plan 2011–2013, UNW 2012/4, Executive Board of the UN Entity on Gender Equality and the Empowerment of Women (UN Women), Annual session of 2012'. Available at <www.unwomen.org/wp-content/uploads/2012/04/EB_UNW-2012-4_ ED-Report-on-Progress-made-on-strategic-plan.pdf>.

2   The three other gender-specific organizations in the UN were: the Office of the Special Adviser on Gender Issues (OSAGI) and the UN Division for the Advancement of Women (DAW) located in the Secretariat, and the International Research and Training Institute for the Advancement of Women (INSTRAW) which had its own governing board.

3   Michelle Bachelet resigned her position as UN Women's executive director in March 2013 and this book went to press before the appointment of her successor was announced.

4   See for instance The Godmothers <www.thegodmothers.org.uk> and the Gender Equality Architecture (GEAR) campaign <www.gearcampaign.org> – a coalition of organizations that advocated for the establishment of UN Women and continue to advocate as it establishes itself. The Godmothers involves UK-based NGOs hosted by Voluntary Service Overseas (VSO), and the GEAR campaign involves over 300 women's rights, human rights, and social justice organizations worldwide. See also Oxfam (2011).

5   There were three co-chairs: Shaukat Aziz (Pakistan); Luisa Dias Diogo (Mozambique); and Jens Stoltenberg (Norway).

6   The Group of 77 – the largest intergovernmental organization of developing countries in the United Nations – provides the means for the

countries of the South to articulate and promote their collective economic interests and enhance their joint negotiating capacity on all major international economic issues within the UN system, and promotes South–South cooperation for development.

7 Secretary-general's statement for the launch of UN Women, 24 February 2011. See <www.un.org/sg/statements/?nid=5106>.

8 See <www.stoprapenow.org/about>.

9 UN General Assembly Resolution GA 39/125.

10 UNIFEM had four executive directors during its existence: Margaret Snyder (1976–88); Sharon Capeling-Alakija (1989–94); Noeleen Heyzer (1994–2007); and Ines Alberdi (2008–10).

11 See for instance <http://feministing.com/2012/02/17/what-if-rihanna-and-chris-brown-get-back-together/>.

12 There are legitimate criticisms from colleagues of the inadequate technical support they receive from gender units and from the former UNIFEM and other specialist organizations. The placement of individuals who lack the knowledge base, networks, and substantive skills to provide high quality and timely expertise on gender equality to those who are asking for assistance, undermines overall efforts to create a conducive environment for advancing gender equality in policies, programmes, and budgets. As one supportive UNDP senior manager once said to me: 'Every time UNIFEM places an adviser or representative who is at too low a level or who has inadequate expertise, you lower the bar for all of the other UN organizations' efforts on gender equality.'

13 UN Women and the UN system have already taken some steps in this direction, including through the chief executive board agreement to the System-wide Action Plan on Gender Equality and the Empowerment of Women (SWAP) which institutes a system-wide accountability framework.

14 This took place about one year after I joined UNIFEM in 1998.

15 Progress Made on the UN Entity on Gender Equality and the Empowerment of Women Strategic Plan 2011–2013, UNW 2012/4, Executive Board of the UN Entity on Gender Equality and the Empowerment of Women (UN Women), Annual session 2012, 29 May–1 June 2012.

16 Comprehensive Proposal for the Composite Entity for Gender Equality and the Empowerment of Women (A/64/588).

References

Mackay, F. and Krook, M. (2011) *Gender, Politics and Institutions: Towards a Feminist Institutionalism*, Basingstoke: Palgrave Macmillan.

Oxfam (2011) *A Blueprint for UN Women*, Oxfam International Policy Brief Available at: <www.oxfam.org/en/policy/blueprint-un-women>.

Rao, A. (2013) 'Feminist activism in development bureaucracies: shifting strategies and unpredictable results', in R. Eyben and L. Turquet (eds), *Feminists in Development Organizations: Change from the Margins*, pp. 177–92, Rugby, UK: Practical Action Publishing.

Rao, A., Stuart, R. and Kelleher, D. (1999) *Gender at Work: Organizational Change for Equality*, Sterling VA: Kumarian Press.

Snyder, M. (1995) *Transforming Development: Women, Poverty and Politics*, Rugby, UK: Practical Action Publishing.

UN (2004) Advisory Panel 'Organizational Assessment: UNIFEM, Past, Present and Future', Report A/60/62 and E/2005/10, New York: United Nations.

UN (2006a) 'Terms of reference for new study on United Nations System-wide Coherence in the areas of development, humanitarian assistance, and the environment', New York: United Nations <www.un.org/events/panel/html/page2.html>.

UN (2006b) 'Delivering as one: Report of the Secretary-General's High-level Panel on System-wide Coherence in the areas of development, humanitarian assistance, and the environment', A/61/583, New York: United Nations.

UN (2009) 'The Status of Women in the United Nations System and the Secretariat', updated December 2009, New York: United Nations.

About the author

Joanne Sandler is a consultant with more than 30 years' experience advancing women's human rights and organizational change strategies. She is a senior associate of Gender at Work – an international NGO that strengthens organizations, to help build cultures of equality and social justice – and a visiting fellow at the Ralph Bunche Institute for International Studies, City University of New York. Between 2001 and 2010, Joanne was deputy executive director for programmes at the UN Development Fund for Women (UNIFEM). She was part of the transition team for the establishment of UN Women (2010–11) and is a current member of its UN Women's Global Civil Society Advisory Group.

CHAPTER 11

Intimate knowledge of the material at hand

Rosalind Eyben

This is the third in the series of chapters about our group of feminist bureaucrats learning and sharing their political craft. The scene moves to an international meeting that exposes how power shapes legitimate knowledge and how strategies may fail. Resilience, subversion, and alliance-building are all necessary to making a difference in politically complex and sometimes hostile organizational environments. This is the continuation of a series of fictionalized conversations begun in Chapters 4 and 8, in which the author is a participant observer.

In Chapter 8 (Eyben, 2013b), Claudia, Ratna, Gillian, Marianne, and Karin spent a weekend together in the countryside. By Sunday afternoon budding friendships had been consolidated and they were looking forward to catching up with each other in Berlin the following spring. In this chapter, each woman is representing her organization at an official meeting on gender and development. On the evening of the first day, our group has supper together. An incident at the meeting that day triggers a discussion about how power operates in international development processes: How do we respond and what are our strategies of resilience? How subversive do we dare to be? In exploring these matters we agree on the importance of friendship as the basis for building and working in alliances that are nimble and opportunistic, and as we learn to find alternative pathways when obstacles block the road ahead. All this requires understanding and responding to the context in which one is working.

Power and knowledge

We are in a wood-panelled room. Heavy chandeliers droop from the ceiling. We sit at pre-assigned seats, separated from each other in a larger gathering of gender specialists from development agencies. We are listening to a public finance management expert speaking about gender-responsive budgeting, and we are told that public sector budgets in aid-recipient countries are increasingly being structured in terms of performance outcomes (rather than inputs). Our strategy, we are told, must be to ensure the inclusion of gender-sensitive indicators for measuring performance in these budgets. Gillian points out to

http://dx.doi.org/10.3362/9781780448046.011

the presenter the difficulties this represents: 'This seems a standard main-streaming approach. But will it work? There are some difficulties.'

She makes the point that, first, performance management indicators require a statistical base, often lacking for gender issues. Thus, because the authorities (and donors) never developed such a base in the first place, it is not just a matter of negotiating the inclusion of an indicator, but also of getting donor organizations to fund the country's national statistical service to include relevant sex-disaggregated data in their household and other surveys. She mentions the case of an aid-recipient country in sub-Saharan Africa where a group of gender specialists in aid agencies were successful in persuading their colleagues to negotiate with the government authorities for increases in women's literacy to be included as an indicator in the Performance Assessment Framework (PAF) agreed between government and donor. This indicator was subsequently removed with the excuse that there were no baseline data.

She takes a breath, speaking slowly to make sure that everyone under-stands her. 'If such a database had existed – and for the last thirty years we have been campaigning for "sex-disaggregated statistics",' she says, clenching her hands, 'the data would probably have been judged as invalid. Every time we do manage to collect data, we are told that it is the wrong data and that we need to collect more data. Even when research has been carried out – for example, time-use studies – policymakers ignore the findings.' There are murmurs of agreement around the room.

Later, a senior official from the host organization comes into the meeting. He is there to demonstrate he cares about gender equality. It is possibly the first time he has been at a meeting of 'gender experts'. He looks at a side-table display of research reports and evaluation material that participants' agencies have commissioned. He is impressed and asks, 'What is the barrier between this evidence and decision-making?' It seemed to us as if this is the first time he has ever asked such a question. There is a moment's silence. How do we answer? 'A five-letter word beginning with P,' Karin replies from the far end of the table, *sotto voce*, so that only those immediately around hear her. Ratna, who is chairing the session, looks politely curious. '*You* tell us,' she says to the senior official. But he says no more, smiles benignly and leaves for his next appointment.

That evening our group meets for supper at a corner table in a small Turkish restaurant. We order a succession of hot and cold *mezze*. 'Don't serve us too fast,' requests Claudia. 'We'll stick with the hummus and olives for some time as we have a lot to talk about.' Karin tears off a piece of pitta bread. 'Let's talk about what happened today, when none of us answered the man's question about evidence. I experienced *power*,' she says with emphasis, 'as a force that kept me silent. All I could do was name that force with a whisper.'

'I felt no explanation would have made sense to him,' says Ratna. 'He wouldn't have understood the points that Gillian was making earlier on in the meeting. I felt that had I tried to explain, he might have reported back to his boss about those "silly women talking a load of philosophical rubbish".'

'Well,' says Marianne, slowly sipping her wine, 'I guess you could have politely replied with some comment like, "there is nobody as deaf as he who does not want to hear".'

'Perhaps, no one answered because we suspect if we start a discussion about this, the challenge will be thrown back to us,' says Claudia. '*We* will be accused of being bad at communication. Oh dear! We've heard this so often before. It is always *our* fault and *our* failure when they ignore the evidence we put before them.'

'I think our silence was a signal that he and we have different *interpretative horizons*,' says Karin, 'and that in the development world it is *his* horizon that dominates. That's how I interpreted Ratna's response to him. I understood it as, *you* tell us why you ignore our evidence.'

Strategies of resilience

'So,' says Marianne, 'what do we do about power? We are working,' she says, banging her hand on the table, 'against a very oppressive bureaucracy that's hostile to our agenda, while the public is indifferent. This can make us cautious because in bureaucracies people are afraid of doing anything.'

'You have to make trade-offs in order to survive in any bureaucratic political body,' says Ratna. 'For example, when writing a policy paper. Do you go for a substantive paper or a simple political one?'

'What's the difference between a substantive paper and a political paper?' Karin asks her.

'You know, what I think it is, is that in a substantive paper you actually take the risk of trying to say things that are real and problematic.'

'OK, and a political one is just positioning yourself?'

'Yes, everything looks good.'

'In the bureaucratic light?'

'Precisely,' says Ratna. 'Well, positioning yourself to be able just to be at that space where you can move without a lot of questions, right?'

Marianne gives one of her warm laughs. 'Yet, making such trade-offs can be very difficult if we feel obliged to play the game in ways that contribute to perpetuating the very structures we are seeking to change.'

'That's me,' says Claudia, looking down at her plate. 'I am definitely contributing to rebuilding and regenerating this present structure. There's no question about it. And at the same time,' she looks up and smiles, 'to get anything done, I subvert it. I break the rules and I subvert it.'

'You remember,' says Marianne, 'how when we last met, I talked about working behind the enemy lines? Well that's how I see it. I feel I am part of an underground cell. I am a guerrilla in a small, nimble band of like-minded people that probes for weak spots in the organizational machinery. We set ambushes and then run away fast, to hide under our desks until things calm down.'

'It's a bit scary,' says Karin, 'but exciting.'

'Yes,' Marianne says, throwing her a sympathetic glance. 'And failure is fascinating. We can learn from what went wrong.'

'Even more intriguing,' says Ratna, 'are the surprise guerrilla successes. I think it is the unexpected allies and friends or unanticipated actions which really move you along.'

The mood around the table lightens. We pass the wine bottle round the table and Ratna catches the waiter's eye to bring another. Guerrillas, we agree, never fight big battles, but their small wins, Karin suggests – referring back to our earlier discussion about success (Eyben, 2013b) – are like miniature experiments that test implicit theories about resistance and opportunity; they uncover both resources and barriers that were invisible before (Weick, 1985).

'I divide people into three types: allies, enemies, and the indifferent majority,' says Karin. 'The indifferent are an important target, because even though they will never be convinced by the arguments, it *is* possible to get them to make space for others to work in. But it can be very disagreeable.'

'I can tell you a story about that,' says Claudia. 'I was meeting the head of the civil service in –'. She names a country in Africa. 'It was a very formal atmosphere, quite intimidating, quite a powerful man. And he started off by saying he didn't want anything to do with gender equality. He said, "Take this woman over here", and he pointed to the only woman – other than me – in the room, who was one of his employees, and he said, "I personally appointed this woman to her job because I thought she was particularly pretty." He was the sort of person that you just despise, although he was basically supporting the agenda and allowing people below him space to act.' Claudia frowns at the memory. 'Then the following week he opened some kind of women's conference and made a speech which hit all the local papers about how the civil service is now promoting women's equality, and you think, that guy's just such a complete shit. Just appalling. How can you possibly even begin to negotiate with a person like this, that you know is the absolute epitome of the problem that you're trying to address?'

'And you realize there's a fundamental hypocrisy and you're forced to mollycoddle someone in that position to create space for people further down who are doing something that's actually quite good.' Claudia's usual cheerfulness has evaporated. 'But despite your best efforts, sometimes the resistance can be overwhelming and nothing works.'

'Just don't give up,' says Ratna, looking around the table. 'When the main door shuts in your face, find a side door that can be opened. If you see failure as a brick wall, then you're saying, well, they don't want to play my game, and so you're left with nothing. Whereas if you interpret it as, well, maybe they don't get it, or maybe they can be persuaded, or maybe they just need to come at it a different way, it keeps many more doors open.' We swap stories of persistence and tenacity.

'We got everything we wanted but we had to fight each stage of the process,' says Claudia.

'My story is a complex history of politicking, setbacks, and opportunism,' says Gillian.

'What we need,' says Karin, 'are strategies of resilience – to not take opposition personally, to be fascinated, instead of being upset, at why individuals are responding in the way that they are – and then we have to find ways of neutralizing the opposition.'

Neutralizing the opposition

'I think when I started I believed that if we had a good idea, and we talked to enough people about it, then people would just do it,' says Karin. 'Then I learnt the importance of securing and broadening political support to neutralize the opposition.'

'And to do that, we need both soft and hard tactics', says Marianne. Pushing aside our empty plates, we brainstorm soft tactics.

'Avoiding unnecessarily making enemies,' suggests Claudia.

'Helping influential actors to find solutions that work for them,' offers Ratna.

'Bypassing middle management blockers by going straight to the top,' adds Karin.

'Of course, all this might have to mean reinforcing the power of the status quo by making important people look good. Everyone has to be massaged,' says Gillian. 'But what about the tougher tactics?'

'These are often a last resort when softer means have failed,' explains Marianne. 'For example, shaming people by making a fuss. But it is risky because it is hard to make friends with those people again. You risk isolating yourself.'

'Yes,' agrees Claudia. 'Tough tactics can misfire. They can be a CLM.'

'What's that?' ask Karin.

'A career limiting move!'

Everyone laughs but it is a serious point. We gossip about a common acquaintance – a gender specialist in an international organization recently dismissed because she named and shamed her boss in a staff meeting for failing to deliver on the organization's gender equality policy.

'But tough tactics *can* work!' exclaims Gillian. She reminds Ratna of when they were both part of an informal inter-organizational network seeking to get representatives from women's groups from a country at war into a peace conference. Despite Security Council Resolution 1325 about the role of women in peace-building, officials from the four governments organizing the conference were blocking their participation. Every official told a different member of the network that they supported women's inclusion and blamed the decision to keep them out on the officials from the other governments. 'Ratna,' says Gillian with an appreciative smile, 'managed to neutralize the opposition by challenging the officials when they were all together in the same room. Because she knew from the network that they had each separately said they welcomed women's participation, now they had no choice but to agree to include them in the conference.'

'Oh, I love this story!' exclaims Marianne, raising her glass to Gillian and Ratna. 'It is about craft. And the importance of networking.'

We pass the wine bottle round the table, and start to talk about allies.

Networks and alliances

'You absolutely need your allies,' says Ratna. 'You need people you can relax with. You need people that you can go to and say, "God, that's just been a complete disaster." And that you can regroup with and who help you feel whole again. Because it's bruising, isn't it? Constantly working on all this.'

'We are most effective,' says Marianne, as Claudia waves to the waiter to bring more pitta bread, 'when we are able to mobilize support through personal relationships that link together NGOs, politicians, and bureaucrats. Alliances are fuelled by sharing information and, very importantly,' Marianne speaks with emphasis, 'we must value them for what they can offer from where they are located, and not expect them to do things beyond what is possible for them.'

'Do you know,' says Karin, 'when I started I spent most of my time outside my organization. That was where I found sympathetic people with whom I could connect intellectually and who understood where I was coming from. But, if you are always doing workshops out there, how are you going to be focusing in here? Inside work is *much* harder.'

'That's interesting', says Gillian. 'It's different from my experience. Where I work there is a relatively friendly environment, especially the externally facing people, but I realized that it was the functional, internal people who were really going to be critical in moving forward. And they struggled. They were asking gender 101 questions. This wasn't a group that was heavily invested in gender politics and gender language, so it wasn't about trying to persuade them. Their questions were about how is this going to translate into fundraising programmes and so on. It wasn't an academic or ideological discussion. But the way that I come into every relationship is to look for the places where we can connect on a positive side.'

'My first six years,' says Ratna, 'were spent building and consolidating internal relationships. It meant time spent servicing other people's agendas in the hope that, in turn, they would support yours. For instance I supported colleagues in the human rights department and helped them get a bigger budget. In turn I got a commitment to include women's rights as a strong element in *their* work.'

We mull over these points. We discuss how our commitment to collaborative ways of working with people on the outside can be frustrated by our organizational identity and our need to be loyal to that identity – on which our internal credibility depends. Inter-organizational alliances need careful crafting.

'Everyone agrees in principle about the value of coordination to achieve visibility, impact, and credibility,' says Claudia. 'Gillian's story of the peace conference shows how effective this can be. But inter-organizational coordination may be difficult if the organizations concerned are to some degree in competition with each other for resources or policy spaces.'

'Once, I was responsible,' says Marianne, 'for an inter-organizational planning group to get women's rights on the agenda of an important conference. People came to the group's meetings with their own personal agendas. There was a lot of bad personal behaviour. There was a breakdown of trust. It was awful. I had to manage the damaging fallout while keeping what happened secret from my own colleagues. I could have done better. It was ghastly not to be working well together.'

Claudia tells us how after getting gender into the organization's programming principles, she began to appreciate the importance of external pressure for putting these principles into practice. 'Of course, every person who's a feminist activist knows this. You build those external alliances because they are what will help you to hold the organization's feet to the fire – not from an ideas perspective but from a power perspective. We can and must have relations of trust with people on the outside.'

Gillian agrees. Working for a big international NGO she not only seeks to put pressure on official organizations to pay more attention to women's rights, but is also struggling to convince her own senior management to continue to keep it a priority. Karin observes that if official organizations *are* influenced to be more receptive to gender then Gillian's NGO may well follow suit, thus – citing Keck and Sikkink (1998) – creating a useful boomerang effect. 'But managing that insider/outsider relationship is tricky.'

We discuss how far we are prepared to take risks in building relations with and providing information to individuals and organizations outside the bureaucracy. There is always a nagging fear of being found out by our superiors. Karin tells of a colleague in another aid ministry who was caught and reprimanded by her line manager for emailing material to an NGO. She has told Karin that while she will not stop doing it entirely, in the future, she will be careful to be more discreet. Around the supper table we debate how to weigh the risk of being caught against the advantage of having strong relationships with people outside the organization. From what Karin has described, it appears that her colleague has not really understood how bureaucracies work.

'Everyone', says Ratna, 'has informal networks – both inside and outside. If we are over-cautious, outsiders won't know that they and we are on the same side. We have to send out signals while not openly declaring our activism to strangers.'

'You know,' says Marianne, 'we can exploit the existence of a women's lobby without actually having to be in direct contact with it. Public demonstrations, parliamentary questions, and media commentary can all be used to support what we are doing on the inside. You can even add to the power and nastiness of the lobby by making it sound more of a menace than it actually is, for example by pointing out that we risk getting some really difficult parliamentary questions unless we change our position on this. Also,' she says, 'it's not just a question of building alliances. You have to be able to judge the political moment if you want to shift something.'

Ripe moments

Marianne tells a story about how in the lead-up to an election in the late 1990s – and a predicted change of government in her country – she and her colleagues had been carefully preparing the ground for a shift to a rights-based discourse, although they anticipated there would be objections from senior officials. Soon after a centre-left government came into power, Marianne was surprised and rather nervous when, exceptionally, the director-general offered her a ride in his official car when they were both going to the same public event. He rapidly made clear to her that he was using this car ride to tell her to back off from proposing a separate policy document on women's rights to the minister, rather than – as he wished – that these be integrated into a forthcoming policy paper on human rights. Various non-specific hints were made to Marianne as to the unfortunate consequences that might arise from her not accepting his suggestion. Continuing working on a policy document on women's rights certainly would appear to be a career limiting move! Marianne did not argue with him but just nodded quietly.

Despite his warning, she continued with the drafting and submitted to the minister a separate paper that was approved. 'In resisting the director-general,' she says, 'I was aware that what one might call the tide of history was, at that moment, on my side. Several other aid agencies had already signed up to rights-based approaches to gender equality. Moreover, there was a politically influential network of women's rights and development activists who had strong connections within the new centre-left government and who were advocating a high profile for women's rights within our development policy. Finally, I knew there was a difference of opinion between the director-general and the minister on this issue. All this led me to believe, correctly, that by not saying either "yes" or "no" to him in the car, I could actually carry on with the drafting, and this was a risk worth taking.'

'The crucial factor in your story Marianne,' says Karin, 'was timing – or what the social movement literature refers to as a *political opportunity window.*'

'But there are always choices to be made in taking an opportunity,' says Claudia. 'Do you look around for a process that is not quite what you want – but is in full flood – and ride with it, to try to turn it into something else, or do you say, well, this isn't our agenda, and go off and do something else?'

Ratna tells us that the first thing she does when spotting an opportunity is to think, 'What is the widest range of possibilities that we can generate around this opportunity? What's going to give us the biggest bang for the buck? And what's going to be the most possible?'

'Also,' says Gillian, 'as well as political judgement, you need courage to act. This is where friendship comes in.'

'That's definitely true,' says Marianne. 'I should have told you about my colleague Paula. We used to take the same train home in the evening and she'd give me lots of advice and support.'

Ratna looks thoughtful. 'Yes, friends are vital. However, as I've become more senior, so my ability to take risks, my ability to send people stronger and clearer messages, has no doubt increased. I think that helps to reduce some of the obstacles but I do know that there were times when I thought, "I don't think we should quite go there yet". And maybe I worry too much about that sort of structure. Maybe there are times when you just need to punch a hole through the plasterboard and go, you know … and hope that everything will stream through after you.'

Claudia reminds us she has previously held other policy briefs and reflects, saying 'There's something I find quite unique about working on women's rights and gender equality, because you do face resistance, and you're forever banging on the door, and it's so obvious to you how things could happen and could be better.'

'But don't forget,' says Marianne, 'what I mentioned earlier about banging on doors. Find a side door that can be opened.'

We laugh. It is late. At Claudia's signal, the owner brings us the bill. We stand up to hug each other. Tomorrow morning is back into the fray.

Conclusion

Along with Chapters 4 and 8 (Eyben, 2013a, 2013b), this chapter has explored how power and relationships shape and inform feminist bureaucrats' craft and their ways of working. These ways of working include creating and nurturing alliances, working with the grain, leveraging external pressure, seizing opportunities for influence, and managing resistance. These strategies are emergent rather than fully planned in advance. Feminist bureaucrats are effective when they learn in action, through iterative probing, analysis, and response.

In our conversations participants reflected much about what it means to be subversive – struck by the metaphors some are using to describe the 'guerrilla' strategies that secure small, sometimes opportunistic wins. Yet collectively there was a feeling that over time these little successes contribute to securing more money for women. There is the hope that this in turn will help the imagined grassroots women – so distant from the global organizations which are the development bureaucrats' arena of action – secure greater representation and recognition.

A recurrent theme of the conversations was the balance between the inside–outside focus. How much effort should be made in changing the entire organization – the aim of gender mainstreaming – or will that be an effort than runs into the sand? Is it more effective to identify some key opportunities to have an external impact – which was Gillian's strategy in supporting women's access to land? But, as Gillian admitted, what she did would not have been possible, had her organization not already formally committed to a women's rights agenda.

Knowing which strategy to choose depends on learning about the organizations one is working with. In Chapter 4 (Eyben, 2013a), Ratna described her work as 'craft', chiming with Mintzberg's analysis of strategy. Mintzberg uses the analogy of the potter at her wheel, shaping and responding to the clay with which she is provided.

> What springs to mind is not so much thinking and reason as involvement, a feeling of intimacy and harmony with the materials at hand, developed through long experience and commitment. Formulation and implementation merge into a fluid process of learning through which creative strategies evolve. (Mintzberg, 1987: 66)

Feminist bureaucrats' materials are the politics, discourses, and procedures within their organization and its environment. Working with these is a process of learning-in-action through an iterative cycle of probing, making sense, and responding to what is at hand (Snowden and Boone, 2007). Without friends, however, it is hard to make sense of, and shape, something so dynamic and complex as the environment of an international development agency; 'Sensemaking is, importantly, an issue of language, talk, and communication' (Weick et al., 2005: 409). A feminist bureaucrat who fails to invest the time and effort in making friends would struggle to understand what is happening, would fail to respond appropriately, and would find doors banging shut in her face. She would soon find herself with the sobriquet of 'gender policewoman'. Thus labelled, she might enter a downward spiral: no one would invite her to meetings unless the office procedures required it, nor would she be copied into emails or invited for a drink after work. Inside the organization she would risk being viewed as a tedious troublemaker, while from the outside, feminist activists would see her as useless and irrelevant.

Only too easily, all this can happen to beleaguered gender specialists in large development bureaucracies. An adept, strategic feminist bureaucrat needs friends with whom she can learn, if she and they are to work politically to make their organization a pathway of women's empowerment. In his classic piece, Mintzberg (1987) explains how strategic learning 'walks on two feet'. It is both deliberate – that is, planned – and emergent – that is, it grows organically and in response to contingency, as in my own story, to which I now return. In the introduction to Chapter 4 (Eyben, 2013a), I described how an unplanned moment – when I began my time in the British aid ministry – became the starting point of a conscious strategy of taking advantage of outside pressure for internal change. What happened next?

By late 1988, I had established cordial, informal links with the WID lobby, playing a brokerage role between them and our male managers. I was also making friends within the organization and they helped me understand its ways of working and thinking. I had to learn that women staff members had to be 'good sports', and to avoid any demonstration of feelings at the risk of being labelled 'hysterical'. At that time, it was an organization where the wives of many senior managers stayed at home and did voluntary work. Women employees knew their place as filing clerks and secretaries; the few who were in senior positions dressed in grey and brown, working quietly in efficient obscurity. The stereotypically masculine environment continued to downplay and even trivialize women's rights and gender justice.

Meanwhile my friends outside were strongly influenced by a group of feminist academics, passionately concerned that only a small percentage of government scholarships to study in Britain were being allocated to women. The gender advocacy lobby opted to make this the key plank of their advocacy with the minister and wrote to him accordingly. How was this to be handled? My managers summoned me to a meeting; I tried to explain to them why the proposal was a good idea. But they disliked anything that smacked of affirmative action or positive discrimination. They were neo-classical economists and playing fields had to be kept level – even when they were clearly not level.

I sat on my boss's cream sofa and looked disappointed. He and his colleague were kind men. They didn't want to discourage me. Out of the blue a thought occurred to me: 'Yes, alright, of course I understand – quotas are out of the question. But might we offer something else instead? Something less controversial, that shouldn't cause any problems for us ...'

'What do you suggest?' they enquired.

'Well,' I replied hesitatingly, the spark of an idea occurring to me as I was speaking, 'we could have a women-in-development strategy for the ministry. Of course no funding commitments. But training and checklists and things like that. We could produce an annual report on how we are doing, and share this with the lobby – so they have a sense of being involved.'

Relieved that I was being a good sport, and not being 'difficult' about the quotas, they quickly agreed with my suggestion. But they had not appreciated the potential dangers of regularly reporting to the lobby that (with my encouragement) was then in a position to hold the ministry accountable for the commitments it had made. I was astonished that I had traded some overseas scholarships for the ministry agreeing, for the first time ever, to an across-the-board plan for how it was going to implement – and, significantly – to monitor its rhetorical commitment to women in development. My managers had fallen into a trap I was not even aware I was constructing until it sprang shut.

Like the other feminist bureaucrats in this book, I had brought to my work an 'intimate knowledge of the material at hand' (Mintzberg, 1987: 66).

References

Eyben, R. (2013a) 'Feminist identities', in R. Eyben and L. Turquet (eds), *Feminists in Development Organizations: Change from the Margins*, pp. 55–66, Rugby, UK: Practical Action Publishing.

Eyben, R. (2013b) 'Finding our organizational way', in R. Eyben and L. Turquet (eds), *Feminists in Development Organizations: Change from the Margins*, pp. 117–26, Rugby, UK: Practical Action Publishing.

Keck, M. and Sikkink, K. (1998) *Activists Beyond Borders: Advocacy Networks in International Politics*, Ithaca: Cornell University Press.

Mintzberg, H. (1987) 'Crafting strategy', *Harvard Business Review* 65: 66–75.

Snowden, D. and Boone, M. (2007) 'A leader's framework for decision making', *Harvard Business Review* 85: 68–76.

Weick, K. (1984) 'Small wins: redefining the scale of social problems', *American Psychologist* 39: 40–9 <http://dx.doi.org/10.1037%2F0003-066X.39.1.40>.

Weick, K., Sutcliffe, K., and Obstal, D. (2005) 'Organizing and the process of sensemaking', *Organization Science* 16: 409–21 <http://dx.doi.org/10.1287%2Forsc.1050.0133>.

About the author

Rosalind Eyben is a Professorial Research Fellow at the Institute of Development Studies, University of Sussex. She is a social anthropologist with a professional background in development policy and practice, and a committed teacher in the IDS doctoral and master's programmes, including on gender and development. She has designed and facilitated numerous workshops for international development practitioners all over the world. Her research interests focus on power and relations in international aid. From 2006–11 she convened the global policy programme of the International Research Consortium on Pathways of Women's Empowerment and is currently developing a new area of work exploring the knowledge/power practices of donors that sustain the invisibility of unpaid care as a development policy issue. In 2010 she launched the Big Push Forward that has created an international network challenging the current audit culture in development. She was awarded a CBE in 2000 and is a board member of UNRISD and ActionAid UK.

CHAPTER 12

Feminist activism in development bureaucracies: shifting strategies and unpredictable results

Aruna Rao

Within the constraints of bureaucratic straitjackets and institutional turf battles, this chapter examines the workings of cross-agency gender theme groups (GTGs) to strengthen the gender equality programming of three UN country teams (UNCTs) through an action-learning approach facilitated by Gender at Work. Looking through the lens of each country context, it examines the importance of safe collective spaces to critically reflect on decision-making and action, the relevance of inter-organizational cooperation between gender equality staff in UN agencies, and why this has been difficult to achieve.

Feminist theorists and gender equality activists have long known that what actually gets done in the name of feminist activism varies widely by institutional context and current gender politics, as well as the actors involved, individual beliefs, skills and influence, or the combined consciousness and skills of activist groups. The intentions underpinning the model of gender equality that feminists or gender equality actors in development bureaucracies pursue, also range widely. They may be promoting equity in pay and working standards, or equality in opportunities, assets, voice, and participation. Some may work to make sure their institutional resources are used to deliver directly to women; some aim to transform gendered institutions. Often, they combine aspects of all. We also know that their choices will be circumscribed by the room to manoeuvre within their organizations and across multiple mandates, capacities, and cultures if they are working in partnerships or through networks. And while global discourses inform country-specific debates, the local contexts and gender politics as well as the priorities of key stakeholders, play a more prominent role in determining what issues are articulated and how. With so many moving parts, gender mainstreaming 'may be understood as the result of essentially contested processes that inevitably produce varying outcomes in different contexts' (Walby, 2005).

Bureaucracies play a limited role in engendering social change and there is a long road to walk from victories for women in bureaucratic spaces to gains for women on the ground. Yet, sometimes the kaleidoscope moves in such

http://dx.doi.org/10.3362/9781780448046.012

a way that significant changes emerge – significant to the actors involved as well as positive for the women they are meant to benefit. This chapter draws on Gender at Work's experience in strengthening gender equality work with UN country teams (UNCTs), to examine the configuration of lenses and processes that led to such changes.[1]

Gender at Work[2] is an international network that strengthens organizations, to build cultures of equality and social justice, with a particular focus on gender equality. We support local and global social change organizations to analyse and change unequal and exclusionary norms and practices in their structures, processes, and programmes by introducing new analytical tools, ways of thinking, and practices. In 2006 we conducted a review of 2005–06 United Nations Development Frameworks (UNDAF) for the UNDG Task Team on Gender Equality led by UNIFEM[3] (now UN Women) and UNFPA. The review highlighted significant gaps between the analysis and proposed action in country programmes relating to gender equality. We recommended *inter alia* an in-depth, action-learning process to build holistic programming for gender equality. This recommendation was accepted by the UNDG and in 2009 we were invited to begin a two-year programme with three UNCTs – from Morocco, Nepal, and Albania. The objective of this UNDG project became: 'To contribute to strengthened knowledge and action on holistic and replicable joint UN programming on gender equality and women's empowerment that, ultimately, support countries to achieve the Millennium Development Goals (MDG) and other international commitments.' Our role was to lead the action-learning process, serving as technical and process facilitators for the UNCTs, and to recommend coordination processes and tools to improve the UNCTs' ability to build a vision of and capacity to support well-coordinated work for gender equality.

Essentially, this was a project about doing better by learning better. The choice of the UNCTs was meant to build knowledge about how to strengthen gender equality work in very specific contexts: in Morocco it was in the context of a large Spanish MDG-funded programme involving multiple stakeholders; in Nepal it was about how to actualize gender equality as an outcome in the UN development framework; and in Albania, it was about how to work specifically in a One UN context[4] where the intent is to strengthen national ownership and enhance development results by bringing together the UN's comparative advantages into one strategic programme with one leader, one budget, one programme, and one office.

The contextual lens

Morocco

The contextual lens in each of the three countries was markedly different, but each provided an opening for action. In Morocco, the women's movement has been active for a long time, and remains deeply rooted in feminist activism, while it operates in the context of Islam. As such, the terms 'equal opportunities' or 'human rights of women' are more frequently used than 'equality between men and women.' Although the principle of equal responsibility for the family is enshrined in law, in practice women and men do not have the same rights and duties at home. In Morocco, women's illiteracy rate remains at 54.7 per cent; maternal mortality is 227 deaths per 100,000 live births, and child mortality is 35 per 1000 live births for children under one year. Cases of sexual and gender-based violence remain under-reported – a problem compounded by a lack of national data on the forms and prevalence of gender-based violence. Existing cultural norms have tended to organize social roles of men and women into a hierarchy and to legitimize gender-based violence. Vulnerability to violence is higher among women from migrant and sub-Saharan communities.

In Morocco the movement towards gender equality was facilitated by several political changes; leadership at the highest levels of governance advanced the fight against gender-based violence. The adoption in 2004 of a new family code, the *Moudawana*, spearheaded by the women's movement, marked the starting point of important legal reforms such as ensuring the welfare of all parties in the case of divorce, especially of children.

The first steps towards achieving gender equality and empowerment in Morocco – led by the feminist movement – entailed raising awareness in the general population of the vulnerabilities faced by women. Next came the institutionalization of mechanisms to facilitate more equitable gender relations, which included the creation of the Ministry of Social Development, facilitated by the work of UNIFEM and strategic involvement of NGOs. The period 2000–5 was marked by legal battles for women's human rights; international agreements like CEDAW led to a debate on national laws. In 2005–8 the gender equality movement entered its operational phase, integrating gender issues into national policies and strategic plans. The political will of the current government to address gender issues has been important to facilitate the movement towards gender equality. The national mechanism to address women's needs – the Ministry of Social Development, Family and Solidarity – was expanded by creating a department to work on gender equality issues.

Nepal

Whereas in Morocco the contextual lens was shaped by an active women's movement and a new political opening, in Nepal political upheaval enabled the articulation of a broad framework of social justice and human rights by a majority Marxist government. Nepal has emerged from ten years of intense political upheaval and violent conflict, rooted in persistent inequalities based on class, caste, ethnicity, religion, and gender. This turmoil nevertheless presented opportunities for change and progress, including for gender equality. The interim constitution has strong provisions on gender equality and the Three-year Interim Plan includes programmes for policy and legal reform on women's participation, gender awareness, and support services. There are several ongoing policies and programmes within the government, UN agencies, and civil society which address different facets of gender equality, including a National Plan of Action on Implementing CEDAW and a Gender Equality Act. In 2002 a major advance was made with the 11th amendment to the Nepali civil code, which expanded women's rights in the areas of abortion, divorce, and property. The Domestic Violence Bill was passed by parliament in 2009. There are also institutional mechanisms, such as the Women's Commission, which are meant to oversee implementation of these policies.

Albania

Albania too has experienced years of political transformation, beginning with the collapse of communism after the death of Hoxha, and moving toward democratic reform since the mid 1990s. EU membership is a high priority for the government and this entails alignment with EU policies, including on gender equality. Years of political, economic, and social instability in the region have given rise to numerous changes which have affected the women's movement in several crucial ways, including the revision of laws to increase the visibility and participation of women in society, and the introduction of anti-trafficking legislation. Equally important is that in 2006 Albania became a One UN pilot country. Regarding women's empowerment and gender equality, the UN in Albania has prioritized improved implementation and monitoring of core legislation and policies (including gender equality and domestic violence), more inclusive participation in public policy and decision-making, increased and equitable access to quality basic services, and regional development to reduce regional disparities.

Although women's educational levels in Albania are on average higher than those achieved by men, their participation falls behind that of men in many areas. Their level of unemployment is substantially higher and women's salaries are lower than men's in both the private and public sectors. At least a third of all women in Albania have experienced physical violence within their homes, although activists repeatedly stress the need for a comprehensive national review of the prevalence of domestic violence and the services in place. Minority women, such as the Roma, face further marginalization and vulnerability to gender-based and domestic violence.

Albania now has its first national law to prevent domestic violence. Further, in July 2008 the government (with UN support) adopted a comprehensive gender equality law. In December 2009 the government incorporated the nation's first women's quota within the national electoral code. In 2007, again with support of the UN, the National Strategy for Gender Equality and Eradication of Domestic Violence (NSGE-DV) was adopted. It encourages a safer and more equal environment for women and girls in Albanian society. Domestic violence is one of the eight main components of the national strategy; the others address various dimensions of gender equality such as health, education, political participation, and institutional and legislative frameworks. The NSGE-DV and the new gender equality and domestic violence laws have laid the groundwork for Albania's gender equality programming.

The institutional lens

Within the UN system, as in many other places, work on women's empower-ment and gender equality has operated in an environment of scarcity. This not only hampers progress but also generates 'territorial' sensitivities among agencies with similar or overlapping mandates and clients. Devaki Jain, who was involved in carrying out an external assessment of the UN's Development Assistance Framework in 1998–9, reports that 'recipient countries felt some-what assaulted by the multiple fingers of UN development assistance thrusting into their countries, often competing for space and legitimacy', and that 'special agencies focusing on women that were set up both as international agencies and as national machineries have suffered from … marginalization, ghettoization, and the demeaning gaze that excluded peoples and women have experienced at all societal levels worldwide'. It has been difficult for feminist activists and gender staffers within the system to nudge what she calls the 'hard rock of entrenched patriarchy' (Jain, 2006). Some years later Thoraya Obaid, the outgoing executive director of UNFPA, underscored this point: 'gender concerns', she said, 'are still considered "soft", marginal issues and because of this they are often pushed down near the bottom of the list of priorities, thereby jeopardizing chances for greater progress' (Obaid, 2005).

This frustrating scenario is not new. Not only has the work on women's empowerment and gender equality been woefully underfunded,[5] but the mechanisms charged with carrying out, coordinating, and monitoring this agenda are toothless. Scarce resources in an uncertain environment breed competition. UNIFEM, which was mandated both to support innovative and catalytic programming in countries and to strengthen gender equality activi-ties across the UN system, was much smaller, both in human and in finan-cial terms, than other agencies which also have a gender equality mandate.[6] Larger agencies such as UNICEF and UNFPA jostled with UNIFEM for leader-ship and visibility on the elastic gender agenda; staffers ardently defend insti-tutional turf and all vie for attention and funding from donor governments, where the same fight repeats itself.

It is not surprising that inter-agency cooperation and coordination on gender equality and women's empowerment is difficult under these circum-stances. Perhaps for this reason there are numerous mechanisms in the UN system, both at headquarters and at the country level, to promote coordi-nation. The UN chief executives board (CEB) is the system's highest-level coordinating body: it leads in coordinating system-wide follow-up activities and highlighting a number of broad principles to guide the elaboration of inter-agency collaborative arrangements. According to the CEB's policy on gender equality, 'gender mainstreaming as a key strategy for achieving gender equality and the empowerment of women is intended to work in conjunction with women-specific actions', and 'coherence and coordination of efforts in the implementation of the gender mainstreaming strategy' are seen to be 'essential for achieving results' (UN, 2006). At the level of the UNCT, the GTG is a key driver of the gender agenda and is usually led by UNIFEM or UNFPA. But the work on women's empowerment and gender equality has some unique features which provide insights into how the turf battles play out on the ground today.

Like other complex social dynamics, there is no common analysis of the causes of inequality or consensus on the actions required to advance equality. This on the one hand encourages creativity, but on the other hand allows mediocrity. Because the field does not have universally acceptable standards for gender expertise, a grab bag of various experiences can masquerade as professional qualifications – a weakness that can result in ineffective negotiation of institutional space and recognition for gender equality work, as well as poor policy analysis and programming. Even worse is the assumption that because one is a woman, one must be knowledgeable about and motivated to effectively address gender equality issues.[7]

When you do find committed and knowledgeable staffers, they have often honed their understandings in the trenches of social movements or critical feminist academic contexts. When opportunities for action come together, with their efforts to open spaces for women's voices, the work sings. For the most part, however, gender equality staffers toil away within the system where this work is only part of their mandate and receives low priority. 'According to a 2002 UNIFEM/UNDP scan, of the 1300 UN staff who have gender equality in their terms of reference, nearly 1000 ... were gender focal points that are relatively junior, have little substantive expertise, no budgets, and who deal with gender as one element of a large portfolio' (Rao, 2006). With few exceptions, addressing gender equality is an add-on job. This was also true for many of the UN staffers involved in the UNDG programme.

The key institutional arrangement for the UNDG project work in Morocco, Nepal, and Albania is joint programming, which involves various UN agencies in partnership with government and civil society. In Morocco, the joint programme on gender-based violence is called Programme Multisectoriel de Lutte contre les Violences Fondées sur le Gendre par l'Autonomisation des Femmes et des Filles au Maroc (Multi-sector Programme to Fight Gender-based Violence by Empowering Moroccan Women and Girls, 2008–10). The Ministry of Social Development, Family, and Solidarity serves as coordinator for all national initiatives, including the joint programme. On the UN side, UNIFEM is the lead agency. The implementation and monitoring of this programme involves many actors: 8 UN Agencies and 13 national partners, as well as NGOs, representatives from the women's movement, and national institutions. The UN GTG acts as a point of collaboration for UN Agencies and often involves national experts and representatives from government ministries. UN Agencies, led by UNIFEM, have been working with NGOs and national institutions for several years. This facilitated the coming together of these diverse groups under one umbrella programme.

Despite the participation of UN staff in the joint programme on gender-based violence, some of the challenges in implementing the programme can be traced to inadequate capacity and knowledge on gender issues, compounded by the different understandings of gender equality and gender priorities, and by lack of a collaborative culture for joint work. With so many partners involved in decision-making, the processes take a long time and programme implementation requires rigorous monitoring. The turnover of representatives also threatens the ownership of the programme, since there are different cultures, interests, and priorities among partners who are competing for money and inputs into programme design. That is why working together, for instance in the GTG, was crucial for sharing visions and creating a common understanding.

In Nepal, when the programme started, the UN agencies were involved in several joint initiatives on gender equality. They were pursuing several target strategies which aimed to empower women, girls, and communities to prevent and address gender-based violence; enhance services and build capacities of service providers; and create a supportive policy and planning environment. The Multi-Sectoral Gender-Based Violence Response at the District Level, for example, involved UNFPA, UNICEF, and UNIFEM. Its objectives were to raise awareness, strengthen availability and quality of services, build the capacity of multiple service providers, and ensure government support via an improved legal framework.

In Nepal it has been difficult, in general, to successfully integrate gender equality into national programmes; even trying to increase the number of women in government ministries has been difficult. Nepal has a strong base of grassroots women's groups and the role of women NGO representatives has been important in joint programming, because they fight to focus attention on grassroots demands and provide real-life examples from the field. Also, because they work directly with communities and can implement programmes more efficiently, their work adds immediate value to gender equality programmes. In the context of joint programmes, various UN agencies have leveraged government and NGO strengths by bringing various actors together on a common platform to complement each other's work. The caretaker government's increasing reliance on the UN system eased this path.

In Albania, the four agencies (UNICEF, UNFPA, UNIFEM, and UNDP) have collaborated to work on gender equality in the country and were the main supporters in the formulation and implementation of the NSGE-DV. All four are involved in Albania's Joint UN Programme on Gender Equality. The aims of this programme are to strengthen capacities, legal frameworks, and systems in government on gender equality; coordinate and service support at the local level; increase women's capacity to hold decision-makers to account (this includes strengthening women's participation to ensure that women as

a 'constituency' can demand certain services and better public sector performance); and support improved coordination between the UN, donors, and
national partners on gender equality.

The process lens

The challenge for us working with the UN system in these three countries
was to create within a non-reflective context a formally recognized space for
reflection, in order to increase the learning, effectiveness, and sustainability
of change. UN agencies and government departments are hierarchical structures built around sectoral and programmatic silos, where decision-making
power is concentrated at the top and where gender equality is one of many
priorities at the bottom of the organizational totem pole.

Creating a 'bubble of reflection' was harder to achieve than in other
organizational contexts. As Standing forcefully argues, 'bureaucracies are not
engines of social and political transformation' and 'the main myth in gender
mainstreaming ... is a mythic relocation of the possibility of political transformation to an inherently non-transformatory context' (2004). Bureaucratic
mainstreaming not only changes the meanings of empowerment, it does not
encourage and motivate a systematic cycle of experimentation and learning,
which is essential to understanding complex social phenomena. But over and
above the obvious characteristics of bureaucracies (hierarchy, routinization,
standard operating procedures, logframe planning, and control mechanisms)
that make them less conducive to organizational learning, we found that UN
bureaucracies have some peculiar characteristics that further complicate the
issue.

Using Pickering's matrix for work settings built on the level of cross-
functional or cross-organizational collaboration required by the job, and the
degree of judgement or improvisation that is required,[8] we believe that the
nature of the work on women's empowerment requires deep understanding
of participants and an ability to improvise rather than carry out routines.
This suggests that a 'network' model with its associated interactive formats,
as well as individual expertise based on reflection on experience, would be
better suited than standardized work planning and 'how to' training. Yet UN
practices reinforce the opposite by emphasizing planning and monitoring
procedures (human rights approach, gender analysis, logframes) to address
complex problems without the requisite investment in helping staff interact
with this information and socialize it to their circumstances. The UN operates with little accountability to women on the ground for delivering results,
but it does require staff to comply with standardized procedures.

Like many other large organizations, UN agencies are 'loosely coupled'
systems (Weick, 1976). This can increase the organization's sensitivity to the
environment, allow local adaptations and creative solutions to develop, and
foster greater self-determination by actors. There is considerable autonomy at
the periphery to manoeuvre a course of action and build supportive alliances.

In such an environment, strong and well resourced advocates who have senior management support might achieve gender equality outcomes. This was our hope in igniting the GTGs as empowered and important drivers of this process within the UNCTs.

The key role of the GTGs was most evident in the case of Morocco, where clear strategizing, integral links to the women's movement, and the feminist activism of UNIFEM wove seamlessly with the genuine ownership and persistent diligence on the part of the lead government agency of the project to keep the programme on track and deliver results. Monitoring of the joint programme was chosen as the entry point for improving the coordination and efficiency of the programme implementation in order to strengthen the efficacy of the UN system's joint assistance and so result in positive programme benefits for women. We developed a simple tool to help the output monitoring committee keep track of the level of participation in coordination meetings and the quality of that participation. Once or twice during every monthly meeting, the meeting monitor made a sketch outlining the different interactions recorded during this time, emphasizing the duration and frequency of those speaking, the interaction between participants (particularly the frequency of exchanges between the lead institution and others), showing to whom the exchange was directed (whether to the wider audience or only to a few); and assessing whether it was facilitating the discussion or blocking it. These data were tabulated into a summary based on the type of interventions – those promoting group work, those strengthening group unity, and individual interventions providing information or blocking it. It enabled an objective assessment of the frequency, duration, and intensity of the interventions made during coordination meetings, mapping the interaction among participants, and analysis of the interventions and the role played by each. It was a seemingly innocuous but in fact quite potent way of mapping how power was practised – and gendered – in that decision-making arena. By consciously observing this pattern, it nudged participants to be conscious of their own roles and encouraged constructive engagement. At a micro level it built on Foucault's conception that power circulates and is exercised rather than held, and that power exercised to dominate or exclude needs to be effectively countered, and structures and practices should be built to allow 'transgressions' (Foucault in Rabinow, 1984).

In Albania, clear and ambitious strategizing on the part of the GTG led by UNIFEM gave the process substance with clear objectives. Using the space provided by the action-learning process, the GTG decided to plan strategically how to comprehensively address gender equality in the upcoming UNDAF, based on an analysis of learnings from the implementation of the joint programme within the One UN context. They agreed that they should organize for a gender audit of the UNCT as part of the UNDAF preparation and cooperate jointly on other activities pertaining to gender equality. But unlike in Morocco and Nepal, the action-learning programme opportunity in Albania was not used for any deep analysis or reflection on power dynamics in the programme, across agencies, or among GTG group members. However, the UN considers the Albania Joint Programme on Gender Equality under the One UN framework a success because it delivered results and improved coordination between the different agencies, which in turn led to improved coordination among national partners and a greater sense of national ownership.

In Nepal, the action-learning process built a sense of solidarity among the GTG members by breaking down the pernicious interagency competition and programmatic silos in which they had been placed. Engagement in action-learning has catalysed the work of the UN GTG and helped it move ahead on the work plan, taking up joint advocacy and leveraging resources. Joint action and 'one voice' by the UN on gender issues contributed to increased visibility of issues and stronger partnerships with national counterparts. The GTG 'think piece' which was developed with our facilitation elucidated the connections between gender equality, human rights, and social inclusion. It was endorsed by the UN system as an intersectional programming tool for testing and application; and the commitment, coordination and personal relationships among core group members became stronger through the process. Personal bonding has helped to overcome territorial tensions – members became comfortable with advocating on gender issues across agency boundaries. Our work in this was critical in helping the group to question assumptions by encouraging people to express their views and their fears, keep the group together, break down barriers, and move the group to consensus building. As a result, the GTG felt that they built a better project using the action-learning process than would have been possible if it had been developed by one agency. Moreover, close coordination of UN agencies, both among themselves and with government partners, put leadership back in the hands of the government. The government now deals with the UNCT as the representative of the whole UN system and no longer asks individual agencies to independently represent the various parts of the UN system.

The outcome lens

What do these experiences of GTGs in three UNCTs tell us about the politics of gender mainstreaming in the UN context? We often separate the picture of feminist strategizing and activism in civil society contexts from the long slog of bureaucratic pen-pushing which we have come to associate with gender mainstreaming in development agencies. Certainly, there is ample evidence to show that gender equality policies get lost in bureaucratic black holes en route to implementation. Yet this experience validates a different picture. We see the potential for organizing for women's empowerment and gender equality by the GTGs. This is the UN parallel to women's organizing in civil society – in other words, for gender mainstreaming to be effective in a bureaucratic context, it needs much the same collective thought and strategy as women's organizing outside it, and can deliver similar results. Rather than burdening GTGs with resource manuals focusing on planning and monitoring mechanisms and processes, it may be far more effective to enable GTGs to organize and develop joint solidarity strategies with government and the women's movement, to enhance their voice within the system and do their part in pushing forward a change agenda.

In all three countries, the GTGs had concrete projects around which to focus their energies, some resources, and senior management support. These were critical success factors, but most important was the experience of collective reflection, relationship building, and strategizing. 'Through learning,' Senge suggests, 'we become able to do something we were never able to do. Through learning we re-perceive the world and our relationship to it' (Senge, 1990). The action-learning process enabled this kind of re-learning which fuelled the collective entrepreneurship of the GTGs within this highly politicized institutional context.

The reflexive lens

What did we do and what did we learn? Going into this process we knew that, unlike much of the work on gender equality in the UN system, these programmes were well resourced and there was a concrete piece of work in all three contexts around which to organize reflection and action. Learning is difficult to do in the abstract. Our work links organizational change, institutional change, and gender equality. We understand institutional change to be multi-factorial and holistic. It should be as concerned with the individual psychology of women and men as with their access to resources and with the social structures in which they live. From the point of view of an organization that intervenes to change gender-biased institutions, change must happen in two spheres – outside the organization and within. Our starting point in this process was to work *within* the organizational system in order for them to effect change on the outside.

There is no dearth of 'how to' training in the UN context and we needed from the start to build something different. How do you help these 'groups' to actually coalesce as groups? How do you help them to move beyond problem solving to asking some of the deeper 'why' questions about existing practices, examining goals and assumptions, relationships (what the organization literature calls 'double loop learning') and beyond that – expanding collective knowledge about underlying paradigms? We used an action-learning process specifically to uncover and challenge informal systemic barriers to gender equality i.e. the invisible beliefs, norms, and practices that underpin and perpetuate gender-based discrimination at the individual and the organizational or societal level. In terms of Gender at Work's framework[9] (Figure 12.1), the action-learning was directed to the lower left quadrant – changing the culture and norms that underpin and perpetuate gender-based discrimination – by supporting people to use analytical tools to highlight these practices and engage collectively in transforming them.

Figure 12.1 What are we trying to change? The Gender at Work framework

By facilitating a reflection on their ideas and values, our interventions with the Nepal GTGs helped them to break down agency silos and end up speaking with one voice. In Morocco, our interventions provided to the joint programme core team the means to collectively analyse power relations. In Albania, they provided an opportunity for the GTGs to collectively analyse their strategies and plan.

Addressing the left side of the framework (Figure 12.1) – particularly the lower left quadrant – is important for moving processes of social change from a minimal compliance, or 'box-ticking' mode toward a results-oriented, problem-solving approach. Capacity-building directed toward individual change is insufficient to shift bureaucratic practice. Although it may permit individuals to perform more effectively, they will continue to battle against norms and ways of working that can obstruct rather than help their efforts.

For us, this initiative highlighted the usefulness of action learning as a means to move a process of building gender equality from the purview of some dedicated and exceptional individuals within a bureaucracy to the expected and accepted practice of the entire bureaucracy. This requires changing the cultural norms, relationships, and work practices that block bureaucracies from paying sufficient attention to gender equality. Just because an agency has a policy on gender mainstreaming does not mean that its staff or the ways it works will automatically change. And just because an agency offers gender awareness or gender analysis training does not mean it will henceforth contribute effectively to gender equality. Similarly, resource allocation alone, although important, is not sufficient. Action-learning processes can build positive synergies between these elements by generating change in organizational beliefs and practice.

However, coming to grips with issues of culture and norms requires certain preconditions. The group members must be ready to engage constructively with their own behaviour and that of their colleagues. Both the cultural context and the bureaucratic context may militate against readiness for engagement: people may feel it is threatening, requiring them to expose their own vulnerability, or they may see it as irrelevant to bureaucratic action, which mainly works with the dimensions on the right-hand side of the framework.

Most of our previous work has involved civil society groups; this was the first time we worked in this manner with the UN system. Consequently, this experience prompted a reflection on the differences between civil society actors and the UN system. Civil society actors who participated had several key characteristics: commitment to change, need for resources, greater flexibility in engaging in 'learning' opportunities, and the participation of individuals within those organizations who had the capacity to make those changes. The UN system, by contrast, does not easily allow for or resource a collective reflective space. Organizational silos and lack of space for reflection perpetuate a piecemeal way of addressing systemic issues of exclusion. By creating spaces for reflection, taking down the walls between agencies and building a framework for coordination, the GTGs were able to work politically and strategically. While every gender focal point (GFP) has a clear analysis of why their issues are marginalized within the UN system, the GTG is traditionally the place where GFPs come together and see that the oppression of their issues is not unique. Therefore by resourcing the GTGs, the space is transformed from being a place for collective victimization to one where the GFPs may be empowered to develop a shared vision, and implement and produce results. In Nepal, the conceptual framework on gender, social inclusion, and human rights is a good example of an integrated product that came out of the willingness of representatives from various UN agencies and government to sit together and work to generate this result.

These reflective processes are also tangled up with complex emotions; emotion drives action and triggers learning. If, in addition, we believe that 'deep meaning can only be made with connection to personal experience' (Fook, 2006), then it is not surprising that the 'personal is political' politics around gender equality issues are deeply felt. People who get involved in such intense processes are forced to re-examine their own personal beliefs and behaviours – to walk the talk – and they do so in an environment which is rife with politics, but where no other issue except human rights is politically framed.

Conclusion

In summary, we have learned that as in any political process, gender mainstreaming in the UN context requires a strong driver – the GTG – to achieve results. GTGs need to have the profile and competence to use the available space to promote gender equality; to develop a sense of collectivity in the team as well as mutual accountability and joint ownership. They also need to actively involve both national and international staff.

Joint programmes can work if they are collectively designed and collectively monitored and if disagreements are ironed out before launching. They tend to be successful when they have strong connections with the women's movement in the country and when gender equality advocates within government are included in the process in pivotal roles.

Collective spaces for learning are essential for building cohesion and programme sustainability. These spaces need to be consciously created, safe, and externally facilitated. The action learning needs to be grounded in experience where the GTG analyses and develops solutions to real programme issues and organizational problems. They need to learn how to ask questions that will bring unstated assumptions to the surface; to learn about themselves as they work on a problem together and be accountable to each other for their decisions and programme implementation.

The spaces of critical reflection we have described above are fragile. When the lens of the kaleidoscope moves again, a new pattern will emerge. These spaces are inherently subversive, both because they unearth deep assumptions that collide with dominant organizational cultural norms, and because they focus on how power dynamics within the institution influence practice. Given the size, weight, and enormous inertia of the development bureaucracies which these activists inhabit, there is no guarantee that these spaces will survive. Members of the groups will move on and the new composition will need to create anew their own voice and cohesiveness. The GTGs and their feminist agendas are constantly at risk of being overwhelmed by their own institutional compulsions, but this programme gave us a glimpse of how collective learning and women's organizing within the system can redefine what gender mainstreaming looks like on the inside, to deliver on women's rights on the outside.

Notes

1 The ideas reflected in this paper are the joint analysis of the Gender at Work team (Aruna Rao, Kalyani Menon-Sen, and Rieky Stuart) involved in the Action Learning for Women's Empowerment and Gender Equality of the United Nations Development Group (UNDG).

2 For more information see <www.genderatwork.org>.

3 As of January 2011, UNIFEM has been merged into UN Women.

4 The United Nations launched the Delivering as One pilot initiative in eight countries in 2007 in order to test how the UN family can provide development assistance in a more coordinated way.

5 Evaluation after evaluation has shown that countries, bilateral donors, and the multilateral system consistently fail to prioritize, and significantly underfund, women's rights and equality work, e.g. UNIFEM Assessment: A/60/62 – E2005/10; UNDP Evaluation of Gender Mainstreaming <www.undp.org/eo/documents/EO_GenderMainstreaming.pdf>.

6   In 2002, UNIFEM's resources totalled $36 million. In comparison, UNFPA's budget for the same year was $373 million, the Office of the High Commissioner for Human Rights' budget was $64 million, and UNAIDS' budget was $92 million. UNICEF's budget in the same year totalled $1,454 million.
7   See for example Torild Skard (2008).
8   See Pickering's 'work styles matrix' in Katherine Pasteur 'Learning for development' in Eyben (2006).
9   See Aruna Rao and David Kelleher (2005).

References

Fook, J. (2006) 'Beyond reflective practice: reworking the "critical" in critical reflection.' Keynote for 'Professional Lifelong Learning: Beyond Reflective Practice', 3 July 2006.

Jain, D. (2006) 'Bringing women's perspectives into UN reform processes', Available at: <http://devakijain.com/pdf/jain_bringingperspective.pdf>.

Obaid, T. A. (2005) Statement by Thoraya Ahmed Obaid, UNFPA Executive Director, 20 January 2005 on Gender Mainstreaming to the Joint Meeting of the Executive Boards of UNDP/UNFPA, UNICEF with the participation of WFP. Available at: <www.unfpa.org/public/News/pid/2637>.

Pasteur, K. (2006) 'Learning for development' in R. Eyben (ed.) *Relationships for Aid* pp. 21–42, London and Sterling, VA: Earthscan.

Rabinow, P. (ed.) (1984) *The Foucault Reader*, New York: Pantheon Books.

Rao, A. (2006) 'Gender equality architecture and UN reforms', Paper submitted to the UN secretary-general's High Level Panel on System-wide Coherence by the Centre for Women's Global Leadership (CWGL) and the Women's Environment and Development Organization (WEDO), 17 July 2006.

Rao, A. and Kelleher, D. (2005) 'Is there life after gender mainstreaming?' *Gender and Development* 13: 57–69 <http://dx.doi.org/10.1080%2F13552 070512331332287>.

Senge, P. (1990) *The Fifth Discipline: The Art and Practice of the Learning Organization*, New York: Doubleday.

Skard, T. (2008) 'Promoting the status of women in the UN system: Experiences from an inside journey' *Forum for Development Studies* 36: 155–91 <http://dx.doi.org/10.1080%2F08039410.2008.9666412>.

Standing, H. (2004) 'Gender, myth, and fable: The perils of mainstreaming in sector bureaucracies' *IDS Bulletin* 35: 82–8 <http://dx.doi.org/10.1111%2Fj.1759-5436.2004.tb00159.x>.

UN (2004) 'Organizational Assessment: UNIFEM, Past, Present and Future', Report A/60/62 and E/2005/10, Advisory Panel to the Consultative Committee of UNIFEM, New York: United Nations.

UN (2006) 'United Nations system-wide policy on gender equality and the empowerment of women: focusing on results and impact', CEB/2006/2, 15 December, New York: United Nations.

Walby, S. (2005) 'Introduction: Comparative gender mainstreaming in a global era', *International Feminist Journal of Politics* 7: 453–70 <http://dx.doi.org/10.1080/14616740500284383>.

Weick, K. (1976) 'Educational organizations as loosely coupled systems' *Administrative Science Quarterly* 21: 1–19 <http://dx.doi.org/10.2307/2391875>.

About the author

Aruna Rao, an Indian national, is the co-founder and executive director of Gender at Work (www.genderatwork.org), an international NGO that helps strengthen organizations, to build cultures of gender equality and social justice. She has over 30 years' experience in pioneering new approaches to gender and organizational change in development agencies, and has consulted widely with a range of government, academic, and development agencies. She has served on several boards including AWID, CIVICUS, and the UN Democracy Fund. She has written extensively on gender equality and institutional change, gender mainstreaming, and human rights. Among Dr Rao's publications are *Gender at Work: Organizational Change for Equality* (Kumarian Press, 1999), and *Gender Analysis and Development Planning* (Kumarian Press, 1991). She holds a PhD in educational administration from Columbia University, New York.

CHAPTER 13

Conclusion: the politics of marginality

Rosalind Eyben and Laura Turquet

In this conclusion, we discuss both the advantages and disadvantages of the marginal position that feminists working in international development bureaucracies find themselves in. Using their creativity and agency as 'tempered radicals' they seek to turn the disadvantages of marginality – such as a sense of powerlessness and reduced visibility – into advantages, as they try to take forward the women's rights agenda. This chapter draws together the insights shared in this book to present a partial checklist for an effective political strategy: building internal and external alliances; leveraging outside pressure; creating win–win situations; preparing for and seizing political opportunities; and coping with bureaucratic pressure. In the end, feminists who believe that international development organizations have a responsibility for supporting pathways of women's empowerment, have to find ways of living with the contradictions of their positions within bureaucracies in order to be effective and to advance the cause in which they so passionately believe.

> When the going gets tough, only a well orchestrated inside–outside political strategy will work.
>
> Sandler (2013: 159)

Engaging directly in counter-hegemonic revolutionary activities that we may think the realization of women's rights merits is impossible from within the international development sector. Thus, radicals will distance themselves from the sector, possibly even avoiding conversations with staff in state machineries and global development institutions, to shield themselves from any risk of cooptation. The contributors to the present volume – including the editors – have chosen a different course. They are 'tempered radicals', seeking a succession of small wins that, accumulatively and over time, they hope may reduce inequity and promote social justice. Their tempered radicalism places them, voluntarily, on the border, the edge, or the periphery of the development agencies that employ them. It is a place where they are neither one thing nor another; neither fully paid-up pen-pushing bureaucrats, nor full-blown feminist activists on the barricades.

Yet despite being a personal choice, the feeling of ambiguity about their location is uncomfortable. One gender adviser in the research project to which this book owes its origins, had started off in women's organizations in Africa and was struggling to understand where she fitted in her bilateral

http://dx.doi.org/10.3362/9781780448046.013

donor agency, especially when she came under fire from activists on the outside – should she be loyal to her organization, or loyal to her deeply held feminist beliefs? Could she do both? For Francesca, in Ghana's women's ministry, any hint of disloyalty to her employer carried the threat of being labelled a troublemaker. You have to work hard to keep from, on one hand, becoming a mainstream bureaucrat working on gender equality or on the other, feeling so antipathetic to the organization you are working for that you have to leave. Tempered radicalism is hard but 'it's worth it' comments Patti O'Neill (Chapter 6). 'That's why I keep on doing it, because it is worth the effort and I see change and I see improvement'.

Although the location is precarious – you are vulnerable to criticism from both sides – it offers distinct advantages for feminist gender advisers committed to making their organizations, and the wider sector, fit for purpose in achieving the women's rights goals to which they are formally committed.

The advantages (and disadvantages) of marginality

The weaknesses of a marginal location become strengths in the hands of a passionate and skilful political feminist capable of living with contradictions. Working from the edge offers four advantages (there may be more that can be identified in the book's case studies): a sense of powerlessness, a relative lack of visibility both inside and outside the sector, an appreciation of different points of view, and the ability to cultivate relationships outside as well as inside. We look briefly at each of these:

A sense of powerlessness

Writing about meetings of women's rights officers from international NGOs, Laura Turquet observes, 'A lot of the discussion was around the trials and tribulations of ... gender mainstreaming ... that sidelined and marginalized gender issues, despite ambitious public proclamations' (Chapter 7). Gender advisers 'are marginalized from mainstream decision-making, and their advice is not taken into account' (Chapter 10), Joanne Sandler writes of the UN system. This sense of powerlessness can be lonely and humiliating but it can also create a passionate desire to be more effective, creating a feeling of solidarity with the hundreds of millions of women that gender adviser's organization is failing to take seriously. A number of contributors to this book say that they hold a fictional grassroots woman in their mind as they work, to test whether what they are doing, albeit in a very indirect way, is helping her to achieve her rights.

Bourdieu's theory of transformative change (Chapter 2) is that it occurs through the actions of a minority among those in privileged and powerful positions, whose identity places them in a relative position of subjection vis-à-vis their peers. In the case of this book's subjects, their identity as gender advisers – often imposed on the organization by external pressure, requirements of the executive board, or insistence from top management – has this effect on their status in organizations whose deeply entrenched and unspoken habits sustain inequitable gender norms. Joanne Sandler observes how bureaucrats who join gender units become radicalized 'after feeling the full weight of institutional gender discrimination' (Chapter 10). It is particularly striking, she writes, to observe how men in this position become feminists as a consequence of the disparaging comments and snide jokes from their colleagues: 'In most cases, these comments strengthen the resolve of my male colleagues to make a difference for women's rights' (Chapter 10).

We have, however, also observed instances where feminists joining the bureaucracy to fight for women's rights find this powerlessness intolerable. Some leave. Others, including some who become directors of gender units as a stepping stone to senior management, opt to play fully by the bureaucratic rules of the game and lose their radical edge.

Reduced visibility

Feminist bureaucrats crave legitimacy from the broader feminist move-ments that help sustain the energy and passionate commitment that are the badge of the feminist gender adviser's craft. The word 'legitimacy' is used in almost every chapter. Yet from the outside, feminist bureaucrat efforts to change their organization are not clearly visible and thus the subjects of our book may not be given the recognition their efforts deserve. To activists on the outside, gender advisers may appear as faceless automatons, unworthy of notice despite possibly – as feminist bureaucrats – playing a pivotal role in securing funds and political space for women's movements. But this is not just about outsiders' ignorance of internal processes, because – as Karin comments in Chapter 8 – 'some of our successes necessarily never get publi-cized because we are resorting to subterfuge. What I do will never be appreci-ated by anyone except myself and some close allies.' Yet given the scale of the challenge, and to be more effective in what they do, feminist gender advisers need those on the outside to better understand their efforts and motivations; this should not just be a one-sided effort. Should they make the effort to establish contact, civil society activists can be agreeably surprised to learn of gender advisers' internal activism. Once they had got to know the staff and to appreciate their perseverance and fortitude, Takyiwaa Manuh and Nana Akua Anyidoho became more optimistic about the potential of feminist bureau-crats to be change agents. Feminists outside the development sector must learn not to be deceived by the bureaucratic cloak of reduced visibility that the feminist insider has to wear.

Reduced visibility inside the organization is another matter that brings its own disadvantages in terms of influencing policies, procedures, and programmes. However, if marginality means not getting invited to every meeting or being asked to comment on every new policy, there is time and opportunity for other activities and relationships. A marginal location offers strategic possibilities for subversive activities –'under the radar' as Patti O'Neill puts it – working away at things management is likely to disapprove of. In Chapter 8 Marianne recounts that at her last meeting with her director-general, shortly before his retirement, he told her that he would have stopped her if he had realized earlier what she had been getting up to. It is, however, a delicate balance; too much invisibility to senior management can risk the job being deemed unnecessary and the post abolished. One also has to be seen to be doing and delivering on the kinds of things that the bureaucracy approves of. Occasions must be sought to make yourself visible: When O'Neill goes to meetings 'she makes herself prominent by walking with a cheerful gait and happy smiles all around the room' (Chapter 6).

Critical consciousness

A marginal location implies staying on the threshold of the organization, one foot in and one foot out, looking both ways like the Roman god, Janus. You see two different worlds and avoid what academic discourse refers to as 'embedded agency' (Chapter 2). Looking both ways enables critical consciousness. It opens our eyes to what might otherwise appear totally natural, to bureaucrats whose jobs have a better fit than that of the gender adviser, with the sector's institutional rules of the game, and the norms and systems of thought accompanying and sustaining these rules, which determine what it is possible to discuss. Looking both ways can create a state of amazement, as for Brigitte Holzner when she realized that the mainstream body of development thinking sees no need to work for coherence between macroeconomic policies and gender equality.

Sustaining critical awareness is easier as a collective activity, both through the kind of informal friendships mentioned in several of the chapters or through more formal processes of reflective practice as Aruna Rao describes in her contribution (Chapter 12). When such spaces are visible, they are fragile – because they are inherently subversive – unearthing 'deep assumptions that collide with dominant organizational cultural norms, and because they focus on how power dynamics within the institution influence practice'. The option then is to use more conventional spaces as a cover for collective critical reflection, as did the composite characters in Chapter 11.

The risk is that critical awareness leads to overly critical speech and bureaucratic sanction, as in the case of a gender adviser known to the project participants, who lost her job in a large multilateral organization when she publicly named and shamed her boss for failing to deliver on the organization's gender equality policy (Chapter 11). A more skilful (manipulative) strategy would be to ventriloquize the criticism, as a supportive and loyal insider informing management of the possibility of external critical voices. 'You can even add to the power and nastiness of the lobby by making it sound more of a menace than it actually is,' Marianne says (Chapter 11).

Two-way relationships

As bureaucrats, gender advisers need credibility to get stuff done, to be taken seriously, to fit in. For advisers coming into the bureaucracy from civil society, there is a temptation to spend time with old friends rather than explore new possibilities for allies within the organization. But internal investments pay off. 'My first six years were spent building and consolidating internal relationships' Ratna says in Chapter 11. 'It meant time spent servicing other people's agendas, in the hope that they in turn would support yours. For instance I supported colleagues in the human rights department and helped them get a bigger budget. In turn I got a commitment to include women's rights as a strong element in *their* work.'

At the same time, every case study in this book stresses the importance of what Ines Smyth refers to as 'keeping the lines of communication open', something that a marginal location can facilitate. The inside–outside quality of working from the edge provides the opportunity to develop alliances and to build up resources from both within and outside the organization. Working with outsiders is easier for gender advisers if they have moved into development bureaucracies after years in social movements and women's organizations, and they see this experience as key to their legitimacy with external allies. But, as Laura Turquet points out in Chapter 7 that for those less well known within the movement – especially those from the North – more proof is sometimes needed, and the relationship can be less easy, requiring honesty about what we can and cannot do. But this also takes confidence – in yourself, and what you stand for – something that your average gender adviser, working in a huge development bureaucracy, might not have in abundance.

The elements of political strategy: a partial checklist

Aruna Rao observes that politics around gender equality issues are deeply felt. People who get involved in such intense processes are forced to re-examine their own personal beliefs and behaviours – to walk the talk. Being clear about one's political goals, Patti O'Neill argues, helps decide when and what kind of trade-offs are acceptable. While political vision tells us where we want to go and reduces the risk of cooptation, political analysis helps identify the kind of organization and sector we are working in, including the wider political environment, the opportunities for making change happen, and the kind of opposition that might be encountered. In Chapter 9, Ines Smyth shows that each development organization has its own character and political context, with different resultant resistances and possibilities. Yet a too common failure of gender advisers is to assume they can employ the same strategy they did in a previous job or in another organization. Political strategy must be context specific and each new context needs patient study and analysis.

The chapters in this book have not all focused equally on power and politics but the experiences recounted and reflected upon have, nevertheless, led us – the editors – to conclude that the tempered radicalism of the book's contributors requires constant conscious political strategy. Partial to being political, we have identified in the book several distinct strategies we suggest could serve as a practical checklist for any feminist gender adviser in a development agency who wants to think and act politically. The items on that list are:

- building internal and external alliances;
- leveraging outside pressure;
- creating win–win situations;
- preparing for and seizing opportunities;
- coping with bureaucratic resistance.

Building internal and external alliances

This is the first and most important item on our checklist. It involves establishing and cultivating personal relationships, and tapping into networks both within and beyond the organization, including collaborating with other gender advisers in the development sector and, importantly, with feminist movements, external lobby groups, and civil society grantees.

Several chapters discuss how working with external women's rights organizations can be effective if built on a relationship of trust, with a clear understanding of what each is able to do from its particular position and they work in a complementary way. Ines Smyth notes, for example, the relative ease with which she collaborated with Filipino feminists from her location within the Asian Development Bank, because they had the 'maturity and confidence to have already established their own relationships (for example as consultants) with ADB without feeling either threatened or compromised by such temporary liaisons' (Chapter 9)

Mutually supportive relations within the sector are also important. Laura Turquet found that her alliance with the gender adviser in another development bureaucracy – a bilateral agency that her own organization was lobbying – worked well because they both recognized what was possible for an INGO like Laura's: she could organize a large public event, bringing together a constituency to demonstrate support for women's rights; the gender adviser could work internally to get the minister to attend the event and to write a speech supportive of their agenda. Neither of them could have achieved what the other did, but together they created an opportunity to put gender equality much more firmly on the ministry's agenda.

Brigitte Holzner observes the practicalities of cultivating inter-organizational relationships within the sector, in attempting to secure a positive change to an EU development policy text. 'Lunches and dinners put everyone in a good mood and provide an informal space for lobbying and advocacy. Such hospitality events are a good base for dialogue and not an unnecessary luxury as outsiders might criticize.'

Cultivating external relationships must be balanced with developing good internal alliances, something that some of the subjects in this book found difficult to manage. Yet spending time on internal relationships is vital to achieving concrete outcomes such as getting gender into programming guidelines, evaluation criteria, budgets, or action plans; it is important to avoid being 'so entrenched in your identity as an activist against a dominant structure that you don't see the opportunities' (Chapter 4). Patti O'Neill comments, 'One of the things that we've really got to think hard about as feminists is how we can sometimes look too much like fundamentalists. We can sometimes be too politically correct and miss the opportunity to make at least some steps towards change.'

Leveraging outside pressure

Good relations with outsiders are important for holding one's organization to account, or 'its feet to the fire' as Claudia puts it in Chapter 11. In the same chapter, Rosalind Eyben explains how when she took on the 'women in development' brief in the UK's international development department, she soon realized that the vociferous external lobby could be used to influence change internally. When someone in the lobby warned her that they were going to apply plenty of pressure, her intuitive response was 'please do, the more the better.' Rosalind was then able to use the threat of this lobby to argue that some kind of concession was needed: a plan would do the trick – no targets or anything – but a plan with a commitment to regularly monitor progress, to keep them quiet. Of course she knew that this was in fact opening the door to greater engagement and a means for the lobby to hold the department accountable. A more extreme example of the power of the external constituency relates to UNIFEM as an autonomous organization. Joanne Sandler shows this constituency to have been a critical factor in its survival (Chapter 10).

Outside pressure can be leveraged more simply by drawing the management's attention to similar organizations whose principles and practices are more progressive; they allow us to hold up a mirror, Ines Smyth comments. These relationships with outsiders are also important for feminists to hold themselves true to their political beliefs, countervailing the internal forces that might incentivize the gender adviser to toe a more conservative bureaucratic line.

Creating win–win situations

O'Neill argues you can use the master's tools to *renovate* the master's house: 'I think that there are things that can be changed and you have to make it in the bureaucracy's interest to make the improvements. This means making the organization look better, making ministers look good' (Chapter 6). It is about working alongside colleagues as mentors, supporting them in their work, and creating a demand for one's advice. A related approach is described by Marianne in Chapter 8 as 'working with the grain' – taking advantage of an organization's instruments, discourses, and procedures and assessing when the opportunities to use them are available.

> I suppose the tactic I've always used is to play the corporate line as strongly as possible in everything that we do. When we put our gender equality plan in front of them, you had people saying, 'This is a really smart plan.' And they weren't talking about the content at all! They liked its presentation and they could see how it just fitted into the work that they have been doing right then. And so that put us immediately in a strong position because departments had been thinking in these ways already. It meant they were being reassured that what we were asking them to do was not new but merely additional – and it was additional within processes and tracks they had begun.

Preparing for and seizing political opportunities

Political effectiveness requires being able to scan the broader political landscape to recognize emerging political opportunities. Patti O'Neill notes how the feminist gender advisers in the DAC had to respond to the aid effectiveness agenda, not as a problem, but as an opportunity: 'We needed to be positioned well to take advantage of that whole different way of working that seemed to be emerging and which the donors and the partners were buying into. This is the groundwork to identifying the action you need to take, including the individuals you need to focus on (Chapter 6). Joanne Sandler makes a similar point in relation to UNIFEM's leadership response to the system-wide effort to reform the UN architecture: By identifying and analyzing an unusual confluence of events, UNIFEM was able to work with its external constituencies to enable the creation of UN Women.

Seizing opportunities means taking risks: Marianne had been busy drafting a women's rights paper for her organization with the minister's approval, but against the wishes of the director-general. However, she felt the tide of history was on her side, and that defying his objection was a risk worth taking; after all, Patti O'Neill notes, you don't usually get found out. However, relative seniority and accumulated experience probably allows for greater risk taking. Ratna notes that as she became more senior, she took more risks and was more prepared 'to punch a hole through the plasterboard … and hope that everything will stream through after you.'

Despite good political analysis and preparation, opportunities can be unexpected and quick decisions are needed on whether to invest scarce time and resources in exploiting these. Using a battle analogy, as some of our project participants did, it is comparable to a guerrilla force discovering an opportunity to ambush an enemy army. Guerrillas secure opportunistic wins and then go quiet, below the radar, until the dust has settled.

Coping with bureaucratic resistance

Participants also compared guerrilla encounters to miniature experiments that test implicit theories about resistance, a major preoccupation of most of the book's contributors. Joanne Sandler notes that in their daily work, all gender advisers must confront systemic institutional discrimination and structures that seek to sabotage their success: 'All must undertake a political analysis that acknowledges the corrosive effects when power, elitism, patriarchy, politics, and gender discrimination join together to hold back progress on women's rights. Confronting this is rarely explicit in their mandates, work plans, or job descriptions, but if left unattended, it is a path to almost certain irrelevance and extinction' (Chapter 10).

Those with prior bureaucratic experience of working on other themes observed the unique challenges of a women's rights and gender equality portfolio: 'I think when I started I believed that if we had a good idea and we talked to enough people about it then people would just do it', Karin says. 'Then I learnt the importance of securing and broadening political support to neutralize the opposition' (Chapter 11). Neutralizing tactics include avoiding making enemies unnecessarily, helping influential actors to find solutions that work for them, and bypassing middle management blockers by going straight to the top. An alternative strategy is to not bang pointlessly on a firmly closed door, but to find a side door that can be pushed open.

Final word: opening up spaces for change

This book and the co-research project which informed it, aimed to discover whether and how feminists working in international development bureaucracies can help to forge pathways for women's empowerment. Some academics are pessimistic about the prospects for feminist bureaucrats. Aruna Rao cites Hilary Standing, who argues that 'bureaucracies are not engines of social and political transformation ... The main myth in gender mainstreaming ... is a mythic relocation of the possibility of political transformation to an inherently non-transformatory context' (Standing, 2004).

Located within these 'non-transformatory contexts', the book's contributors still see their work as feminist activism, even if not regarded as such from the outside. Perhaps we are deluding ourselves about the possibility that gender advisers in development organizations can play a part in paving pathways of women's empowerment, but as Joanne Sandler says, 'it is absolutely essential that women's rights activists are located in these bureaucracies. It is one of the ways that change happens' (Chapter 10). In her interview with Laura Turquet, Everjoice Win – who came from the women's movement in Zimbabwe to head the women's rights unit at ActionAid International – argued that feminists 'must invade these spaces ... We must take the power that these organizations have and use it to advance women's rights.'

However, to take advantage of these spaces feminist bureaucrats must learn to live with contradiction; as one of the project participants remarked, 'I am definitely contributing to rebuilding and regenerating this present structure. There's no question about it. And at the same time, to get anything done, I subvert it. I break the rules and I subvert it.' They are subversively accommodating.

Feminist bureaucrats see their work as urgent, essential, and a necessary contribution to bringing about change. None of the people who took part in this project doubted that this work is needed. The stories in the book make visible the strategies and tactics that feminist gender advisers use, and the challenges that they face in their work. We hope that by going public about what they really do, more effective alliances will be built between feminists in different spaces, to foster greater change within international development bureaucracies.

Reference

Standing, H. (2004) 'Gender, myth, and fable: the perils of mainstreaming in sector bureaucracies', *IDS Bulletin* 35: 82–8 <http://dx.doi.org/10.1111%2Fj.1759-5436.2004.tb00159.x>.

About the authors

Rosalind Eyben is a Professorial Research Fellow at the Institute of Development Studies, University of Sussex. She is a social anthropologist with a professional background in development policy and practice, and a committed teacher in the IDS doctoral and master's programmes, including on gender and development. She has designed and facilitated numerous workshops for international development practitioners all over the world. Her research interests focus on power and relations in international aid. From 2006–11 she convened the global policy programme of the International Research Consortium on Pathways of Women's Empowerment and is currently developing a new area of work exploring the knowledge/power practices of donors that sustain the invisibility of unpaid care as a development policy issue. In 2010 she launched the Big Push Forward that has created an international network challenging the current audit culture in development. She was awarded a CBE in 2000 and is a board member of UNRISD and ActionAid UK.

Laura Turquet has worked as an advocate and researcher on gender equality and women's rights for the past decade, with experience in diverse settings – from a small feminist campaigning organization to the newly established United Nations Entity for Gender Equality and the Empowerment of Women (UN Women), where she manages the organization's flagship publication, *Progress of the World's Women*. She has published many reports on gender equality issues including violence against women, access to justice, and the Millennium Development Goals. Laura has master's degrees in history and international relations from the Universities of Edinburgh and Sussex.

Index